EVERYTHING BRITISH COLUMBIA

THE ULTIMATE BOOK OF LISTS

By Bethany Lindsay and Andrew Weichel

MACINTYRE PURCELL PUBLISHING INC.

MacIntyre Purcell Publishing Inc.
194 Hospital Rd.
Lunenburg, Nova Scotia
B0J 2C0
(902) 640-3350

www.macintyrepurcell.com
info@macintyrepurcell.com

Printed and bound in Canada by Friesens

Cover design: Mikaela Whitney
Book design: Denis Cunningham

ISBN: 978-1-77276-135-1

Library and Archives Canada Cataloguing in Publication
Title: Everything British Columbia : the ultimate book of lists / Bethany Lindsay and Andrew Weichel.
Names: Lindsay, Bethany, author. | Weichel, Andrew, author.
Identifiers: Canadiana 20190112328 | ISBN 9781772761351 (softcover)
Subjects: LCSH: British Columbia. | LCSH: British Columbia—Miscellanea.
Classification: LCC FC3811.6 .L56 2019 | DDC 971.1—dc23

MacIntyre Purcell Publishing Inc. would like to acknowledge the financial support of the Government of Canada and the Nova Scotia Department of Tourism, Culture and Heritage.

Dedicated to all the family and friends who make B.C. feel like home, and to the best cats the province has ever seen:

1. *Andrew Jr.*
2. *Fred Spaghed*
3. *Catticus Finch (RIP)*

TABLE OF CONTENTS

INTRODUCTION: 10 THINGS WE LOVE ABOUT BRITISH COLUMBIA .... **page 8**

GEOGRAPHY .... **page 11**
Roy Henry Vickers' List of 10 B.C. Places That Inspire Me . . . 50 Stops on a Very Bleak
Tour of B.C. . . . 10 Places to Visit on a Pretty 'Blah' Trip to B.C. . . . 10 B.C. Places that
Sound Absolutely Disgusting . . . 10 B.C. Locations that Make up a Complete Breakfast . . .
The Sad Story of One Dog's Life in 10 B.C. Place Names . . . 10 Tales of Personal
Misfortune in B.C. Place Names . . . 12 B.C. Place Names Pulled from a Word of the
Day Calendar . . . Drag Queen Shanda Leer's List of 10 *Camp*-sites . . . 10 B.C. Places
for People with One-track Minds . . . 10 B.C. Locations that Look Like They Were Named
by 12-year-olds . . . 5 B.C. Locations that Look Like They Were Named by 4-year-olds . . .
Nature's Best: A List of 9 Geographical Superlatives

HISTORY .... **page 19**
A List of the 7 Best B.C. Ghost Towns, As Unilaterally Determined by Justin McElroy . . .
The Vancouver Historical Society's List of 10 Turning Points in the City's History . . .
6 (Very Justified) B.C. Government Apologies for Historical Wrongs . . . 5 Epidemics That
Ravaged B.C. . . . 6 B.C. Riots That Had Nothing To Do With Hockey . . . Rick James' List of 5
Enduring Characters From B.C.'s Rum Running Days . . . 10 Lasting Reminders from Expo 86

POLITICS .... **page 35**
Rob Shaw and Richard Zussman's List of 10 WTF Moments in B.C. Politics . . .
The Highly Suspicious or Downright Illegal Activities of 8 B.C. Politicians . . .
Legislature Linchpins: B.C.'s 5 Longest Serving Premiers . . . The Seat-Warmers:
B.C.'s 5 Shortest Serving Premiers . . . 5 Facts About B.C.'s First Premier,
John McCreight . . . 10 Much More Interesting Facts About B.C.'s Second Premier,
Amor De Cosmos . . . 10 B.C. 'Boondoggles' (According to the Vancouver Sun)

CRIME .... **page 55**
Eve Lazarus's List of 10 Bizarre Murders . . . 3 Failed Terror Plots With Ties to B.C.
— And 5 That Succeeded . . . 3 Times 'Severed Feet' Appeared on B.C. Beaches
But Turned Out to be Disgusting Pranks . . . Devils Among Us: 5 Serial Killers Who
Haunted B.C. . . . 10 Haunting Missing Persons Cases From B.C. . . .
Bonus: 1 Person Who Was Found Safe After 52 Years . . . 8 Remarkable B.C. Prison Breaks

PEOPLE .... **page 71**
Bif Naked's List of Tremendous and Brilliant B.C. Women . . . Fred Lee's List of 10
British Columbians I'd Love to Have a Drink With . . . 10 Stories That Will Make You
Wish You'd Known Joe Fortes . . . 11 Lesser-Known Facts About Terry Fox . . .
10 B.C. Memories I'll Carry With Me Forever, by Rick Hansen . . . 10 Times Kim Campbell
was Delightfully Candid on Twitter . . . The Moneybags Brigade: A List of B.C.'s 9 Richest
People . . . 10 Outrageous Stories About B.C. Billionaire Chip Wilson . . . 11 Crotchety
Quotes From Legendary Newspaperwoman 'Ma' Murray

FLORA AND FAUNA .... **page 87**
No Really, You Shouldn't Have: 7 Invasive Species We're All Stuck With Now . . .
10 Famous Trees: A List That Could Only Be Written in B.C. . . . Paula Wild's List of
10 Things You Didn't Know About B.C.'s Apex Predators . . . 10 Facts About the Whales

and Dolphins of B.C. . . . 5 Disturbing Stories About B.C.'s Most Beloved Wildlife . . .
10 Times Exotic Animals Ran Wild in B.C. . . . 8 Dinosaurs (And Dinosaur-Like Creatures)
That Roamed B.C.

THE GREAT OUTDOORS .... **page 99**
Stephen Hui's 10 Long B.C. Hikes Worthy of Your Bucket List . . . 10 Beautiful B.C. Beaches . . .
Bow-Wow! Darcy Matheson's List of 10 Extremely Scenic and Dog-Friendly B.C. Beaches . . .
The Top 7 Ways to Die While Snowmobiling in B.C. . . . 10 Devastating B.C. Natural Disasters

SPORTS .... **page 107**
Ashleigh McIvor's 10 Favourite B.C. Ski Runs . . . Kat Jayme's List of 10 Reasons to Bring
Back the Vancouver Grizzlies . . . 10 Memorable Moments From the 2010 Vancouver
Olympics . . . Daniel Wagner's List of 10 Devastating Moments That Define Being A
Vancouver Canucks Fan . . . 10 Defunct B.C. Sports Teams

PROGRESS .... **page 117**
Rod Mickleburgh's List of 10 Key Moments in the History of the B.C.
Labour Movement . . . David Suzuki's List of 10 Environmental Gains in B.C. . . .
8 Made-in-B.C. Inventions . . . 10 Pre-Colonial Innovations from B.C. First Nations

CULTURE AND COMMUNITY .... **page 125**
Shanda Leer's List of 10 B.C. Drag Queens Who Could Drain the Strait Out of Georgia . . .
10 Outdated, Unnecessary, or Downright Disturbing B.C. Laws . . . 8 Times Someone
Tried to Create a Utopia in B.C. . . . 7 New Religions, Sects, and Straight-Up Cults in B.C. . . .
10 Words From the Witsuwit'en Language and Their Meanings . . . 10 Familiar (Or Just
Plain Fun) Chinook Jargon Terms . . . 10 Guinness World Records Set in British Columbia

THE PARANORMAL .... **page 137**
Greg Mansfield's List of B.C.'s 10 Most Haunted Places . . . UFO*BC's 10 Most
Compelling Close Encounters . . . 10 Facts About the Ogopogo—Most of
Them True . . . Thomas Sewid's List of 8 Facts about B.C.'s Rich Sasquatch History

HOLLYWOOD NORTH .... **page 143**
Lainey's List of 4 Celebrity Scandals That Happened in B.C. . . . The Star Treatment:
8 Actors Who Had a Bad Time in Vancouver . . . 11 Cities (And 1 Planet) Vancouver Has
Played in the Movies . . . 10 B.C. Actors Who Hit It Big . . . 10 Highest-Grossing Movies
Filmed (At Least Partly) in B.C. . . . 10 Box-Office Bombs Filmed in B.C. . . .
10 B.C.-Filmed TV Shows That Didn't Make It To Season 2

THE ARTS .... **page 153**
Best of the West: Terry David Mulligan's 10 Favourite B.C. Musical Artists . . . From Strip
Clubs to Shopping Malls: 8 Gigs Michael Bublé Played On His Long Path To Stardom . . .
12 Songs By B.C. Artists That Topped The Billboard Charts . . . Nathan Sellyn's List Of The
8 Unquestionably Greatest Video Games Developed in B.C. . . . Kevin Chong's List of 10
Essential Books Of Fiction Set In Vancouver . . . 3 Books By B.C.-Based Authors That Won
The Giller Prize . . . 4 Books By B.C.-Based Authors That Won The Governor General's
Award For Fiction . . . 11 Books By B.C.-Based Authors That Won The Governor General's
Award For Non-Fiction

FOOD AND DRINK .... **page 163**

Inez Cook's List of 9 Friggin' Delicious Indigenous Foods to Try in B.C. . . . . Chef Tojo's Top 10 Delicious Sushi Ingredients From B.C. . . . Must-Try Dishes From B.C.'s Top 10 Restaurants . . . And Selections From 4 Non-Vancouver Restaurants That Made the Top 100 . . . Glen Mofford's List of 10 Strange But True Stories From B.C. Bars . . . John Schreiner's List of 10 Wineries That Put B.C. On The Map . . . The 10 Most Expensive Local Wines at the B.C. Liquor Store . . . Joe Wiebe's List of 10 B.C. Craft Beer Stories

TOURISM .... **page 175**

10 Gigantic B.C. Roadside Attractions . . . Teresa The Traveler's Top 10 List of Historical Spots to Visit in B.C. . . . 10 Weird and Wonderful B.C. Museums . . . 5 B.C. Transportation Wrecks to Explore

THE CONCIERGE RECOMMENDS .... **page 181**

Karin Schwagly's List of 10 Things To Do in Vancouver . . . Deborah Sleno's List of 10 Things To Do in Victoria . . . Coast Inn of the North's List of 10 Things To Do in Prince George . . . Toby Kolada's List of 10 Things To Do in Kelowna and the Okanagan . . . Antoine Gay's 10 Things To Do in Tofino and Pacific Rim National Park Reserve . . . The Four Seasons Concierge's Guide To 10 Things To Do in Whistler and the Sea-To-Sky Corridor

FOR YOUR REFERENCE .... **page 189**

8 Official Symbols of B.C. . . . B.C. By The Numbers: 25 Basic Facts . . . B.C.'s 10 Most Valuable Homes . . . The Living Wage For 10 B.C. Cities . . . Most Popular Baby Names of 1918 . . . Most Popular Baby Names of 1968 . . . Most Popular Baby Names of 2018

PHOTO CREDITS .... **page 199**

INTRODUCTION: 10 THINGS WE LOVE ABOUT BRITISH COLUMBIA

1. THE DRIVES: Having driven across Canada from coast to coast, we can tell you this: when it comes to scenery, not all provinces were created equal. (There's truth to the old joke that in the flatlands of the Prairies, you can watch your dog run away for three days.)

Sure, road trips can be tedious. But once in a while, being surrounded on all sides by B.C.'s natural beauty and listening to a favourite song—we have an unironic love for Mission's Carly Rae Jepsen (page 159)—verges on transcendent.

Just ask someone who's taken the winding drive down the Pacific Rim Highway to Tofino, the Sea-to-Sky up to Pemberton, or Highway 3 to Osoyoos. Shimmering lakes, towering mountains (page 17), and glorious trees (page 90) abound.

2. THE ROADSIDE FRUIT STANDS: One more reason to love zig-zagging across B.C. is the abundance of roadside fruit stands. When you're on a long road trip, they can feel like an oasis of nutrients in a desert of gas station pepperoni sticks.

And whether you're picking up Fraser Valley blueberries or Okanagan cherries, you know you're in for something juicy and delicious. Local strawberries in particular can make the imported stuff you find at major grocery chains taste like watermelon rinds.

Plus, if you're in the Southern Interior, you don't have to worry about encountering the dreaded apple maggot (page 88). The invasive insect hasn't reached the region—at least not yet.

3. THE SCANDALOUS POLITICS: Did you ever hear the one about the politician who tried to replace the word "sex" with "BOLT"—as in "Biology On Life Today"? It sounds almost too crazy to be true, but in B.C., that's just politics as usual (page 39).

This, after all, is the land of former premier Bill Vander Zalm, the Dutchman who lived in a biblical theme park. It's also the place where a group of tipsy female lawmakers burst into the legislative chamber in the midst of a debate in order to present a male colleague with a tiny wind-up penis.

In B.C. politics, anything truly is possible—one day you're robbing people at gunpoint, the next you're embarking on a decades-long career as a representative of the people (page 44).

4. THE PROTEST CULTURE: People joke that it's next to impossible to get anything built in B.C., whether it's something as big as a pipeline to the ocean or as small as one building that might replace two trees. No matter what change you're trying to make in this province, there's going to be a protest. They're not always justified and they can sometimes be annoying, but each one gives us a chance to take a step back and consider what we want British Columbia to look like.

Protests are behind some of the biggest steps B.C. has taken toward protecting the natural world (page 120), and have helped secure the rights and safety of workers across the province (page 118). Protests have also stopped a freeway from being built through the centre of Vancouver, a project that would have drastically altered the city—though they were too late to save the historic black neighbourhood in Hogan's Alley (page 24).

5. THE PET OBSESSIONS: They say you can tell a lot about a person by how they treat animals, and we tend to agree. That's why some people think British Columbians are absolutely *nuts*.

We don't just treat pets like children, we helicopter parent them.

On a sunny afternoon in this province, you might see a pampered little pug being pushed around in a baby carriage, or an orange tabby headed to an acupuncture appointment. We outfit our pets in high-tech GPS collars, buy them stylish denim jackets from specialty boutiques, and drive great distances to show them the perfect dog-friendly beaches (page 102).

And our crazy pet bonding extends to all kinds of animals. There's at least one B.C. city that felt it necessary to cap how many pet snakes or rats could be kept in a single home (page 126).

So yes, when it comes to our furry, scaly, or feathered companions, we might be a little bit nuts. But we do it out of love, and because we know that in one crucial way, pets are a lot like people: when they're treated well, they can bring a whole lot of joy into this world.

6. THE CASCADIA CONNECTION: Don't get us wrong, we love being part of Canada. But there's something heartwarming about the cross-border kinship British Columbians have with our neighbours in Washington and Oregon.

And whenever the ruling federal party of the day feels particularly corrupt, incompetent or wrongheaded—or all of the above—the idea of like-minded Pacific Northwesterners breaking away to form a quaint little nation-state is perfect daydream fodder*.

Back in the '90s, someone even designed a Cascadian flag, "Old Doug," made up of blue, white, and green horizontal stripes and the silhouette of a Douglas fir.

But the idea of a great Cascadian secession has never been all that popular on either side of the border, and we'd put the odds of it actually happening at approximately 3,720 to one. Fortunately, we can still hop on the Amtrak Cascades any time and know that whether we step off in Bellingham, Everett, Seattle, Tacoma, Vancouver, or Portland, it'll be teeming with friends we haven't met.

Technically, Cascadia wouldn't be all that little. It's been calculated that B.C., Washington, and Oregon would form the 20th biggest country on Earth.

7. WHITE SPOT ON THE FERRY: If you live on the South Coast like we do, it's easy to feel like you're doing something wrong if you don't eat some sort of paleo-organic-keto-vegan-raw food dish at every meal. There's something so sweet about hopping on the BC Ferries, shrugging your shoulders, and saying "Well, I guess I'm stuck with this delicious Spicy Ultimate Crunch Burger." And then there are the desserts—those towering slices of chocolate cake, or even better, the soft serve ice cream.

But best of all are those early morning visits to the Coastal Cafe. Really, is there anything that cures a long weekend hangover better than a greasy ferry breakfast?

8. THE WILD WEST HISTORY: To be completely transparent, neither of us knew a whole lot about the history of B.C. before we started writing this book, but boy, are we ever glad we got a chance to learn a bunch more. This province's history is woven together by stories of life on the Western frontier, from the Indigenous peoples who invented countless uses for cedar and just as many ways to catch a fish (page123), to the Gold Rush hopefuls who swarmed the province looking to make their fortunes.

Want to know what makes this place so special? Read some of the wild hijinks that took place inside B.C. bars, like Mike the Dog, who served drinks at the Bowser Hotel, or the mysterious skeleton buried beneath the floorboards of the Pony Saloon (page169). If you really want to get up close to B.C.'s history, check out the eerie remains of once-booming communities in one of our province's many ghost towns (page 20).

Some of B.C.'s history, unfortunately, is quite shameful—like the treatment of the Indigenous Peoples and people of Japanese, Chinese, and Indian descent (page 25). We're thankful that more and more of this history is coming to light, thanks to the tireless efforts of the people who were affected, and the families that came after them.

9. BEARS IN THE BACKYARD: Let's face it, there are bears pretty much everywhere in the province. They're not just in your backyard, they're taking a dip in your hot tub or passing out drunk on fermented fruit from your apple tree. Sometimes they hitch a ride downtown on a garbage truck or climb onto your second storey balcony to steal seeds from the birdfeeder. (Yes, these are all real stories about bears in B.C.)

And bears aren't the only large predators you're likely to see if you spend enough time in B.C. You might wake up one morning to find your pet cat teasing the bobcat on your back porch, or run into a cougar in the parking garage of Victoria's ritziest hotel (page 92). We've seen a coyote walking down our street, right in the middle of Vancouver's most densely populated neighbourhood.

If you're really, really lucky, you might even run into something truly wild and unexpected, like a Siberian tiger by the highway or a wallaby watching you enjoy your morning coffee (page 95).

10. THE PEOPLE: Fun fact: the reputation Vancouverites have for being quiet, guarded, and unapproachable actually goes back at least six decades. A *Vancouver Sun* article from the 1950s cites "shyness of the people" as one of the main complaints among tourists.

But there's more to Vancouverites than their reputation lets on, and there's a whole lot more to British Columbia than Vancouver.

Our province has produced some of Canada's all-time greatest people, like Terry Fox (page 77), and been home to some of its biggest oddballs, like Amor de Cosmos (page 49). At various points in our history, B.C. residents have threatened to secede, rioted over a sold-out Rolling Stones concert, and passed a law making it legal to treat "dumb animals" with liquor (page 127).

And though there might be some truth to Vancouver's timid reputation, the two of us still managed to meet some of our favourite people in the world right here. We wouldn't change it for anything.

(Opposite) Desolation Sound, one of many beautiful B.C. locales with depressing names.

GEOGRAPHY

ROY HENRY VICKERS' LIST OF 10 B.C. PLACES THAT INSPIRE ME

Roy Henry Vickers is a celebrated artist from Hazelton with roots in the Tsimshian, Haida, and Heiltsuk Nations. He holds a hereditary chieftainship and has been appointed to the Order of British Columbia and the Order of Canada. Vickers was nominated for a 2019 Grammy Award for his design work on a Grateful Dead box set.

1. RIVERS INLET: A long fjord on the west coast—the Great Bear Rainforest begins here. Rivers Inlet is home to two places I love, Wuikinuxv and Good Hope Cannery.

2. HAZELTON: Old Hazelton is at the junction of the Bulkley and Skeena Rivers. It is a famous place where the paddle wheelers used to travel to and from the mouth of the Skeena. It's an absolute jewel of B.C. frontier towns.

3. MOUNT HOSMER: The Ghostrider legend* of Mt. Hosmer is one of my favourite stories. This mountain overlooks the city of Fernie.

4. CHESTERMAN BEACH, TOFINO: This beautiful beach in Tofino is one of my favourite beaches on the coast. It's beside Long Beach in the Pacific Rim National Park Reserve.

5. BUTEDALE: Butedale is a privately owned piece of property on the Inside Passage. It is a ghost town with a beauty that is recognized by BC Ferries, as it's the only scenic site that the ferry slows down and announces. The 300-foot waterfall is gorgeous. I'm a shareholder in the Inside Passage Marine Company that owns Butedale today.

6. KISPIOX/SKEENA RIVER JUNCTION: This river junction is where the ancient village of Kispiox is situated. A beautiful sandy beach is a favourite fishing spot for generations of fishermen.

7. GITXAALA (KITKATLA): Gitxaala is one of the oldest continuously inhabited village sites in Canada, dating beyond 5,000 years! It is situated in a pristine area of the northern section of the Great Bear Rainforest. It's my home village.

8. TOBACCO PLAINS: This area is known today as Grasmere. It's my favourite place to harvest elk in B.C. The area is rolling hills of open grasslands along the Koocanusa Lake. It is the home to relatives of the Chief in the legend of the Ghostrider*.

9. GREAT WHALE SEA: This area incorporates Whale and Squally Channels, and my grandmother's ancestral fishing area at the Estevan Islands. White sand beaches and good fishing in this wilderness area.

10. HAIDA GWAII : This area is another example of the beauty of B.C.'s west coast. Home of my great grandfather, Amos Collinson, these islands are a rare example of pristine beauty.

The Ghostrider legend of Mount Hosmer begins in the late 1800s, when it's said that William Fernie agreed to marry a young Ktunaxa woman to learn the source of the coal necklace she wore around her neck. After the woman's father, a local chief, divulged the secret location of the Morrissey Coal Seams, Fernie reneged on his promise and the chief put a curse on the town. Fernie was beset by a series of tragedies in the early 20th century that were blamed on the curse—two fires, flooding, and a mining explosion that killed at least 128 men. In 1964 at the request of the town, members of the Ktunaxa, led by Chief Ambrose Gravelle, held a ceremony to lift the curse.

11 LISTS OF B.C. PLACE NAMES

The Gazetteer of British Columbia lists more than 40,700 official names for places in B.C. Here's just a small sample.

50 STOPS ON A VERY BLEAK TOUR OF B.C.

1. Abyss Glacier
2. Affliction Creek
3. All Alone Stone
4. Anger Anchorage
5. Assault Glacier
6. Assimilation Lake
7. Badman Point
8. Beware Passage
9. Bleak Bay
10. Blessing's Grave
11. Burial Cove
12. Calamity Bay
13. Casualty Creek
14. Crying Girl Prairie
15. Damnation Creek
16. Deadman Falls
17. Deception Gulch
18. Defeat Point
19. Delusion Bay
20. Desolation Sound
21. Despair Pass
22. Devastation Island
23. Disappointment Lake
24. Disintegration Ridge
25. Dismal Glacier
26. Doom Mountain
27. Fatigue Pass
28. Graveyard Lake
29. Hardship Mountain
30. Isolation Glacier
31. Lonesome Creek
32. Menace Rock
33. Misery Summit
34. Murderers Bar
35. Outcast Hill
36. Parasite Creek
37. Pathetic Glacier
38. Poison Hill
39. Purgatory Ridge
40. Quarantine Cove
41. Rage Reefs
42. Rapids of the Drowned
43. Slaughter Bay
44. Slum Lake
45. Sob Creek
46. Sorrow Islands
47. Starvation Peak
48. Toil Mountain
49. Tombstone Mountain
50. Worthless Creek

10 PLACES TO VISIT ON A PRETTY 'BLAH' TRIP TO B.C.

1. Big O.K. Lake
2. Unnecessary Mountain
3. Duplicate Glacier
4. Bland Island
5. Boring Ranch
6. Useless Inlet
7. No Name Lake
8. Fizzle Mountain
9. Another Lake
10. And Another Lake

10 B.C. PLACES THAT SOUND ABSOLUTELY DISGUSTING

1. Reeks Island
2. Garbage Creek
3. Mount Ick
4. Roach Rock
5. Ugly Creek
6. Scuzzy Rapids
7. Nevertouch Lake
8. Foul Bay
9. Spoil Rock
10. The Wart

10 B.C. LOCATIONS THAT MAKE UP A COMPLETE BREAKFAST

1. Coffee Crater
2. Milk Lake
3. Orange Juice Creek
4. Frying Pan Slough
5. Fried Egg Lake
6. Bacon Cove
7. Flapjack Lake
8. Whipped Cream Peak
9. Butterworth Rocks
10. Caesars

THE SAD STORY OF ONE DOG'S LIFE IN 10 B.C. PLACE NAMES

1. Pup Lake
2. Dog Pond
3. Big Dog Mountain
4. Fat Dog Creek
5. Mad Dog Glacier
6. Lost Dog Canyon
7. Water Dog Lake

8. Toodoggone River
9. Killdog Creek
10. Dead Dog Creek

10 TALES OF PERSONAL MISFORTUNE IN B.C. PLACE NAMES

1. Footsore Lake
2. Gash Creek
3. Splinter Hill
4. Tentfire Creek
5. Broken Leg Lake
6. Scar Mountain
7. Emergency Lake
8. Cut Thumb Creek
9. Split Toe Gulch
10. Lost Shoe Creek

12 B.C. PLACE NAMES PULLED FROM A WORD OF THE DAY CALENDAR

1. Obstreperous Ridge
2. Asperity Mountain
3. Salubrious Bay
4. Prudential Mountain
5. Solifluction Ridge
6. Melanistic Peak
7. Surfusion Glacier
8. Recumbent Peak
9. Iconoclast Mountain
10. Metacarpus Peak
11. Poignant Creek
12. Sophist Mountain

DRAG QUEEN SHANDA LEER'S LIST OF 10 *CAMP*-SITES

1. Bear Lake
2. Dome Creek
3. Topley Landing
4. Fanny Bay
5. Beaver Creek
6. Mount Jimmy Jimmy
7. Lone Butte
8. Pink Mountain
9. Fruitvale
10. Queens Bay

10 B.C. PLACES FOR PEOPLE WITH ONE-TRACK MINDS

1. Climax Col
2. Concubine Peaks
3. Flirt Island
4. Kink Creek
5. Lust Subdivision
6. Saucy Creek
7. Shag Rock
8. Nude Creek
9. Minx Reef
10. Younghusband Ridge

10 B.C. LOCATIONS THAT LOOK LIKE THEY WERE NAMED BY 12-YEAR-OLDS

1. Family Humps
2. Cumsack Creek
3. Jackass Mountain
4. Sperm Bay
5. Toodick Lake
6. Gooch Island
7. Suck Creek
8. Hump Mountain
9. Kumeon Bay
10. The Nipples

5 B.C. LOCATIONS THAT LOOK LIKE THEY WERE NAMED BY 4-YEAR-OLDS

1. Poopoo Creek
2. Ipoo Mountain
3. Kaka Creek
4. Ta Ta Lake
5. My Lake

Osoyoos boasts the hottest average daytime temperatures in all of Canada. It's also very easy on the eyes.

NATURE'S BEST: A LIST OF 9 GEOGRAPHICAL SUPERLATIVES

1. BIGGEST LAKE: WILLISTON LAKE. Sure, Williston Lake is man-made—a reservoir in the Northern Interior created by the W.A.C. Bennett Dam—but it is still far and away the biggest lake in the province, with a surface area of 1,761 square kilometres and a volume of *74 trillion litres.*

2. DEEPEST LAKE: QUESNEL LAKE. Shuswap Lake may be more popular, but Quesnel Lake is deep and mysterious. Shuswap's deepest point is less than halfway down Quesnel's dark depths, which reach 610 metres into the Earth. (For context, that's about the length of six Canadian football fields.)

3. TALLEST MOUNTAIN: MOUNT FAIRWEATHER. Much of B.C.'s tallest mountain, Mount Fairweather, is actually located in Alaska. But we have the summit, which most people agree is really the high point of any mountain. At an elevation of 4,671 metres, Fairweather is roughly half as tall as Everest, but taller than both Matterhorn and Fuji.

4. WETTEST PLACE: HENDERSON LAKE. Located southwest of Port Alberni on Vancouver Island, Henderson Lake is not only the most rain-drenched place in B.C., it's actually the wettest place in North America, recording an average of *6.9 metres* of rainfall annually.

5. HOTTEST PLACE: OSOYOOS. Tourism companies will tell you Osoyoos is an oasis in the desert. Nitpickers like to say it's actually more of an oasis in a shrub-steppe. But when you're basking in the highest average daytime temperatures in all of Canada (17°C), does it really matter?

6. COLDEST PLACE: FORT NELSON. Despite having fairly warm summers, Fort Nelson has the coldest winters in the province, with an average low of -24.6°C in January. Its record low is -51.7°C, which is the equivalent of a bad day in the Arctic.

7. SNOWIEST PLACE: MOUNT FIDELITY. Found near the Alberta border in Glacier National Park, Mount Fidelity is actually said to be the snowiest place in all of Canada, recording well over 13 metres of snow a year. That's enough to bury a brachiosaurus, although the snowfall is not cumulative and brachiosauruses are, to the best of our knowledge, extinct.

8. LONGEST RIVER: FRASER RIVER. From its source in the Rocky Mountains to its mouth in the Strait of Georgia, the mighty Fraser River—or Stó:lō, to the Halkomelem-speaking peoples—runs 1,375 kilometres. As impressive as that is, the Fraser is only about one-fifth the length of the Nile.

9. SHORTEST RIVER: NAUTLEY RIVER. The Nautley River, which connects Fraser Lake to the much longer Nechako River, is just 800 metres—which means Kenyan Olympic runner David Rudisha could potentially get from one end to the other in a couple minutes.

(Opposite) Expo 86 helped turn Vancouver into a global destination.

HISTORY

A LIST OF THE 7 BEST B.C. GHOST TOWNS, AS UNILATERALLY DETERMINED BY JUSTIN MCELROY

Justin McElroy is a reporter with CBC Vancouver and an obsessive ranker of pretty much everything in British Columbia.

British Columbia is a place full of mountains and lakes, of rivers and inlets, of small towns and gleaming metropoles, and everything in between. It's also a place full of ghost towns.

This province was settled by Europeans in a predictable pattern through the 19th and the 20th centuries—someone realized A Thing could be taken from the ground, and then a town was formed to make a profit from That Thing, with a big mine or mill right next door.

What happened when a company decided it wasn't economically feasible to sell That Thing anymore? Well, if it had diversified or grown to a large enough size, it would probably stumble along, waiting for the next big resource boom while trying to create a tourism/service sector.

But for towns overly dependent on That Thing (and usually, That Company that employed everyone to take That Thing), it would spell doom.

There are dozens and dozens of ghost towns around B.C. Some had a mass evacuation, while others had a slow decline. Some remain with a number of buildings still in fine condition, some are just a few structures in various states of a decay, and some are little more than a few wooden foundations.

From townsites in northern B.C. to settlements a day trip from Vancouver, they remind us of the province's past, the precarious and hazardous nature of the resource economy, and the inescapable fact that nothing lasts forever. (Mostly though, they're just cool to look at)

Here are my seven favourite B.C. ghost towns.

7. ANYOX: For about 20 years there were around 3,000 people living in this company town, about 140 kilometres north of Prince Rupert. It was created to mine the surrounding copper, but if you visit today the most distinctive feature is the massive hydroelectric dam, the tallest in Canada when it was built.

Its most lasting contribution may be hundreds of lightbulbs that were etched with the word "STOLEN" on them. In an isolated town where supplies were sometimes low, employees with the Granby Consolidated Mining and Smelting Company often resorted to stealing lightbulbs from work—so Granby etched those bulbs with "STOLEN" to dissuade people from *actually* stealing them.

Spoiler alert: it didn't really work. Employees would either blatantly display the lightbulbs, or try sanding over the evidence of their thievery.

6. PHOENIX: Known today for a small ski hill nearby, 100 years ago there was another mining town owned by Granby, in this case in the area between Grand Forks and Greenwood. Phoenix closed up shop in 1919 when the price of copper crashed.

That's a pretty generic story, though. What wasn't generic about Phoenix's demise was that when the end came, people were already in the middle of raising funds for a memorial, honouring town citizens who fought in the First World War.

To get the money to make that happen, lumber and iron from the skating rink were auctioned off. By the time the memorial was erected, the town was deserted. Today, the only structures still standing in Phoenix are the memorial and a graveyard.

5. BARKERVILLE: Well that was dark! Let's talk about a ghost town with a happy ending.

If you grew up in British Columbia, chances are you learned in school about Billy Barker, the huge windfall of gold he found in a place on the outskirts of the Cariboo Gold Rush, and the town formed around it, which for a while was the largest community in North America west of Chicago and north of San Francisco.

A century later, it was mostly abandoned and with no real prospects of revitalization—until the provincial government decided its restoration would be a key part of celebrating B.C.'s centennial as a colony.

Today, you can travel back in time when you visit Barkerville, sort of: the architecture, roads, exhibits and in-character guides are designed to evoke the feel of 1860s British Columbia, all thanks to continual funding from the government (extensive historical recreations hours from any major city don't come cheap, people.)

It's a facsimile to be sure, but it allows us to experience what a ghost town actually felt like, and for the majority of folks who would prefer that over a few derelict structures, it's a welcome tradeoff.

4. BRADIAN: Want to buy your very own ghost town? Just a couple hours from Whistler sits the former mining community of Bradian, available for sale for just over $1 million. The area fell into disrepair for decades, until the 1990s, when it was bought by a couple who spent every summer repairing the 20 or so homes that make up the town.

In 2014, the story of this ancient B.C. community took a very modern turn—a group of Chinese investors bought it with hopes of using it to gain Canadian citizenship, via a program that gave a fast track immigration process to people who created small businesses. When a feasible business plan couldn't be figured out, the town went back on the market, where it has been ever since.

3. OCEAN FALLS: A large pulp and paper mill was the reason Ocean Falls grew to around 5,000 people in the middle of the 20th century, despite its relative inaccessibility on the Central Coast.

When it shut down in the 1970s, the province took it over for a few years, so great was the desire to avoid the type of ghost town exodus that was once common in B.C. But the government gave up after a few years, and since then Ocean Falls has slowly faded away.

At least, it sort of has: because Ocean Falls was so big, and because a few dozen residents continued to make it home, and because in the summertime it's an incredibly picturesque location, BC Ferries continues to service the town—giving the remaining denizens a lifeline, and the rest of us a chance to see what happens when nature has a few decades to take over a mid-sized community.

2. SANDON: You know the drill by now—there was a town centred around a resource (silver), in a less-populated part of B.C. (West Kootenay, in a hard to reach valley), which had a bustling yet mysterious past. (It's been called the "alcohol, gambling, and sex capital of Canada's own Wild West.")

What makes it truly unique today are a couple of factors: first, you can still visit Sandon and see a few of the buildings that have stood for over a century, along with a train from that era. Second, it's more than just a discarded historical curiosity: the Silversmith powerhouse, built in 1916, continues to generate hydroelectric power and is available for the public to see. But the weirdest and most delightful quirk of Sandon is the collection of vintage Vancouver transit buses from the middle of the 20th century that sit in the middle of town. Rescued by Sandon's protector a couple of decades ago, it's a strange combination of heritage from two different parts and two different eras of B.C., all available for the public to breathe in (and inevitably Instagram) for free.

1. KITSAULT: Yes, there's still an entire mining town in B.C.'s Interior that was kept in good condition after it was evacuated in 1983. Yes, there's a shopping centre, pub, apartments, and a school, all frozen in time, with a crew of employees keeping buildings and lawns in good condition every summer. Yes, it's owned by an eccentric millionaire who has proposed any number of uses for the town since he bought it a decade ago, none which have come anywhere close to fruition. Yes, you can visit it.

Everything about Kitsault today defies any reasonable expectation for what happens to a community after the people leave, which is why so many articles have been written about it.

Still, the next time you come across pictures of Kitsault, spend a second thinking not of the eerie buildings themselves, but of the people who once inhabited them—miners, doctors, teachers and nurses, young families and restless adventurers, most believing that this brand new purpose-built community would be their home for decades.

The dream lasted just three years. There hasn't been an attempt in this province to replicate Kitsault since. Large companies now create temporary work camps when a new rush on a resource happens. It's efficient. And it marked a definitive end to the frontier days of British Columbia.

Which means Kitsault is both the biggest—and most likely, last—monument to a very particular part of our history.

THE VANCOUVER HISTORICAL SOCIETY'S LIST OF 10 TURNING POINTS IN THE CITY'S HISTORY

Madeleine de Trenqualye is vice president and Michael Kluckner is president of the Vancouver Historical Society.

1. INDIGENOUS PEOPLES RESTRICTED TO RESERVE LAND: In 1869, the Squamish, Tsleil-Waututh, and Musqueam First Nations, who had lived in this region for 10,000 years and never ceded their land to colonizers, were restricted to small Indian reserves. The creation of the reserve system decimated Indigenous access to traditional territories and resources and paved the way for settlers to develop on the land without interference from Indigenous interests. It was one of many colonial actions—along with residential schools, and banning spiritual practices—that had a devastating impact on the Indigenous way of life. Unlike the rest of Canada, very few treaties were negotiated in B.C., and when the province joined Confederation in 1871, it did not recognize Aboriginal title. Today, the struggle for land, rights, and equality continues.

2. THE CPR MOVES ITS TRANSCONTINENTAL TERMINUS FROM PORT MOODY TO VANCOUVER: The Canadian Pacific Railway—a nation-building project linking Canada from coast to coast—was slated to terminate in Port Moody. But at the last-minute, CPR officials decided to move the end of the line to Coal Harbour. They had negotiated a secret deal with the province that gave them 6,000 acres of land, including 200 acres in downtown Vancouver.

The No.16 streetcar heads down Cordova Street in Vancouver in the year 1890.

The switch guaranteed Vancouver's future as Canada's most important West Coast city and leading Pacific port, and caused Port Moody to fade into the background. The CPR was the most powerful company in early Vancouver and shaped the city we know today, swinging the centre of commerce from Gastown to Granville.

3. STREETCAR SYSTEM CREATES VANCOUVER'S NEIGHBOURHOODS: Vancouver received a state-of-the-art electric streetcar system in 1890. It marked the arrival of modern public transportation and was critical to the city's early growth. Chewing its way through rugged bushland, the streetcar line spurred settlement outside the downtown core, effectively creating the neighbourhoods of Kitsilano, Kerrisdale, Marpole, and Mount Pleasant. The rail system saw its demise in the 1950s, but its skeleton left a lasting mark on the city. Many of the original streetcar lines formed the basis of today's liveliest streets including Robson, Davie, Denman, Hastings, Broadway, Fourth Avenue, Granville, and Main Street.

4. THE 1907 RACE RIOT: On Labour Day in 1907, a white supremacist mob swept through Chinatown and Japantown attacking residents, looting stores, and smashing windows. The riot followed an anti-immigration rally organized by the Asiatic Exclusion League, at which prominent labour leaders and politicians delivered speeches blaming non-whites for taking their jobs. Some 10,000 people attended, carrying banners that read "Keep Canada White" and "Stop the Yellow Peril." By the time the damage was done, every window in Chinatown had been smashed. News of the riot was broadcast around the world. The federal government ordered an inquiry, ultimately compensating Chinese and Japanese merchants for the damage. But they also tightened restrictions against Asian immigration, implementing quotas on Japanese migrants and eventually barring entry from China. Incidentally, the riot also led to Canada's first drug law (the inquiry into compensation claims, some of which came from opium manufacturers, had aroused concern among government officials.)

5. VANCOUVER AMALGAMATES WITH POINT GREY AND SOUTH VANCOUVER: The city had expanded from its original 1886 boundaries of Burrard Inlet, Alma, 16th Avenue, and Nanaimo, and in 1929 it absorbed the municipalities of South Vancouver and Point Grey. Overnight, Vancouver became Canada's third-largest city. The merger brought together the working-class suburb of South Vancouver (east of Cambie) and the wealthier municipality of Point Grey (including Shaughnessy Heights, which itself had wanted to separate and become its own municipality). Following amalgamation, the west side dominated civic politics for 70 years through the Non-Partisan Association, formed in the late 1930s to counter the rise of radical labour during the Great Depression.

6. THE TRIUMPH OF THE AUTOMOBILE: 1932-1958: Vancouver was slow to adopt car culture, partly due to its excellent B.C. Electric Railway Co. transit system, partly due to the impacts of economic depressions in 1913 and 1929 and the lingering effects of the First World War. The Burrard Bridge, opened in 1932, was the first piece of publicly funded infrastructure to make no provision for rail transit. It was followed by regional and local road improvements including the Pattullo Bridge in 1937; the Lions Gate Bridge, built privately in 1938 to give access to Guinness Company lands in West Vancouver and prompting the demise of the West Vancouver ferry service in 1946; the dismantling of the streetcar and interurban systems from 1950-55; the Granville Street Bridge in 1954; the George Massey Tunnel and Oak Street Bridge in 1957; and the Ironworkers Memorial Bridge in 1960, two years after the North Vancouver car-ferry system shut down.

7. NEW IMMIGRATION LAWS CHANGE THE FACE OF VANCOUVER: Early Vancouver was an explosive mix of different ethnicities and nationalities. But by the turn of the twentieth century and up until the 1960s, the bulk of the population was of British origin. That changed in the 1960s, after the federal government abandoned its discriminatory immigration laws and established a point-based immigration system that was blind to race and country of origin. The 1970s-90s brought a huge influx of immigrants from China, the Philippines, India and Hong Kong. Today, Vancouver is the most Asian city outside Asia—with nearly half the population of Asian origin and 40 per cent foreign-born.

8. POWER TO THE PEOPLE, 1967-1975: The so-called "long decade" of the 60s, which began in the USA with civil rights actions, continued through the mid-1970s with protests against the Vietnam War and in favour of minority rights. In Vancouver, hippie "flower power" changed the face of Kitsilano in 1967 and morphed into a protest culture rejecting conspicuous materialism, neighbourhood redevelopment, and laws against marijuana, while embracing environmental politics, most notably with the founding of Greenpeace. Chinese-Canadian residents in Strathcona led the battle against urban renewal and found common cause with activists fighting plans for a freeway through East Vancouver, Chinatown, and Gastown. As a result of their efforts, Vancouver is the only major North American city without an inner-city freeway.

1972 marked a sea change in Vancouver's civic culture. That year, voters defeated the development-oriented NPA party, which had held power for three decades, and replaced it with a moderate, more human-focused council led by Mayor Art Phillips that, amongst other changes, developed the south shore of False Creek for co-ops and family housing. In provincial politics, voters elected an NDP government headed by Dave Barrett that delegated power to Vancouver to designate heritage buildings and, regionally, established the Agricultural Land Reserve to preserve farmland and control urban sprawl.

9. THE PROVINCIAL GOVERNMENT PASSES THE STRATA TITLES ACT: Few single pieces of legislation have had such an impact on Vancouver as this 1966 legislation. It allowed for "the condo"—a new kind of ownership in multi-family buildings that previously could be controlled either by an individual who rented to tenants or a corporation which, during the 1940s-1960s, sold shares to individuals who would reside in its suites (the "for-profit co-op" or "apartment corporation.") On the plus side, it spurred the densification and urbanization of areas such as Downtown South and the north side of False Creek, and made home ownership possible for many who could not afford a detached house. On the minus side, when combined with changes to the Income Tax Act in 1972, it removed investor incentives from rental housing. The huge transformation of the city since the 1970s, both in new construction and, for example, in the conversion of large heritage buildings into suites, could not have happened without it.

10. EXPO 86 LAUNCHES VANCOUVER AS A GLOBAL DESTINATION: Expo 86, the six-month world fair that coincided with Vancouver's 100th birthday, brought millions of visitors to the city and launched Vancouver as a global destination. Originally pitched as "Transpo," it prompted the creation of the first SkyTrain line, now the Expo Line—the first significant investment in mass transit in many generations. One of its goals was to promote Vancouver to an international audience and encourage foreign investment. Following the fair, the Expo lands were privatized and sold to Hong Kong developer Li Ka-Shing in the largest real estate deal in Vancouver's history.

Expo 86 left the city with many public amenities including Canada Place, Science World, and the Dr. Sun Yat-Sen Garden. But in the Downtown Eastside, an estimated 500-850 long-term residents were evicted as hotels prepared for a flood of visitors. Expo 86 also marked the point at which Vancouver became a gateway city for flows of global capital. Over the next 20 years, housing prices would soar to extraordinary levels, decoupling from local incomes.

6 (VERY JUSTIFIED) B.C. GOVERNMENT APOLOGIES FOR HISTORICAL WRONGS

1. THE REFUSAL OF THE KOMAGATA MARU: In 1914, the steamship Komagata Maru arrived in Vancouver, carrying 376 people from India's Punjab state. They were hoping to make a new life in Canada, but just two dozen passengers—mainly Canadian residents returning home—were allowed to disembark. The rest were turned away and sent back to India, where about 20 were killed by British gunfire upon arrival.

The B.C. government offered a formal apology in the legislature in 2008, acknowledging that racism was at the root of the refusal to embrace fellow citizens of the Commonwealth. "Forgive us, you are welcome," then-house leader Mike de Jong said in Punjabi.

2. THE HANGING OF SIX TSILHQOT'IN CHIEFS: The Chilcotin War of 1864 exploded around colonists' plans to build a road through Tsilhqot'in territory without the Nation's permission. One major trigger was reportedly a threat from the road-building team's foreman to unleash smallpox on the Tsilhqot'in as punishment for stealing flour—the community had just come out of an epidemic that devastated Indigenous peoples across the province. War was declared, and a Tsilhqot'in war party killed most of the road crew.

Five chiefs were later summoned to what they were told would be peace talks to end the war, but they were hanged instead. A sixth chief tried to offer reparations, and he was hanged as well. In 2014, then-premier Christy Clark apologized for the mass execution, saying the chiefs "are fully exonerated for any crime or wrongdoing."

3. JAPANESE INTERNMENT DURING THE SECOND WORLD WAR: Japanese-Canadians have a long history in B.C., but after the bombing of Pearl Harbor, Canadian governments tossed all that aside and rounded up 22,000 people of Japanese descent, forcing them into internment camps. More than half of those interned were people who'd been born in Canada, but none of that mattered—everyone was stripped of their homes and property, which would be sold off to pay the costs of their internship.

The B.C. government formally apologized in 2012 for its role in the forced incarceration. Then-minister of advanced education Naomi Yamamoto, whose father was 14 and a Canadian citizen when he was sent away to the camps, said her dad remembered his high school principal telling him "We are at war with your people." Yamamoto continued, "My dad suddenly realized that 'we' did not include him and 'your people' were the Japanese."

4. ABUSE OF CHILDREN AT JERICHO HILL SCHOOL: The deaf children who were sexually, emotionally, and physically abused at Vancouver's Jericho Hill School in the 1970s and 80s tried to communicate what was happening to them, but few of their caregivers understood sign language. Police and Crown counsel weren't much help either. But abuse was endemic at the school—children were hurt both by staff and older students.

In 2004, about 350 abused former students won a $15.6-million settlement from the province. Part of that settlement included an official apology.

5. WRONGS AGAINST THE CHINESE COMMUNITY: This apology wasn't just about one thing—it was about seven decades of racist laws and policies targeting Chinese-Canadians beginning at Confederation. These abuses included segregation, forced labour, restrictions on education and employment, and denying people of Chinese descent the right to vote or own property. It also included the federal head tax, the heavy fee that all Chinese migrants were forced to pay on entering Canada. The province received about 40 per cent of the $23 million that Canada collected from the tax.

B.C. offered an omnibus apology in 2014 for all of those practices, calling them "unacceptable and intolerable."

6. VIOLATIONS AT WOODLANDS INSTITUTION: When Woodlands first opened in 1878, it was called the Provincial Asylum for the Insane. By the time it closed its doors in 1996, it mainly housed the mentally disabled. The true story of what happened inside Woodlands would become clear in the decade after it closed: residents were beaten, sexually assaulted, forced to take cold showers or scalding hot baths, and kept in extended isolation. Parents weren't informed, and in most cases, neither were the police. A provincial ombudsperson's report said Woodlands employees maintained a "code of silence" to hide the systemic abuse.

The province officially apologized in 2003 for the treatment of former Woodlands residents, but did not acknowledge any abuse.

5 EPIDEMICS THAT RAVAGED B.C.

1. SMALLPOX, LATE 1770s: B.C.'s First Nations were largely spared the exotic disease outbreaks that devastated the eastern seaboard of North America until the 1770s. But when smallpox hit B.C., it hit hard. It's estimated the disease killed about 30 per cent of the Indigenous people who lived in the Pacific Northwest. The story goes that when the explorer George Dixon arrived on the coast of Haida Gwaii in 1787, his ships were met by the surviving Haida dancing on the shore, signalling at these unwanted spirits of the pestilence to turn back and sail away from their land. Dixon and his crew ignored them.

2. MEASLES, 1847-50: The arrival of the Hudson's Bay Company was a bad omen for many Indigenous peoples across Canada. In B.C., the company's trading routes on land, by river, and along the coastlines all became pipelines for disease. According to an account from the historian R.M. Galois, the measles outbreak of the late 1840s began with the arrival of the steamship *Beaver* and the establishment of trading posts in places like Fort Victoria. Within just a few years, the disease had spread from the southern coast to the North, and deep into the Interior. Some historians suggest about 10 per cent of the population was killed during the epidemic.

3. SMALLPOX AGAIN, 1862-1863: The smallpox outbreak of the 1770s was just a taste of what was to come for members of First Nations in B.C. In 1862, the brutal disease arrived from San Francisco, carried by a single ambitious miner looking to cash in on the Gold Rush in the Cariboo. The sick man was quarantined upon arrival in Victoria, but the colonial government failed to take proper measures to contain the disease. Instead, infected Indigenous people were towed out of town on canoes, carrying smallpox up and down the coast. Wide swaths of the province were almost completely depopulated and whole villages were abandoned. At least 30,000 Indigenous people died in the epidemic, slashing the total population by nearly two thirds.

4. SPANISH INFLUENZA, 1918-1919: This wasn't just an epidemic. The "Spanish flu" was a pandemic that infected 500 million people around the world, killing up to five per cent of the world's population. British Columbia was not spared. The flu arrived in Vancouver and Victoria first, then spread by steamship and rail. And, once again, the Indigenous population suffered the heaviest blow. Federal agents recorded that 1,139 Indigenous people died of the flu, though that's believed to be a gross underestimate. But even based on that flimsy data, the death rate for B.C.'s Indigenous population was more than seven times that for the rest of the province. In all, about 4,000 people in B.C. had died of influenza by the end of 1919.

5. POLIO, 1927-1953: Canada had only seen relatively low numbers of poliomyelitis infections before 1927. Then suddenly, B.C. had 182 polio patients in one year. By 1934, about half of all disabled people in the country could blame their condition on the disease. For the country and for B.C., 1953 was the climax of the polio epidemic. In British Columbia, there were 797 cases that year, and 500 people died across Canada. Of those who survived, many were left partially paralyzed. Some former patients alive today still struggle with post-polio syndrome, a neurological disorder that can lead to trouble swallowing, weakness, and severe mobility problems.

6 B.C. RIOTS THAT HAD NOTHING TO DO WITH HOCKEY

Everyone remembers the riots that erupted when Vancouver Canucks fans' Stanley Cup dreams were dashed in 1994, and then again in 2011, but those weren't the only times British Columbians took to the streets in shocking displays of mob violence—and while the hockey riots were embarrassing, some of the previous riots represent much darker blotches on the province's history.

1. THE 'ANTI-ORIENTAL' RIOTS, SEPTEMBER 7-9, 1907: Back in 1907, resentment toward growing populations of Chinese, Japanese, and South Asian immigrants was festering from B.C. down to California. Vancouver was a powder keg of racial tensions, and a protest organized by the Asiatic Exclusion League—a group of xenophobes that counted the city's mayor and several councillors among its ranks—provided the spark.

A damaged building is seen in the aftermath of the 1907 race riot in Vancouver.

Several thousand people attended the event and were whipped into a fury by its speakers, until someone finally hurled a brick into the window of a Chinese storefront. What followed was three shameful days of roving violence that saw angry mobs attack homes, shops, and human beings.

Though no one was killed and the government later offered reparations for much of the damage, there was little in the way of justice for the victims. Only one person was ever convicted for their involvement.

2. MAY RIOT, MAY 8, 1915: The streets of B.C.'s capital city are rich with history, and back in May 1915, in the midst of the First World War, they were crowded with vengeful mobs seeking to punish local Germans for the crimes of their countrymen. The May Riot began one day after the infamous sinking of the RMS Lusitania, an ocean liner bound for Liverpool that was downed by a German torpedo, killing nearly 1,200 people on board.

Outrage spread swiftly across Canada, but nowhere was it more explosive than Victoria— home to 15 of the fated Lusitania's passengers. Rioters began targeting German-owned businesses and buildings with German names, including the former Kaiserhof Hotel, smashing glass and looting whatever they could find inside.

Several hundred people took part, while more than a thousand looked on. The riot continued into a second day before Victoria police and the military could ultimately disperse the crowds, leaving the affected business owners—German and non-German alike—to survey the needless destruction.

3. BLOODY SUNDAY, MAY 20, 1938: The devastation of the Great Depression is hard to imagine today—it left millions of Canadians unemployed, homeless, and desperate, and in the early 1930s the government responded by setting up relief camps for men across the country.

But conditions were terrible, and private businesses exploited the residents for cheap labour, paying them just 20 cents a day—which is equivalent to about $2.86 today. Not long after the government decided to cut off this most meagre of safety nets, hundreds of the homeless and unemployed descended on downtown Vancouver to protest. They spent weeks occupying Sinclair Centre, which was then a post office, until RCMP officers decided to move in with tear gas and batons.

Protesters in the building smashed windows to let in oxygen, and made a futile effort to hold their ground against the Mounties. By the time officers managed to clear the building, dozens of people were injured, including a few police officers. But despite the heavy-handed response, which prompted a much larger protest against police brutality, no one was ultimately arrested for taking part.

4. GASTOWN RIOT, AUGUST 7, 1971: Vancouver's burgeoning counterculture scene of the 1960s was full of hippies who abandoned traditional values, opposed war, embraced their sexuality, and experimented with drugs—all before it was cool. They also had contempt for the city's police, and the feeling was certainly mutual. In 1971, after years of antagonism on both sides, those tensions would come to an infamously savage head in the Gastown Riot.

Outraged over Operation Dustpan—a systemic crackdown on drug users—an estimated 2,000 hippies gathered for a "smoke-in" at Maple Tree Park. When mounted officers decided to charge the crowd, they unleashed what even the Vancouver Police Museum described as "a level of extreme and unnecessary brutality" toward the protesters.

According to news reports from the time, officers wailed on hippies, including youths, with riot sticks and dragged one screaming woman over 100 metres of broken glass. The hippies took part in the violence as well, lobbing bottles and chunks of cement at law enforcement. When it was over, the streets of the now-trendy neighbourhood—which was then part of skid row—were splattered red with blood.

5. THE ROLLING STONES RIOT, JUNE 3, 1972: When The Rolling Stones decided to kick off their 1972 American Tour in Vancouver, local fans were over the moon. They descended on Pacific Coliseum by the thousands on June 3, happily paying $6 (equivalent to roughly $38 in 2019) to see one of the biggest bands in the world in their hometown.

But there was only so much space at the venue. Anger festered as wave after wave of arriving concertgoers realized they weren't going to be concert-seers, and eventually, around the same time the band was opening the show with "Brown Sugar," the crowd erupted into violence. As the front page of the *Vancouver Sun* put it: "The Rolling Stones and an ecstatic crowd of 17,000 were inside, flying stones and an unruly mob of 2,500 were outside."

And the crowd threw more than just rocks. They lobbed Molotov cocktails, including one that burst onto a police patrol car. Nearly 300 baton-wielding cops responded, and, to their credit, kept their cool better than they had the previous year in Gastown, even as dozens of them suffered various injuries ranging from cuts and bruises to a cracked breastbone.

By some miracle, police managed to disperse the crowd by the time the show let out at 11:45 p.m., arresting a handful of people, including a man who was carrying "a four-foot logging chain with a hook on one end," according to the *Sun*. The Rolling Stones packed up and left, with another concert scheduled the next night across the border. Things were so comparably serene the show was summed up with the headline "Seattle has quiet time."

6. PENTICTON RIOT, JULY 28, 1991: Let's end this list on a lighter note, free from racial hostilities or social upheaval, with the unnamed riot that erupted during Penticton's 1991 Peach Festival—following a concert by none other than MC Hammer. The rapper had just finished performing when hundreds of youths decided they were feeling 2 Legit 2 Go 2 Bed and began looting stores and overturning cars.

At one point, the mob turned their attention to the iconic peach-shaped concession stand at Okanagan Lake, which they rolled into the water. Police eventually had to use tear gas to disperse the crowds, and dozens of people were injured during the fracas.

But time heals all wounds, and decades later, the owner of The Peach offered an olive branch to those involved with a pun-filled public message. "MC Hammer sang 'Can't Touch This' at the festival that year and the lyrics did not apply to me," it read. "And so they rocked and I rolled, and then there I was, floating in the lake feeling … impeached."

BY JING, THE OLD CEILING LEAKS!

—Morris for the George Matthew Adams Service.

Editorial cartoon from The Literary Digest, 1920.

RICK JAMES' LIST OF 5 ENDURING CHARACTERS FROM B.C.'S RUM RUNNING DAYS

Rick James is a maritime historian and the author of Don't Never Tell Nobody Nothin' No How: The Real Story of West Coast Rum Running, *as well as other works about B.C.'s oceangoing history.*

It was the radio operator Fraser "Sparky" Miles, aboard the distributor boat *Ryou II,* who pointed out that rum runners as a group made the Sphinx sound like a chatterbox. "It allowed the business to flourish in obscurity at the time, but left an impossible job for later historians trying to research Pacific Coast rum running, especially as the active participants didn't write anything down either."

Sparky was indeed correct in his assessment, since there were literally thousands involved in the endeavour who all kept their mouths shut long after U.S. Prohibition was all over and done with in December 1933. Still, thankfully, there were a handful who did step forward much later in life to tell tales of their fascinating adventures, and even went into some detail in explaining how the whole operation was run and operated.

1. JOHNNY SCHNAAR: (Source: *Rumrunner: The Life and Times of Johnny Schnaar*. Orca Book Publishers, Victoria, B.C., 1988)

Johnny Schnaar's niece, Marion Parker, finally got her uncle, who was working out of Victoria harbour throughout the Prohibition years, to open up and then set down on paper all his tales and adventures back in the 1980s. As a result, in collaboration with publisher Robert Tyrell, they were able to work up a particularly insightful biography with many a quote from a gentleman who excelled at "jumpin' the line."

As it was, Johnny was able to make himself a handsome dollar during the U.S. Prohibition years, regardless of the fact that it was outright illegal and required taking on a lot of risk crossing into American waters, what with the U.S. Coast Guard and, more particularly, dangerous and often violent hijackers about. He proved particularly adept at running across the border into Washington state waters on dark and moonless nights, with his fast black-hulled launches, which he designed and had built locally. Overall, he noted that "...as much as anything else—the money and excitement and all—I enjoyed the whole challenge of the game that was involved in the rum running: the challenge of not getting caught."

2. HUGH GARLING: (Source: *Rum Running on the West Coast: A Look at the Vessels and People*, *Harbour & Shipping*, Vancouver, B.C., November 1988 – July 1991)

Hugh "Red" Garling was able to land himself a job in January 1931 at the age of 19 crewing aboard the "mother ship" and "Queen of Rum Row," the five-masted auxiliary schooner *Malahat*. In a series of articles in Vancouver's monthly *Harbour & Shipping* magazine, Garling not only provided his own personal account of what transpired down there on Rum Row just south of Ensenada, Mexico, in the early 1930s, but also delved into and explained how the whole rum running trade operated on both coasts of North America throughout the Prohibition years.

As he recounted in his introductory article, he was quite excited when he first signed on. "I would be serving in sail, getting my sea time, and receiving pay above the scale for deep-sea sailors and … no doubt the *Malahat* would be calling in at exotic foreign ports with many adventures awaiting me…. It sounded adventurous, but I didn't have any clear idea of what rum running was all about." He soon discovered that, "...when you signed two-year articles on a rum runner's mother ship, it was much the same as a voluntary two-year sentence of penal servitude. ...there was the endless day-after-day and week-after-week of waiting, drifting into month-after-month, for the day you would be homeward bound. On one voyage, I was at sea for an entire year without shore leave."

Life aboard a ship of sail, what with the continual maintenance of sails, rigging and the hull, entailed a lot of challenging and hard labour. Then there was all the work dealing with the thousands of cases aboard, which required hours upon hours of hands-on work. Once all the cases were broken open and the bottles repackaged in burlap sacks, they were passed up or thrown along from one crewman to another in a line, and then passed over to a vessel loading alongside. But there was one benefit to all this tedious labour: "It was the fastest way of handling cargo and rarely did someone miss his catch. It was hard work and kept you in good shape."

3. FRASER MILES: (Source: *Slow Boat on Rum Row*. Madeira Park, B.C., Harbour Publishing, 1992)

As for Fraser Miles, he finally worked up a definitive book on rum running when he was well into his 70s, regardless of the fact that the brotherhood's strict code of silence made it particularly difficult for later historians to research. Back when he was a young man trying to figure out how he was going to get by, he was offered a job in December 1931 as the radio operator aboard a boat, after just completing a wireless telegraph course at Sprott-Shaw Wireless School in Vancouver. All he knew was he had a job on the *Ruth B*, a fish packer that apparently hadn't carried fish in years. What he didn't know didn't seem all that important, like what she would be carrying, where they were headed, when they'd be returning to port, or even the name of the company.

It didn't take long for him to catch on from his tight-lipped crew members that "...the less anyone knew about our other activities the better, and I followed instinctively the rum runner's motto: 'Don't never tell nobody nothing, no how.'" That being said, Mile's book was a major accomplishment since he went beyond the sharing of his own adventures and was able to ferret out a few other personal accounts, which were provided in appendices. Also, along with a number of charts, he compiled a 16-page list of West Coast vessels that took part in the trade while providing background on their owners, specifications and, for some, a line or two on their history.

4. CAPTAIN STUART S. STONE: (Source: *My Dad, The Rum Runner*. North Waterloo Academic Press, Waterloo, Ontario, 2002)

A particularly fascinating and insightful look into West Coast rum running was provided by Jim Stone in the biography of his father, Captain Stuart S. Stone. Stuart Stone was out working on boats in the early 1920s with his own father, Jim, and brother Chet, first on the 37-foot work boat *Tofino*, and then on the 75.5-foot converted fish packer *Roche Point*, transporting passengers, mail, and general freight from Port Alberni out Barkley Sound to Bamfield, Ucluelet, and waypoints. But seeing an opportunity to make better money, the Stone brothers were quick to jump into rum running. Stone and his brother Chet started out by smuggling bottles of whiskey in the *Roche Point* from the west coast of the Island by hiding it under cargos of rotten chum salmon they were packing into Seattle harbour for use as mink feed.

The well-seasoned mariner finally moved into rum running big time when he took charge of the 190-foot freighter *Principio*. In February 1927, he was in command of the steamer *Federalship* when they were captured off the California coast in international waters. When captain and crew were found innocent after a short trial, they re-boarded their ship and headed out on their merry way. Captain Stone continued to be a persistent thorn in the side of the U.S. Coast Guard right into the twilight years of Prohibition.

Once he was recognized as an astute sea captain and able sailor who could be counted on to be a clever daredevil when the occasion warranted, he was given the command of the most important ship in Consolidated Exporters Corporation's fleet, the big mother ship *Malahat*, in March 1929. He got to enjoy the best year of the trade in the early 1930s with his recent bride, Emmie May (nee Binns), aboard ship down at Rum Row, just south of Ensenada, Mexico, but unfortunately he passed away in July 1933—only a few months before Prohibition was put into the dumpster of history. As Jim Stone pointed out in his preface, once he was well into his biography he no longer felt ashamed of his dad's occupation since "he and most of the other adventurous young involved in rum running truly believed they were twentieth-century Robin Hoods maintaining the right of American citizens to drink alcoholic beverages without government interference."

5. CAPTAIN CHARLES HUDSON: (Source: *Rum-running interviews: tape 1*. Sound Records: Ron Burton interviews: T4407:0001; Imbert Orchard 1967 Interview. T4255:0039. British Columbia Archives and Record Services)

Surprisingly, the first one to open up and share his take on all that went down was none other than Captain Charles H. Hudson, the managing director of Consolidated Exporters Corporation Ltd., the big liquor export consortium made up of local brewers, distillers, and hotel liquor buying agents, which operated out of Vancouver during the U.S. Prohibition years. Captain Hudson was most gracious and very open to being interviewed by oral historians Imbert Orchard and Ron Burton for CBC, and today these aural history tapes are available at the British Columbia Archives. Listening to them, one gets a good sense of how well organized and generally peaceful the whole operation was.

As Hudson recounted in his charming and sophisticated British accent, "Vancouver was in the midst of a real depression, with logging, fishing, mining, etc. in the doldrums. It took rum running to keep industry going, especially on the waterfront. The tremendous moneys paid out to industry in Vancouver were never known to the average citizen. We spent a fabulous amount of money building boats; purchasing and overhauling engines; buying food and supplies for our ships; using the shipyards for overhaul and in wages for the crew and fuel..." Overall, he said, "We had a wonderful, wonderful time!" And that, "The people down below, our (American) customers, trusted me implicitly."

10 LASTING REMINDERS OF EXPO 86

1. SKYTRAIN: Twenty-two million people came to Vancouver over the six months of Expo, and they all needed some way to get around. This was just the kick in the butt the city needed to finally get some rapid transit in place.

2. SCIENCE WORLD: It's pretty hard to imagine Vancouver's skyline without it. The big, shiny geodesic dome on False Creek actually opened a year before Expo as a preview centre for the world's fair, and then housed the Futures Theatre during the event.

3. MCBARGE: A floating McDonald's on False Creek—what a dream of the 1980s. For decades after Expo, the now-derelict barge was anchored in Burrard Inlet, where it became a destination for illicit parties and the stuff of urban legends. In 2015, it was towed to Maple Ridge to be retrofitted—the plan is to turn it into a floating museum dedicated to the deep sea.

4. INUKSHUK: Inuit artist Alvin Kanak created the stone sculpture for the Northwest Territories' pavilion at Expo, but it was given to the City of Vancouver and placed at English Bay once the fair was over. Now it's one of the city's most photographed pieces of public art—it even became the inspiration for the 2010 Winter Olympics logo, despite the fact that B.C. Indigenous peoples don't build inukshuks.

5. CHINA GATE CAFE AND MCDONALD'S SPACESHIP: The fate of these two restaurants is really a testament to the spirit of recycling that pervaded the province after Expo. When the world's fair ended, a businessman in Sechelt bought the China Gate Cafe and shipped it, piece by piece, on a ferry to the Sunshine Coast. It was rebuilt as the Lighthouse Pub on Porpoise Bay. The lighthouse that sits on top of the pub is actually a repurposed spaceship from a space-themed McDonald's at Expo—yep, people sure loved McDonald's back then.

6. CHINA GATE: The ornate gate once welcomed visitors to China's pavilion at Expo '86, but the country's government donated it to Vancouver at the end of the fair. Now it stands over Pender Street as the symbolic entryway to Chinatown.

7. WORLD'S LARGEST FREE-STANDING FLAGPOLE: The original Canadian flag that waved atop this 86-metre pole is long gone, whipped to shreds by the wind decades ago. But the pole and its replacement flags now hold a place of pride outside a car dealership in Surrey. The pole is so tall and the 15 x 24 metre flag is so big that it costs more than $40,000 a year to keep it flying, the dealership once told the *Surrey Now-Leader.*

8. BC PLACE: The famous white marshmallow roof is long gone, but when BC Place opened in 1983 in preparation for the fair, it was the world's biggest indoor structure with an inflated roof. Then as now, the stadium was home field for the Vancouver Whitecaps soccer team and the BC Lions football team, but during Expo it played host to the opening and closing ceremonies.

9. CANADA PLACE: The sails of Canada Place, now home to a wing of the Vancouver Convention Centre, are another enduring featuring on the city's waterfront. During Expo, it was the Canada Pavilion, where visitors were wowed by the Hystar, a remote-controlled "flying saucer," and a Haida war canoe.

10. UFO H2O: Anyone who was a kid at Expo might remember this water park, designed to look like a Martian spaceship. Once the fair was over, it was shipped all the way north to Terrace to be part of the Mount Layton Hot Springs Resort, which was supposed to be a grand destination for family fun, fine dining, and golf. But the resort has never really lived up to those promises, and the water park has fallen into disrepair.

(Opposite) W.A.C. Bennett speaking on stage at the 1966 P.N.E. opening ceremonies.

POLITICS

ROB SHAW AND RICHARD ZUSSMAN'S LIST OF 10 WTF MOMENTS IN B.C. POLITICS

Rob Shaw is the B.C. legislative columnist for the Vancouver Sun; *Richard Zussman covers the legislature for* Global News. *They are the co-authors of* A Matter of Confidence: The Inside Story of the Political Battle for B.C.

1. ONE NIGHT WITH YU: An obese Taiwanese billionaire who conducted business in his underwear, a flamboyant Chinese realtor with ostentatious hats, a defiant Dutch premier who lived in a fantasy theme park, and a shady deal in which $20,000 cash in an envelope exchanged hands. In the long history of B.C. political scandals, none have ever been quite as colourful as Bill Vander Zalm's sale of Fantasy Gardens.

At the height of his career, in 1986, Vander Zalm was a rock star in B.C. politics. With his chiseled chin and charismatic smile, "The Zalm" and his Social Credit party swept the election over the NDP in a burst of popularity known as "Vandermania." But his freewheeling style and controversial social stances, such as attempting to cut funding for abortions that weren't medically necessary, quickly dulled his shine.

By 1990, Vander Zalm was looking to sell his home—a flower garden and Christian theme park known as Fantasy Gardens. The Richmond attraction, with its Dutch windmill, medieval castle, and miniature railroad, had become a political and debt-ridden financial albatross for Vander Zalm.

The premier tried to cut a deal with Taiwanese billionaire Tan Yu. He used his premier's office to broker a meeting with the prospective buyers and senior government officials, as well as set up a luncheon at Government House with Lt.-Gov. David Lam. The deal culminated August 3 with a bizarre evening at the Westin Bayshore Hotel, where the province's 27th premier spent all night in a top-floor suite scribbling offers and counter-offers on hotel stationary while Yu—who had just enjoyed a $600 Chinese buffet in the dining hall—sat in his underwear with his feet up in a different bedroom and played hardball on the price.

Running the offers from room to room was Faye Leung, a Chinese real estate agent who was known for always wearing colourful and outrageous hats. Unbeknownst to both men, Leung surreptitiously squirreled away the written notes from the premier and the billionaire—evidence that would document the transactions for investigators and give her a media platform for years in the resulting scandal.

After eight hours of bartering, Yu emerged in a kimono to shake hands on the deal with the premier. Fantasy Gardens would be sold for $16 million. But before he left, Yu counted out $20,000 USD in crisp $100 bills and handed them to Vander Zalm in a manila envelope.

"It didn't feel good," Vander Zalm said in an interview years later. "When somebody comes out and counts cash, you don't like it.... But then, if I'm dealing with people from another country who have their ways and their customs, am I to walk away...?"

He took the cash. The move would end his premiership. Within a year, Vander Zalm found himself embroiled in controversy and attacks over the extent he used the premier's office to facilitate the sale. Under pressure, Vander Zalm asked then-conflict commissioner Ted Hughes—a former judge, deputy attorney general and widely-respected jurist—to investigate. The 1991 Hughes report found Vander Zalm had deliberately withheld evidence from the inquiry, and that the premier had violated B.C.'s conflict of interest guidelines by mixing his public office with the private sale of Fantasy Gardens.

Lt.-Gov Lam watched the scandal unfold carefully and said in a later interview he was prepared to fire Vander Zalm as premier if he did not resign. It would have been the first time since 1903 a vice-regal representative intervened to oust a premier.

Vander Zalm did eventually resign. The RCMP investigated the sale and Vander Zalm was later charged with breach of trust but acquitted of criminal charges in the case. Judge David Campbell said while some of Vander Zalm's activities "might be considered foolish, ill-advised, and in apparent or real conflict of interest," his ethical lapses fell short of criminal wrongdoing.

2. THE NIGHT OF THE DANCING PENIS: Strange things happen at the B.C. legislature when MLAs gather for late-night sittings. Such was the case on a Wednesday night at the rockpile in July 1997. Inside the chamber, a boring debate unfurled on the Ministry of Forestry estimates. But outside the chamber, in the nearby MLA lounge, a group of female legislators and women staffers—led by the NDP's Joy MacPhail—started partying.

As the alcohol flowed, NDP Children and Families Minister Penny Priddy made a grand entrance into the party carrying a tray of burning candles that surrounded a covered object. With dramatic flourish, she tore away the sheet to reveal a small plastic toy penis with two little feet. The women debated who that year's recipient would be of the annual prize they'd created: "Dick of the Year."

Shortly thereafter, Liberals Bonnie McKinnon and Linda Reid snuck into the chamber, where Forests Minister David Zirnhelt was debating his budget with Liberal critic Ted Nebbeling. As the Hansard cameras rolled, McKinnon plopped the wound-up penis on Nebbeling's desk. Reid delivered a quick curtsey to the camera. Both women fled, giggling.

"I don't know what's going on around me, but I have been surrounded by women who want to do something," Nebbeling said in a line forever recorded in the legislature's records. The little toy penis promptly began bouncing in front of the minister on its little toy legs.

"They were giggling a bit and I knew something was up, but then I saw this dancing penis on my desk—it stunned me for a moment," Nebbeling later recalled to reporters. The prank was at first greeted with much laughter by politicos. But, as the days unfolded, many began to question whether the women were picking on Nebbeling, who was openly gay. Then, there was considerable debate over whether the prank was sexist. Eventually, the women involved apologized, which Nebbeling accepted.

As for the toy penis? "I don't know where it is," said Nebbeling. "I assume Joy MacPhail and Penny Priddy are digging a deep, dark hole in the forest somewhere to bury it and it won't ever be found."

The entire affair gave new meaning to the phrase "women's caucus." And it sparked this excellent letter to the editor in *The Province* newspaper, written as a poem:

Those legislative ladies of quaint Victoria
Led a lewd gathering full of euphoria
They pulled a mischievous prank
With a plastic bouncing frank
Now they're subpoenaed to political Siberia

Members of the Legislative Assembly take part in the last sitting of the legislature in the old B.C. Parliament buildings.

3. THROWN FROM THE CHAMBER: Former premier Dave Barrett is best remembered as the father of some of British Columbia's most recognizable institutions—the Agricultural Land Reserve, the Insurance Corporation of B.C. and the Labour Relations Board, among others. But after Barrett was defeated by Social Credit leader Bill Bennett in the snap election of 1975, he would quickly earn another place in the history: The first MLA ever physically dragged out of the legislative chamber.

It came early in the morning of October 6, 1983. The legislature was debating Bennett's controversial austerity measures that targeted the civil service, union and labour rights. Taking a page from his father's book (former premier W.A.C. Bennett) the younger Bennett resurrected the practice of "legislation by exhaustion" through all-night sittings designed to break the spirit of the opposition.

But Barrett would not be broken. At around 4 a.m., he began picking a fight with Social Credit MLA John Parks, who was sitting in the chair as deputy Speaker. The two duked it out verbally over procedural matters relating to why Parks had declared a motion to adjourn the house out of order. Parks grew frustrated at Barrett's deliberate provocation and eventually ordered Barrett to leave the chamber, which Barrett refused to do.

Video cameras had yet to be installed in the chamber, but the incident appears in the text of Hansard thusly:

> DEPUTY SPEAKER: Hon. member, I reluctantly direct the Sergeant-at-Arms to remove you from this chamber.

(Interjections.)
DEPUTY SPEAKER: Sergeant-at-Arms, remove the hon. Leader of the Opposition from this chamber.
[Interruption.]

That "interruption" was Parks conscripting three members of the sergeant-at-arms staff to eject Barrett from the chamber. Normally, these security officers spent their days filling glasses of water, checking hallway passes and attempting to stay awake while monitoring the proceedings. Now, faced with ejecting an uncooperative former premier, they first tried to lift his chair, with him in it, in an attempt to carry him out of the room. It failed when the chair tipped over and Barrett fell to the red-carpeted floor of the house. He then crossed his arms and lay there. The staffers, now thoroughly perplexed, took the only course of action left: they grabbed his limp frame and dragged him across the carpet before hurling him out of the side doors of the chamber and into the corridor.

This would have been one of the great photographic moments of B.C. history, were it not for Speaker Walter Davidson, who was already standing in the hallway and threatened to revoke the press pass of any journalist who filmed the scene. Shamefully, none defied him. And so, the moment was lost to time.

4. A BAN ON SEX: The MLA who tried to ban sex has become, over the years, one of the more colourful stories of legislature lore. Sex isn't usually a topic up for debate in the B.C. legislature. But in the afternoon of February 19, 1970, backbench Social Credit MLA Agnes Kripps plunged the legislature into a discussion about reforming the way sex education was taught in classrooms with her idea for the government to forbid "that nasty little three-letter word, sex, which carries with it a stigma and a distorted connotation."

"I hate the word sex, and I propose that we throw it out of the vocabulary of education," she told the house. "Let's find a substitute and start all over again."

Kripps suggested BOLT, which she said stood for "Biology on Life Today." "Let's call it the word BOLT," she said. "Then we can tackle the problem afresh so that when we talk about BOLT education in schools we're not going to become involved in moral or religious aspects of its meaning."

The mostly-male legislature hooted and hollered during her speech. "On behalf of all of us I would certainly welcome you, Mr. Speaker, to our BOLT new world," Socred MLA Herb Capozzi said after Kripps finished her address. "And I will certainly say, that if nothing else, she had everyone BOLT upright in their chairs."

Kripps only served one term in the legislature, from 1969-72. But what a term. She sat on the legislative committee charged with reviewing B.C.'s film classification system. MLAs decided they were obliged to view the softcore porn film *The Stewardesses* before it was allowed in B.C. The 3D film had already drawn fines for obscenity in Saskatchewan.

The special MLA screening, covered by the *Vancouver Sun*, was recounted by veteran political columnist Vaughn Palmer: "Some of those in attendance squirmed in silence. Others walked out. Kripps heckled. 'Disgusting,' she groused during the first sex scene. Then as one of the female characters began to disrobe for a repeat performance, Kripps fretted, 'Oh dear, hasn't she finished yet?' When a subsequent scene depicted an attempt at sexual congress with a lamp (who could make this up?) Kripps was heard to say: 'Oh, why doesn't it just blow a fuse.'"

The committee also watched *A Clockwork Orange*, during a session that journalist Iain Hunter later recounted: "The groans from Kripps revealed her pain. 'Oh no, not again,' she exclaimed in the darkness, then: 'What's he doing now?' and 'What's he going to do with that?'"

Kripps was often referenced in the house, long after her departure. In 1987, 15 years after leaving politics, she visited the legislature and was introduced by MLA Bob Williams. "I'd like to welcome Agnes Kripps, the former member of the legislature from Vancouver South, who has arrived here like a BOLT out of the blue this morning," deadpanned Williams.

Kripps remained active in the Social Credit Party until the 1990s. Though she also helped push for anti-smoking rules and the creation of B.C. Day, the headline in the newspaper when Kripps passed away in 2014 captured her succinctly: "The BOLT lady left a memorable legacy."

5. STEALING FROM CHARITIES: In the long history of dastardly deeds done by politicians, perhaps none is as dastardly as the scheme cooked up by NDP MP and MLA Dave Stupich to steal money from charities that were supposed to help children and the disabled. "Bingogate," as it has come to be known, was a long and convoluted scam perpetrated over decades. It involved the Nanaimo Commonwealth Holding Society, an organization set up by the BC NDP in the 1950s and run by Stupich, as well as a series of related registered charities that together raised about $18 million over the years through licensed "charity" bingo games.

The money was supposed to go to legitimate charities like the Boys and Girls Club, local food banks, and the Handicapped Workshop Society. Instead, Stupich helped cheat those charities out of more than $1.5 million, funnelling the money to himself and the BC New Democratic Party, and using it to repay loans due after the society invested in several failed Nanaimo building projects. As much as $2.9 million was stolen, defrauded or misdirected by the society.

Stupich kept meticulous notes, but the crime was so complicated forensic auditors were never entirely sure where all the money went once it hit his maze of accounts and societies. The audacity of the fraud was compounded by Stupich's status as an NDP heavyweight, one of the party's elder statesmen and a former party president. He was a former agriculture minister (father of the Agricultural Land Reserve) and briefly a finance minister under NDP premier Dave Barrett's government in the 70s. He served 22 years in the legislature and went on to be Nanaimo's MP.

The son of a coal miner, with humble beginnings, Stupich soon found himself rich from politics and Bingogate. He personally took at least $1 million from the society. His $650,000 Gabriola Island home had a $75,000 swimming pool and spectacular ocean view.

The jig was up in 1992 when whistleblower Jacques Carpentier, head of the Nanaimo Commonwealth Bingo Association, went public with his concerns about Stupich's society. The resulting scandal was immense. Then-premier Mike Harcourt resigned in 1996—not because he was personally implicated, but in an attempt to save the NDP from the public backlash.

It didn't work. Several societies run by the NDP were convicted of fraud and the publishing arm of the NDP was fined for operating an illegal lottery scheme. New premier Glen Clark started a public inquiry before the 1996 election. It would go on to reveal damning new information, including how the NDP secretly channelled donations to the society from corporations and people. And it raised questions about whether officials in both NDP and Social Credit governments knew of the wrongdoing but failed to act.

The RCMP laid 64 charges against Stupich in 1998, but they were eventually rolled into two fraud charges that Stupich pleaded guilty to in 1999. Then 77, and suffering dementia, Stupich was sentenced to two years of house arrest—not in his lavish Gabriola residence but at his daughter's modest Nanaimo home. "He approaches the latter stages of his life a broken and disgraced man," the judge said at Stupich's sentencing.

The full Bingogate story was never truly known. When the BC Liberals took power in 2001 they cancelled the public inquiry just before it was set to release its final report, citing the wasted cost of continuing the investigation. Stupich died in 2006.

6. THE CITIZEN REVOLT OVER THE HARMONIZED SALES TAX: An arrogant premier. A surprise new tax that raised prices on common goods. And a recall law that was designed to never actually work. Combine all these elements and you get the most remarkable citizen uprising in B.C. political history.

Premier Gordon Campbell was riding high after the 2009 election, when British Columbians voted his Liberal party back into office for a third term. Despite the worldwide recession, Campbell had promised voters mid-campaign that B.C. would run a relatively small deficit. "The deficit will be $495 million, maximum," he declared.

But he knew it wasn't true. The recession had blown a $1.5-billion hole in his revenue forecasts. To salvage his reputation, Campbell quickly signed a new deal with Ottawa to get $1.6 billion by merging the GST with the PST into a new 12 per cent HST. Voters were outraged, not just because the tax came 10 weeks after an election in which it was barely mentioned, and then only as something not on the radar screen, but also because it applied to items that had been previously exempt from provincial tax, raising the cost of things like school supplies, cable television and restaurant meals.

Disgraced former Social Credit premier Bill Vander Zalm seized the opportunity to rehabilitate his reputation following his resignation two decades earlier. He became the new anti-HST crusader, whipping the public into a frenzy with his trademark rhetorical flourish.

He and NDP activist Bill Tieleman turned to B.C.'s Recall and Initiative Act. If they could gather signatures from 10 per cent of registered voters in each of B.C.'s 85 ridings within 90 days, they could force government to debate changing or scraping the tax. The recall law was the only one of its kind in Canada and it was widely considered to have such high thresholds as to be functionally designed to fail. Yet Vander Zalm's populist touch and Tieleman's organizational know-how accomplished the seemingly impossible in 2010. They needed 299,611 signatures. They got 557,383.

The overwhelming success, and public anger, set in motion Campbell's resignation as premier. In a resulting referendum, voters killed the HST. It remains the only successful initiative petition, and one of the most hated, bungled tax measures in B.C.'s history.

7. CHRISTY CLARK'S NON-CONFIDENCE VOTE: Sixteen years of Liberal rule came to an end with a simple vote in the B.C. legislature. A motion by NDP Leader John Horgan that said "the present government does not have the confidence of this House," passed 44-42 on June 29, 2017, with all NDP and Green members of the legislature voting in favour, and all Liberals voting against.

But the reaction was delayed. The decorum of the house still needed protecting. For a few moments the NDP and Green MLAs, along with supporters who packed the chamber, remained quiet. Then as speaker Steve Thomson dissolved the legislature and Clark left her chair as premier for the last time, the chamber erupted in cheers. The thundered applause, desk banging and in some cases foot stomping reverberated through the legislature, shaking the walls. The Liberal collapse had been months in the making, first after the province's closest election ever in May 2017, and then after a confidence and supply agreement signed between the Greens and the NDP opened the door for Horgan to become premier.

But Clark's day wasn't done. She left the legislature to the applause of her staff and caucus colleagues. With a news helicopter hovering overhead, Clark drove from the legislature to Government House, her every move tracked by television viewers. Once inside Government House it became quickly apparent to Clark that she wasn't going to get what she wanted from then-lieutenant governor Judith Guichon: a new election. Still, she spent an hour with Guichon trying to convince her to send voters back to the polls. Clark eventually gave up and left, still hopeful she might get her election.

Guichon, however, had received advice that the correct course of action was to ask Horgan to govern, with the support of the Greens. And so before the day was done, Horgan was asked to become the province's 36th premier. It was a history-making day—the first time in 65 years that a B.C. government had been defeated on a confidence vote and the first time in 134 years that an opposition party had replaced the government following such a vote, without a new election.

8. THE HOME RENOS THAT DEMOLISHED A PREMIER: A leaky roof, a casino licence and a new sundeck so poorly built it had to be torn down—this was all enough to force NDP Premier Glen Clark to resign in one of B.C.'s oddest political scandals.

It started with water dripping out of a pot light in the kitchen of Clark's East Vancouver home in 1997. A neighbour, Dimitrios Pilarinos, offered to fix it and to expand the master bedroom in the premier's house. At one point, Pilarinos ripped up a cheque for $5,000 and said all that Clark owed was $3,200. Pilarinos also built Clark a new sundeck at his summer cottage in Penticton in 1998— a job so thoroughly botched it had to be rebuilt after failing to pass a building code inspection.

But Pilarinos wasn't an ordinary handyman and neighbour. He happened to have a lucrative casino application up for government consideration in Burnaby. According to court testimony, he began bragging to his friends of his connections and insider influence and that he had "pull" with a "big shark" to get the casino licence approved.

Then-gaming minister Mike Farnworth approved the licence at Clark's urging, but the process was later deemed to have been fair. Adrian Dix, Clark's principal secretary, was forced to resign after admitting to backdating a memo in an attempt to insulate Clark from questions about the casino licence. Some of Dix's termination papers were signed by then-staffer John Horgan. The names are notable because 20 years later, Horgan would become premier, with Dix and Farnworth as two of his top cabinet ministers.

Eventually, a whistleblower took a memo to then-opposition Liberal leader Gordon Campbell. Police raided Clark's home on March 2, 1999. A Global TV (then BCTV) cameraman spotted an undercover police car and set up to catch Clark's wife Dale answering the door for the waiting RCMP officers.

The police investigation sparked an enormous public uproar and backlash against the NDP government. After he resigned, Clark was charged with breach of trust and defrauding the government for accepting an improper benefit of $1,800 worth of free labour from Pilarinos on the home renovation. He said he didn't know about the free labour, and had nothing to do with approving the casino licence.

Clark was cleared of any criminal wrongdoing in 2002—though the judge noted the former premier had exercised poor judgment. But he was found guilty of conflict of interest by conflict commissioner H.A.D. Oliver—a conclusion Clark complained was "manifestly unfair." Pilarinos was convicted on six of nine counts as part of a conspiracy to try to influence government decision-making on the casino licence.

9. DRUNK CAMPBELL: To Maui police, the rented silver Honda CR-V speeding down the highway on January 10, 2003 was just another drunk driver. The SUV was travelling 70 miles per hour in a 45 mph zone, veering over the centre line and cutting through bike lanes. The police officers arrested the 54-year-old driver, who had bloodshot eyes and slurred speech, failed to walk a straight line in the roadside sobriety test, had to grip the SUV with one hand just to keep from falling over, and recorded a blood alcohol level of 0.161—more than double the legal limit.

It wasn't until the man's mugshot hit the news wires that police realized they had an international incident on their hands. The drunk driver was British Columbia Premier Gordon Campbell.

One picture showed the bespectacled premier smiling into the camera. The second a more serious looking Campbell holding a placard reading the date. Unlike B.C., where drunk driving is a criminal offence, Hawaii prosecutes drunk driving as a misdemeanour. The premier was fined $913 USD, underwent a substance abuse program and lost driving privileges for 90 days.

Campbell's more immediate problems were back home in the province he led, where opponents called on him to resign. But Campbell refused. Instead, he apologized in a nationally-televised press conference and promised to stop drinking. His tearful address saw his popularity actually increase in the polls. He attended Alcoholics Anonymous, and met privately with Mothers Against Drunk Driving, embarking on a long road to forgiveness. For some, it would have been a career-killer. But Campbell survived. Voters, in fact, re-elected him two more times. He'd go on to serve nearly eight more years as premier.

10. BUD SMITH'S CAR PHONE: Back when cellphones were the size of shoe boxes, and car phones were an extraordinary luxury, a bizarre B.C. politics scandal played out involving the mobile devices of Social Credit Attorney General Bud Smith.

It was 1990, and Victoria radio reporter Brian Graves was routinely scanning the airwaves with his radio scanner looking for stories when he started to pick up telephone conversations. It didn't take long for him to realize he'd inadvertently tapped into the car phone of the attorney general. Graves began recording the calls.

In one call, Smith discussed ways to discredit a lawyer who was investigating his former cabinet colleague, Bill Reid. Reid stood accused of inappropriately awarding lottery grants to a project run by a family friend and a former campaign manager. Smith's ministry had declined to prosecute Reid. But the NDP had hired its own lawyer to attempt a private prosecution of Reid—and Smith was now looking for ways to smear that investigation.

In another, Smith spoke with CKVU-TV reporter Margot Sinclair about planting stories to discredit the lawyer, as well as handle the media on the case. The two bantered about late-night meetings for wine.

Graves leaked the tapes to *The Canadian Press* legislative reporter Debi Pelletier. But her stories never made it to print after CP lawyers vetoed them because the conversations were illegally recorded.

Then things got even wackier. NDP justice critic Moe Sihota picked up copies of the tapes left in Pelletier's office. She denied leaving the package for him and claimed she was simply acting in an intermediary role. Sihota took maximum advantage of the legal protection afforded MLAs when they speak in the house, and tabled the phone calls and transcripts. In a bombshell private member's point, he alleged Smith was in contempt of parliament.

The scandal exploded. Speaker Stephen Rogers struggled to get order in the house. Smith was forced to resign.

But the situation continued to spiral into absurd new directions. A second tape was leaked to the media. *Vancouver Sun* legislative bureau chief Keith Baldrey got a call to look for a package underneath a car in a nearby government parking lot. The Social Credit government, stung by the recordings, ordered its offices be swept for secret recording devices.

CKNW reporter Kim Emerson tried to out Graves as the leaker, attempting to interview his former radio colleague wearing a hidden microphone while a BCTV cameraman hid in the bushes nearby, camouflaged for an ambush. The credibility of the legislative press gallery took such a beating that news outlets began flying in replacement reporters to cover the story.

Sinclair, caught on tape talking to Smith, resigned from CKVU. Pelletier, whose employer had failed to publish one of the biggest B.C. scandals in years, was transferred to Vancouver. Sihota faced criticism he was unethical in making the tapes public. "One guy tried to give money to his friend. I didn't do that; I just blew the whistle on it," he told reporters at the time. "Another guy tried to tamper with the administration of justice. I didn't do that; I blew the whistle on that. And now they are trying to say the guy who blew the whistle blew it a little bit too loud and let's charge him with disturbing the peace."

In the end, no one was charged with any crime. However, ombudsperson Stephen Owen recommended government hire special prosecutors to handle future accusations of criminal wrongdoing against politicians. The recommendation gave rise to B.C.'s modern day special prosecutor system, where attorneys general and politicians are cut out of the process of administering justice.

THE HIGHLY SUSPICIOUS OR DOWNRIGHT ILLEGAL ACTIVITIES OF 8 B.C. POLITICIANS

1. THE ILL-GOTTEN RUG: It was a not-so-proud distinction for British Columbia: the first cabinet minister in the entire British Commonwealth to be sent to prison for accepting bribes related to his office. Robert Sommers was minister of forests in W.A.C. Bennett's Social Credit government of the 1950s when the opposition began asking questions about a forest management licence that had been awarded to a company called B.C. Forest Products. As it turned out, Sommers was a drinker and a gambler, with all the money problems that tend to accompany both vices, and something fishy was indeed going on with that licence.

According to reports in the *Vancouver Sun*, Sommers had accepted bribes including a $607 rug, $1,300 in travel expenses, and $7,000 in cash and savings bonds in return for granting the licence. Sommers was convicted in 1958 of conspiracy and accepting bribes, and sentenced to five years behind bars. After his release, he started up a new career in tuning pianos—a skill he'd learned in prison.

2. THE EX-CONVICT: Unlike the other rascals and alleged scoundrels on this list, Frank Howard's criminal history preceded his time in office, when by all accounts he played it strictly by the books. His early life was another matter altogether. As the story goes, Howard was the son of a sex worker and her pimp, and a troublemaker from the very beginning. At age 12, he was sent from his foster home in Kimberley to an orphanage in Vancouver after he was caught stealing a butterscotch pie from the Sullivan Hotel, according to an obituary in *The Globe and Mail*. As an adult, he spent a month in the summer of 1943 trying out a career as a stickup man before he was sent to prison for armed robbery.

Somehow, this shady past didn't shut him out of politics. After his release, Howard worked his way up as a union organizer, and eventually won a seat in the legislature in 1953 as a

Co-operative Commonwealth Federation MLA for Skeena. From there, he moved on to federal politics, spending 17 years as an MP with the CCF and then the NDP. Though he lost his seat in 1974, he returned to provincial politics five years later, spending another seven years in the legislature.

3. THE JEWELRY HEIST: What a fall from grace. Svend Robinson was the first member of Parliament to come out as gay while in office, acted as a leader in the push for physician-assisted death in the 1990s, and successfully sponsored legislation to include sexual orientation in federal hate crimes law. The NDP stalwart represented his Burnaby constituents for 25 years before things fell apart spectacularly in 2004.

In a tearful press conference, Robinson admitted he'd stolen a pricey ring at an auction. He said he'd been dealing with severe stress and "something just snapped in this moment of total, utter irrationality." A local jeweller told *The Canadian Press* he helped Robinson design a diamond ring for his partner Max Riveron two days after the theft.

Robinson later pleaded guilty to theft, receiving a conditional discharge that required him to receive psychiatric counselling and do 100 hours of community service. He attempted a political comeback in the 2006 election, running in Vancouver Centre, but lost handily to Liberal incumbent Hedy Fry. Thirteen years later, Robinson announced he was trying yet again, gunning this time for the Burnaby North seat in the 2019 polls.

4. THE JAILBIRD MAYOR: Scott Young had a rocky seven years in office as mayor of Port Coquitlam, but by any measure, those years were much worse for his ex-girlfriend. Young was arrested twice in 2007 because of his unwanted contact with her—first for allegedly harassing her, and then for breaking into her garage and beating her and a friend. He was charged with seven criminal counts and eventually pleaded guilty to two charges of assault.

It wasn't the first time the mayor had gotten into trouble for his treatment of the women in his life. In 2002, early in his career as mayor, Young was charged with assault against his then-wife. That charge was stayed when he agreed to a peace bond.

None of this was enough for Young to give up the mayor's seat, however. Even after he was convicted of assault in the 2007 break-in and forced to abide by an 8 p.m. curfew, he ignored voters' calls to step down. He even tried to run for council again in 2008, but was handily defeated.

5. THE GOLDEN WHISTLE: To be clear, what Prince George city councillor Brian Skakun did wasn't criminal. In fact, many called it heroic. In 2008, Skakun leaked a confidential report about the local RCMP detachment to CBC, revealing allegations that a manager at the Prince George detachment was harassing city employees. The move earned him a Golden Whistle Award from a national non-profit group, but the courts saw things in a very different light. Skakun was convicted in 2011 of violating the Freedom of Information and Protection of Privacy Act and fined $750, a decision that was upheld three years later by the B.C. Court of Appeal. "I always maintain I did the right thing, but I did it the wrong way," Skakun later told *The Prince George Citizen.*

6. SOUR GRAPES: Flamboyant former premier Bill Vander Zalm might have narrowly escaped a criminal conviction in the shady sale of Fantasy Gardens, his biblical theme park, but his 1992 acquittal didn't exactly leave him a chastened or more humble man. Twenty years later, fresh off his unexpected victory in the battle against the Harmonized Sales Tax, Vander Zalm found himself back in court. Once again, he was in the role of defendant, and once again the topic at hand was Fantasy Gardens. This time, it was a defamation suit brought against Vander Zalm by the well-respected former conflict of interest commissioner Ted Hughes.

Way back when, Hughes had found Vander Zalm had a conflict of interest when he sold his Richmond amusement park to Taiwanese billionaire Tan Yu. That essentially ended the Zalm's political career, and the former premier was still smarting by the time he released his self-published autobiography in 2008. The book accused Hughes of being biased, and suggested he'd produced his negative report on Vander Zalm to curry favour with the NDP in anticipation of their imminent election. A jury found those allegations to be libellous and ordered Vander Zalm to pay Hughes $60,000 in damages—legal costs would add another $40,000 to the bill.

7. THE PIPELINE PROTESTERS: It's not often you see the leader of a federal political party being taken into custody by the RCMP. But if it was going to happen to anyone, it's no surprise it was Green Party Leader Elizabeth May. In the spring of 2018, the Vancouver Island politician joined protesters outside Kinder Morgan's Burnaby Mountain facility to voice her objection to the planned Trans Mountain pipeline expansion project. That demonstration violated a court injunction barring activists from the worksite, and May was arrested.

NDP MP Kennedy Stewart—just months away from being voted mayor of Vancouver—was arrested the same day. But the two federal leaders received only fines after they pleaded guilty to criminal contempt, which was nothing compared to the fate of Jean Swanson. The activist, who would also be voted onto Vancouver city council later that year, spent four days in jail for her role in the protest.

8. 29 CRIMINAL CHARGES: This is by far the most disturbing entry on this list. When Luke Strimbold was elected mayor of Burns Lake at age 21, he was the youngest person in B.C. history to hold the top spot on a municipal council. Five years later, he resigned, saying he wanted to focus on his studies and spend more time with family.

But in 2018, it was revealed that a handful of boys and young men had gone to police to report they'd been sexually abused by the young mayor while they were under the age of 16. Strimbold would eventually be charged with 29 sex-related crimes involving six alleged victims. Some of the alleged offences took place while Strimbold was in office, and according to the prosecution, the alleged abuse often took place after alcohol had been consumed, while the boys were asleep. Strimbold pleaded guilty to four counts of sexual assault in May 2019.

LEGISLATURE LINCHPINS: B.C.'S 5 LONGEST SERVING PREMIERS

1. W.A.C. BENNETT: (20 years and 45 days; August 1, 1952 - September 15, 1972)
As it turns out, W.A.C. isn't actually an abbreviation for "Wacky." British Columbians may forever remember Bennett by that nickname, but his parents called him William Andrew Cecil. It's true, Bennett's plans were sometimes a bit out there and he *did* have ambitions of annexing the Yukon Territory, but he also won seven straight elections for the Social Credit Party against what he called the "godless socialists" on the left. He acted as his own finance minister for almost his entire term as premier, and brought us BC Ferries and BC Hydro. As the journalist Peter Murray said, Bennett may truly have been "Wacky like a fox."

2. RICHARD MCBRIDE: (12 years and 197 days; June 1, 1903 - December 15, 1915)
That's *Sir* Richard McBride, if you please—the first B.C.-born premier in the province's history, and the leader who brought us UBC. Before he seized power in 1903, the B.C. legislature had traditionally been non-partisan, but McBride thought that was silly, and after his election as premier, he announced that he would run the province as a Conservative.

Though his longevity suggests a certain political savvy, geography might not have been his strong suit. On the first day of the First World War, McBride's government bought two submarines to protect B.C. from the Germans. The federal government confiscated them within two days.

3. BILL BENNETT: (10 years and 227 days; December 22, 1975 - August 6, 1986)
The Bennetts are something like B.C.'s Trudeaus. Bill Bennett took over the Social Credit leadership from his dad, W.A.C., in 1973 and was elected premier two years later—successfully blocking the NDP from power for 16 years. He oversaw some of the events and landmark projects that ushered British Columbia into modern times, including Expo 86 and the construction of the SkyTrain and Coquihalla Highway. At the same time, he cut thousands of jobs from the public service, doubled ferry fares and bumped up the PST by 40 per cent. Even so, when he retired from politics in 1986, he remained undefeated at the polls.

4. GORDON CAMPBELL: (9 years and 282 days; June 5, 2001 - March 14, 2011)
There aren't a heck of a lot of politicians who can hold onto power after their mug shots show up in the newspaper, but Gordon Campbell did it. Less than two years into his first term as premier, the BC Liberal leader was jailed for drunk driving in Maui, and yet somehow he survived the scandal and won two more elections for the party.

In the end, it was a sales tax that brought Campbell down. The controversy wasn't about the Harmonized Sales Tax, exactly, but about the way the Liberals introduced it, as any HST opponent will tell you. Why would Campbell's government say the tax wasn't on the radar before the 2009 election when their emails suggested they'd been talking about it for months? The uproar was so loud that Campbell resigned in a televised address, saying it was in the "best interests" of B.C.

5. JOHN OLIVER: (9 years and 164 days; March 6, 1918 - August 17, 1927)
"Honest John" Oliver was a bit of a rough sort. He was a farmer before he was a politician, and he continued to dress like one even after he was elected to the legislature. One newspaper column described him as "a good farmer and a weak politician, given to long-winded and very ungrammatical attacks upon anyone who does not agree with him." Oliver became premier after his predecessor died in office, and continued to wear his folksy tweed and heavy boots in the ledge. He oversaw the end of Prohibition after a provincial referendum, bringing in a government-controlled system for selling booze that has frustrated British Columbians for almost a century. In the end, it was cancer that put a stop to Oliver's political career. He died in office after his caucus refused to accept his resignation.

THE SEAT-WARMERS: B.C.'S 5 SHORTEST SERVING PREMIERS

1. JOSEPH MARTIN: (106 days; February 28, 1900 - June 15, 1900)
"Fighting Joe" sure got around. He sat in not one but four legislatures during his feisty political career, holding seats in Manitoba, Canada, B.C., and Britain. His very short stint in the B.C. ledge began after he'd already made his fortune in that timeless Vancouver trade, property development.

Martin was elected as an MLA in 1898 and spent two uneven years as attorney general, introducing legislation in favour of an eight-hour workday (good) and preventing Chinese people from owning mining claims (bad). In the end, "Fighting Joe" turned against Premier Charles Semlin and then took his place after a non-confidence vote. The Martin government lasted for just three months before he and most of his supporters were soundly defeated in the election of 1900.

2. DAN MILLER: (183 days; August 25, 1999 - February 24, 2000)
Miller was always something of a reluctant premier, and if you don't remember him, it's probably because his time in office was pretty unremarkable. He took over leadership of the NDP

after Glen Clark resigned in the face of a criminal investigation over whether he'd helped his neighbour and handyman get a casino licence. From the beginning, Miller said he had no intention of remaining as party leader or premier, and he only stayed in power long enough for Ujjal Dosanjh to be voted in at a convention as his replacement.

3. EDWARD GAWLER PRIOR: (192 days; November 21, 1902 - June 1, 1903)
Now this guy was a bit more interesting. Prior was the leader of B.C.'s last ever non-partisan government, though it didn't last very long at all. He'd barely made it half a year before he was accused of a pretty blatant conflict of interest for awarding a major government contract to his own hardware business. The lieutenant governor fired him—he was the last premier that's ever happened to. And yet somehow Prior would later be appointed as lieutenant governor. He died within a year of assuming that role.

4. RITA JOHNSTON: (217 days; Apr. 2, 1991 - November 5, 1991)
It's true—for a few brief seasons, a woman who wasn't Christy Clark was in charge of B.C. Johnston broke the legislature's glass ceiling in 1991, another beneficiary of a major scandal involving her predecessor. She took on the premiership after that rascally Bill Vander Zalm resigned because of a damning report on his conflicts of interest, and became the first female premier in the country. Johnson was selected as leader of the Social Credit Party amid promises to fight violence against women, children and seniors. But she didn't get much of a chance to fulfill that promise; her badly wounded party was defeated in an election later that year.

5. ROBERT BEAVEN: (230 days; June 13, 1882 - January 29, 1883)
Beaven was born an Englishman, but spent a whopping 23 years as an MLA for Victoria, beginning in 1871—the year B.C. joined Canada. His brief time as premier is probably best remembered for his bold but not necessarily well-planned attempt to declare independence for Vancouver Island. Just before his minority government was defeated in a vote of non-confidence, Beaven hosted the Marquess of Lorne and his wife, Princess Louise. As the royal pair was leaving Victoria, Beavan proposed that the princess become queen of Vancouver Island. As you may have already guessed, she said no.

5 FACTS ABOUT B.C.'S FIRST PREMIER, JOHN FOSTER McCREIGHT

1. HE WAS AN IRISH LAWYER: McCreight was born the son of a Protestant clergyman in the village of Caledon, in what is now Northern Ireland, in 1827. He studied law at King's Inns in Dublin before sailing to Australia, where he practised for years before deciding, for reasons unclear, to switch colonies.

2. HE WAS (POSSIBLY) EMBROILED IN A SEX SCANDAL: There has been speculation it was an extramarital affair that drove McCreight to ditch Australia for pre-Confederation British Columbia. And since you can't defame a dead person, let's just say the rumours were 100-per-cent true, and *even more scandalous than you can imagine.*

3. HE WAS A FREEMASON: Like many famous Canadian politicians—including Sir John A. MacDonald and John G. Diefenbaker—McCreight enjoyed the privileges and connections of membership in the Freemasons. (So did Tim Horton, though that really has very little to do with British Columbia.)

4. HIS TEMPERAMENT MADE HIM AN ODD CHOICE OF LEADER: McCreight's moods, according to B.C.'s first attorney general, Sir Henry Crease, fluctuated between "extremely credulous," "extremely suspicious," and "excessively obstinate." While those traits might remind the reader of a few modern politicians, most would agree they're hardly premier material.

5. HE LOST THE CONFIDENCE OF THE LEGISLATURE: Following a speech from the throne, mere days into the second session of the B.C. legislature, McCreight lost a confidence vote and resigned. Given his glowing personality, it was presumably a surprise to no one. McCreight's defeat paved the way for one of the most intriguing politicians in B.C. history, Amor de Cosmos.

10 MUCH MORE INTERESTING FACTS ABOUT B.C.'S SECOND PREMIER, AMOR DE COSMOS

British Columbia's well-earned reputation for wacky politics goes back a lot further than Bill Vander Zalm. Case in point: Amor De Cosmos, who was premier for one year, one month and 17 days until an angry mob ran him out of the legislature in 1874.

There's an unfortunate dearth of information about De Cosmos's personal life, but the public records that are available paint quite an odd picture. He was intellectually curious, but also terrified of electricity. He fought for B.C. to join Confederation, but threatened to secede just a few years later. He opposed efforts to force Christianity on Indigenous populations, but was also despicably racist.

Here are some of the ways he lived up to his unique name.

1. HE CHOSE AMOR DE COSMOS: Believe it or not, B.C.'s second premier was not born Amor De Cosmos. (Suffice to say, that would have made his parents some of the hippest people in their hometown of Windsor, Nova Scotia, when he was born back in 1825.) Instead, he entered the world as William Alexander Smith, a name that was both perfectly respectable and completely unsuited to the kind of eccentric he was destined to become.

William Alexander Smith changed his name to Amor De Cosmos before becoming B.C.'s second premier.

Explaining his decision to adopt Amor De Cosmos—a mix of Latin, French and Greek words that he initially spelled with an epsilon—he said it represented the things he loved most: "order, beauty, the world, the universe."

He was living in California at the time, and local newspapers, perhaps understandably, had some difficulty with the spelling. One particularly egregious misprint dubbed him "Amos de Bosmos."

2. HE HAD RUMOURED RUN-INS WITH MORMONS IN SALT LAKE CITY: William Smith travelled to California to join the Gold Rush, and along the way he came across the Mormons of Utah. He was intrigued by the upstart religion, and spent months learning more about their ways in Salt Lake City. Unfortunately, this stop sparked a few strange rumours that would dog him for years, and which earned him the nickname "Mormon Bill."

According to Gordon Hawkins' book *The De Cosmos Enigma*, one such rumour is that Smith was forced to flee Salt Lake City because none other than Brigham Young "tried to make him marry and settle down there." Another is that Smith made off with "precious Mormon memorabilia" before skipping town.

3. HE FOUNDED WHAT'S NOW THE TIMES COLONIST NEWSPAPER: Less than six months after leaving California for Victoria, Amor De Cosmos founded the *British Colonist* newspaper, a scrappy publication he used as a platform to push for confederacy and self-government.

From the very first issue on December 11, 1858, De Cosmos announced his intentions to shake things up loud and clear. He argued government should be run "according to the well-understood wishes of the people," and slammed the constitution of the day as "radically defective."

"We shall counsel the introduction of responsible government—a system long established in British America, by which the people will have the whole and sole control over the local affairs of the colony," De Cosmos wrote.

At least four other newspapers launched in Victoria the same year, but De Cosmos's paper managed to outlive them all. It merged with the *Victoria Daily Times* in 1980 and remains in print today as the *Times Colonist*, making it Western Canada's longest-running paper.

4. HE WAS MOODY AND WORE ALL-BLACK CLOTHES: He may have been a revolutionary thinker, but De Cosmos was not what you'd call a people person. He never married, and his personality was often described as humourless, grouchy, arrogant and impatient. (Fellow B.C. politician George Anthony Walkem once described him as having "all the eccentricities of a comet without any of its brilliance.")

De Cosmos' wardrobe matched his antisocial tendencies, and he was known to dress himself head-to-toe in black. A retrospective on his life published in *The Province* newspaper in 1921 recalled that he never "seemed to alter in appearance," even in his later years, with his hair and whiskers "kept black to the last."

5. HE HELPED B.C. JOIN CANADA, THEN THREATENED TO SEPARATE AGAIN: De Cosmos had a major hand in bringing B.C. into Confederation, through tireless public advocacy and, eventually, by helping to organize the 1868 Yale Conference that formalized the colony's demands.

His dream came true in 1871, but just eight years later, when he was an MP for Victoria, he threatened to secede from Canada. Why? De Cosmos was frustrated over the state of transcontinental railway negotiations, and, true to his reputation, was probably just being petulant.

6. HE WAS CHASED OUT OF THE LEGISLATURE : De Cosmos was appointed premier in 1872, the year after B.C. joined the rest of Canada, and his time in office was uneventful—for the most part. There was, of course, the time in early 1874 when an angry mob stormed into the legislature chanting, "We're going to hang De Cosmos on a sour apple tree," sung to the tune of "John Brown's Body."

De Cosmos had just returned from a trip to Ottawa, where he negotiated new funding for various public works projects. The deal might well have been popular, had it not required updating the Terms of Union, the document that joined B.C. to Canada and ensured the railway would reach all the way to the province.

Some of his constituents were nervous. De Cosmos tried to address their concerns at a public meeting, but it became so rowdy the reporter at his old paper, which he'd sold by that point, couldn't hear him speak over cries of "Traitor!"
The premier eventually called the shouters "hoodlums," "scum of society," and "skunks," the *Colonist* reported, which didn't exactly lower the temperature. Days later, the mob came for him at the legislature. De Cosmos was forced to hide in the Speaker's chamber, and resigned as premier shortly after.

7. HE TRIED (UNSUCCESSFULLY) TO MODERNIZE DIVORCE LAWS: During his time as a Member of Parliament, De Cosmos pushed to modernize Canada's divorce laws—an interesting pet cause for a lifelong bachelor. At the time, divorces could be granted by act of Parliament, which meant MPs were sometimes lobbied to vote yay or nay on a particular couple's relationship. De Cosmos wanted to end that practice, arguing divorces should be decided in a provincial courtroom instead of the House of Commons.

He was unsuccessful, unfortunately, and divorce remained a rare and difficult process in Canada until the late 1960s.

8. HE WAS RACIST AGAINST CHINESE IMMIGRANTS: In his later years in politics, De Cosmos wasted a lot of breath railing against Chinese workers, even pushing to have them banned from working on government projects, including the railway.

Even worse, he apparently harboured these racial resentments despite owing much of his livelihood to immigrants. A "large portion of his income" at the time came from renting out Chinatown shanties, according to *The De Cosmos Enigma*.

And though he steadfastly opposed forcing Christianity on Indigenous peoples, writing in the *Colonist* that religion should "work its way among the Indians on the voluntary principle, as it does among us," his attitudes toward Aboriginal populations weren't exactly enlightened either. He referred to them as "inferior" and "irrational."

9. HE ONCE RAN AGAINST PRIME MINISTER JOHN A. MACDONALD: Though the Conservatives won the 1878 federal election, John A. Macdonald suffered a bruising defeat in his hometown riding of Kingston, Ont., which he'd represented for more than a decade. Fortunately for him, ridings voted on different days back then, and there was still time to pick up a seat out west in Victoria.

"He sent a hurry-up call to his friends here, asking to run," according to a look-back in the *Vancouver Sun*. "Victoria was impressed. One after another, the candidates withdrew in favor of the Prime Minister."

But not everyone dropped out. Two candidates stayed in the race, including Amor De Cosmos, who was running for the Liberals. Because the riding then had two seats, both Macdonald and De Cosmos managed to secure a place in Parliament, even though Macdonald had actually never been to Victoria, and never bothered to visit at any point in his term.

10. HE WAS DECLARED INSANE AND LOCKED UP: In 1895, Amor De Cosmos tried returning to politics. Sadly, his declining mental state had rendered him unelectable. He was known to wander the streets of Victoria ranting and waving a cane, and was reportedly so afraid of electricity he wouldn't set foot in an electric streetcar.

Shortly after his failed comeback, he was declared "of unsound mind" and locked up in an institution, where he died two years later at the age of 71.

Diagnosing mental illness wasn't exactly a precise science at the time. Hawkins noted the chemicals De Cosmos would have handled for his photography, which included mercury, bromine and chlorine, could have potentially contributed to his diminished mental capacity. Whatever the case, it was an odd, sad end for an odd, fascinating man.

10 B.C. 'BOONDOGGLES' (ACCORDING TO THE VANCOUVER SUN)

Maybe you prefer the term "white elephant" or something simpler like "swindle," but "boondoggle" is the preferred nomenclature of newspaper columnists—it's shorthand for "an unnecessary, wasteful, or fraudulent project," according to the Oxford dictionary. Here are just a few illustrative examples from the pages of the *Vancouver Sun*.

1. THE FAST FERRIES FIASCO: It's practically impossible to find the words "fast ferries" in the pages of the *Sun*, or any B.C. newspaper really, without a "boondoggle" in close reach. And it's even more unlikely you'll read anything about Glen Clark's NDP government of the 1990s without a mention of the fast ferries fiasco. Columnist Vaughn Palmer wrote in 1997 that, in light of this latest NDP folly, B.C. needed a more specific term than boondoggle. "Maybe it should be 'the Glendoggle,' after the premier who is the principal author of the government's trail of broken promises and reckless spending of tax dollars."

To make a long story slightly shorter, the fast ferry scandal was a government plan to build three custom-designed high-speed vessels to run between West Vancouver and Nanaimo. The ferries cost about $450 million to build, but a raft of mechanical problems, the huge wake they created and their high fuel consumption meant they were only in operation very briefly. When they were finally sold off to the Washington Marine Group, they brought in a paltry $19 million—just four per cent of what they cost to build.

2. AIR FARCE ONE: Some called it the Flying Folly. Others, the Flying White Elephant. Whatever the nickname, the province's Challenger jet was a $7.3-million mistake. Then-premier Bill Vander Zalm and his Social Credit government bought the luxury plane in 1987 (exactly why isn't clear) but soon discovered it was virtually useless for official purposes. It was too big to land at most airports in B.C., so it couldn't be used as an air ambulance. In fact, it was so big, it couldn't fit into the government hangar until a hole was cut in the door. The Socreds tried using it as a biweekly shuttle between Victoria and Ottawa, but it was more expensive than flying commercial and few bureaucrats were interested.

"Critics said from the outset that the jet was a boondoggle," Vaughn Palmer wrote in 1990. The province put the Challenger up for auction just two years after buying it, promising the returns would be worth it. One cabinet minister estimated it would bring in $10 million. Instead, the government discovered a market saturated with Challengers, and the jet failed to sell. When it finally sold to a Germany buyer in 1992, the price was just $5.9 million.

3. THE MUSEUM THAT BLED MONEY: The B.C. Transportation Museum was "the kind of borderline project that was pushed along as a pet of the [Social Credit] party and eventually plunked down in a Socred riding. And now, sure enough, the thing isn't working out as planned," columnist Jamie Lamb wrote in 1992. The "enormous cavern-like facility" was lightly occupied by antique cars and trucks, and stranded in the farming community of Cloverdale, far from the usual routes that tourists take through Metro Vancouver.

Opened in 1987, the museum "tended to be identified with politics as least as much as it was identified with as a transportation facility," Lamb wrote. By the time the NDP closed it in 1992, it was bringing in less than $75,000 in revenue annually, while losing an estimated $1 million.

4. A BEACON OF THE FUTURE IN SURREY: The vision for TechBC was of a university where students could learn the skills they needed to enter the high-tech workforce of the future. Opened in a former Zellers store in 1999, it was meant to sprawl across 500,000 square feet in a revamped Surrey Place Mall, then a rundown complex in Whalley. The NDP government of the 1990s spent $253 million to redevelop the mall, building a new 20-storey tower that was supposed to become the headquarters for the Insurance Corporation of B.C.

But both the university and the mall failed to deliver on their promises. TechBC attracted some top talent to its faculty, but by 2001, there were just two students for every teacher. The Liberals closed the school in 2002. The same year, ICBC revealed the new tower at Surrey Place was worth just $112 million, less than half what it cost to build. ICBC never moved in, and sold off the property in 2007.

5. THE (THEORETICAL) THIRD CROSSING: Many North Shore commuters will probably read this and wish they had a time machine to travel back to 1972 just so they could slap some sense into every single member of the B.C. legislature. And, it must be said, they'd likely save a slap or two for venerable *Sun* columnist Alan Fotheringham. The federal and provincial governments, and the City of Vancouver, were all on board to build a $177 million tunnel across Burrard Inlet, easing some of the pressure on the Lions Gate and Second Narrows bridges. But Fotheringham scoffed at the idea as "certainly premature and ... probably an unnecessary political boondoggle. Some day a transit crossing may be required. But the urgency of an auto crossing has been overstated." Modern commuters would disagree.

Of course, that crossing would have been part of a freeway running through downtown Vancouver, a deeply unpopular project that would have altered the city forever. In the face of public opposition, the freeway and the crossing were never built. Instead, the new NDP government elected into power in September 1972 offered the North Shore an alternative option, the SeaBus, and promised to prioritize public transit. A worthy goal, to be sure, but governments at all levels have failed to deliver on that mass transportation infrastructure, and the daily gridlock on the bridges has only gotten exponentially worse.

6. THE NORTHERN TRAIN TO NOWHERE: "W.A.C. Bennett had a dream—an ambitious railway that would exploit the vast resource potential of the province's northwest," reporter Larry Pynn wrote in 1991. "But the dream became a living nightmare, the province's biggest, costliest and most controversial boondoggle of the 1970s." The Social Credit government of the day approved the 600-kilometre track extension north from Fort St. James to Dease Lake in 1969, hoping to open up resource-rich northwestern B.C. to the rest of the province.

Initial estimates put the price tag for building one 540-kilometre stretch of the railway at $69 million, but a 1978 Royal Commission report revealed the cost had soared to $360 million. The commission called the extension "an unplanned, reckless, astonishingly naive, in the end utterly disastrous mistake." Meanwhile, worldwide demand for the resources of the northwest, including asbestos and copper, was dropping. The province ended construction of the railway in 1977, and mothballed it in 1981.

7. PHOTO FINISHED: "Our radar detects a boondoggle," the *Sun*'s editorial board declared in a December 14, 2000 headline. Another project of the 1990s NDP, photo radar was supposed to discourage speeding. Instead, the editorial argued, it was an inefficient "cash cow." "Victoria has extracted $100 million in fines from photo radar over four years, but it has done nothing to make roads safer." As it turns out, "cash cow" might have been a generous description. One hundred million dollars in fines sounds like a lot, but that's how much the program cost to implement in the first place—not including the cost of enforcing the fines. By 1999, three years into the program, there was already a 16-month backlog of tickets.

The Liberals killed the program in 2001, but the courts would still be dealing with the leftover tickets for months and even years to come. Fifteen months after photo radar was cancelled, the province was forced to throw out 170,000 ancient photo-radar tickets, some dating back five years. They were no longer enforceable in court, but if they'd been dealt with in a timely manner, they could have brought in $22 million.

8. A MARSHMALLOW ON FALSE CREEK: "Welcome, conventioneers, to world-class Vancouver, B.C.—'B.C.' standing for Boondoggle Capital of Canada, with the most extensive herd of white elephants outside Quebec," columnist/playwright/novelist John MacLachlan Gray wrote in 1999. In his mind, BC Place led the pack. Back then, the stadium was an unmistakable marshmallow-like structure plopped down in the middle of Vancouver's rapidly modernizing skyline, completed in 1983 at a cost of $126 million to welcome visitors to Expo 86. But after that, Gray lamented, the "Big Commode" sat empty most days.

When the roof was refurbished a decade later at a cost of $563 million, the boondoggle descriptor was dragged out once again. But today, it must be said, BC Place is a slightly more happening stadium, home to the Lions football team, the Whitecaps soccer team, and more frequent concerts, festivals, and trade shows.

9. BC HYDRO'S MISADVENTURE IN PAKISTAN: Another "Glendoggle," but this one was known more specifically as "Hydrogate." In the 90s, BC Hydro decided to get into the Asian energy market, and bought shares worth 15 per cent of the Raiwind power project in Pakistan. The project blew up into scandal six months later, just before Glen Clark was sworn in as premier, when the Liberals held a press conference alleging major financial misconduct—specifically, an insider scheme for buying shares in the project. Later came allegations of bribery in Pakistan.

Clark promptly fired BC Hydro's president, John Sheehan. Chairman John Laxton resigned when it was revealed he'd secretly invested in the project through family members. The RCMP opened an investigation and a special prosecutor was assigned, but in the end, both the prosecutor and the police agreed that no charges should be laid. The utility was forced to pay Sheehan, its former president, $1 million for wrongful dismissal. To add to the losses, BC Hydro sold its stake in the project in 1999 for about $7 million less than it had originally paid.

10. CARS, IN GENERAL: To be fair, writer Alan Morley's gripe wasn't specific to B.C., but is there anywhere else in the country where you could imagine a mainstream newspaper columnist taking on the mighty automobile in 1976? "The automobile is the biggest boondoggle in the history of the industrial era," Morley wrote, throwing his support behind a proposal to raise vehicle insurance rates by 300 per cent.

He and his wife, he explained, hadn't driven or owned a car in 25 years—they couldn't afford it, and preferred to walk. And yet their taxes went toward ever-widening highways, ugly parking lots, healthcare for car crash victims and traffic police. "We are just sick and tired of making welfare payments for the benefit of car owners of all classes, from VWs to Rolls Royces."

(Opposite) Serial killer Clifford Olson leaves provincial court in Chilliwack on August 8, 1981.

CRIME

EVE LAZARUS'S LIST OF 10 BIZARRE MURDERS

Eve Lazarus is a crime historian, blogger, podcaster, and author. Her passion for history and fascination with murder has led to six books of non-fiction including the B.C. bestsellers Sensational Vancouver; Cold Case Vancouver; Blood, Sweat, and Fear; *and* Murder by Milkshake: An Astonishing True Story of Adultery, Arsenic, and a Charismatic Killer.

1. BABES IN THE WOODS: The Babes in the Woods case—the story of two young children found dead in Stanley Park—is one of Vancouver's oldest unsolved murder mysteries. While the murders likely happened in October 1947, the story starts in January 1953, when a Vancouver Park Board employee stepped on a skull in a remote area of Stanley Park. For the next half century, police searched for a missing brother and sister, and it wasn't until 1996, when DNA profiling became part of the forensics toolkit, that investigators reopened the file and found they were dealing with two brothers. The children remain unidentified.

2. VANCOUVER'S FIRST GANGLAND KILLING: On September 15, 1954, Danny Brent's body was found on the 10th green at UBC's golf course. He'd been shot once in the back and twice in the head. On the night of his murder, Danny had finished his shift at the Press Club, and headed over to the Mayling Supper Club. He was seen leaving with a woman and two men through the back door. Four days after his murder, police opened a locker and found 30 ounces of heroin with a street value of $175,000. It was quickly apparent that there was more to Danny than bartending. Either he was killed by a gang trying to take over the heroin industry or murdered by a hit team for an outstanding drug debt.

3. THE JAMES BAY MURDER: A few years after the Bests bought their home in James Bay, Victoria, a young woman knocked on the door and asked if she could come and take a look inside. She told them that her grandparents had lived in the cottage in the 1950s and she'd grown up believing they were killed in a car crash. It was only recently that she'd discovered that her grandfather Chester Pupkowski had died in a hospital for the criminally insane, more than 40 years after stabbing and bludgeoning her grandmother Cecelia to death in the Bests' kitchen in 1956, and later trying to drown himself at Holland Point.

4. VANCOUVER'S FIRST TRIPLE MURDER: David Pauls was shot three times in the head by the back door of his family's South Vancouver home. The killer went upstairs and clubbed 11-year-old Dorothy Pauls to death in her bed. When Helen Pauls returned from work, she was shot and then beaten with a blunt instrument. The Pauls were Russian Mennonites. The year was 1958. David worked as a janitor for Woodward's and Helen worked the afternoon shift at the Home Fancy Sausage Shop on East Hastings. Police investigated several theories including connections to Russia, a botched robbery, and a peeping Tom, but no evidence was found and the murders remain unsolved.

5. MOUNT PLEASANT AXE MURDER : On December 9, 1965, 17-year-old Thomas Kosberg made chocolate milkshakes for his mother, father, and four younger brothers and sisters, added some sleeping pills, waited for them to go to bed, and then hacked them to death. Only a baby survived. Tom had a history of mental illness, but no one could imagine him plotting a murder, let along killing his own family. The court ruled that he was not guilty by reason of insanity, and Thomas was shipped off to Riverview. He was released 12 years later, married and worked at Vancouver Children's Hospital for the next 30 years. He died in 2016.

6. MURDER BY MILKSHAKE: In 1965, Rene Castellani, a CKNW radio personality who was known for his crazy promotional stunts, murdered his wife Esther so he could marry Lolly, the station's 20-something receptionist. He poisoned Esther with arsenic in her food and-

Rene and Esther Castellani were married on July 16, 1946, at the Holy Rosary Cathedral in Vancouver.

milkshakes over several months, and, if not for Esther's doctor, who was determined to find out how she died, he would have gotten away with it. Castellani was charged with capital murder, but managed to avoid the death penalty when it was commuted two weeks before he was scheduled to hang. The couple had an 11-year-old daughter called Jeannine.

7. A POETIC MURDER: Noted poet Patricia Lowther, 41, died in September 1975, beaten to death in her Vancouver home. The *Vancouver Sun* published Pat's first poem when she was 10. She published her first collection of poems in 1968 and taught at the University of B.C.'s creative writing department. At the time of Pat's murder, husband Roy Lowther was a failed poet and teacher. They had four children—two were from her first marriage. Pat's body was found by a family hiking at Furry Creek, three weeks after she was reported missing. Roy was convicted of murder and died in prison. In 1980, the League of Canadian Poets established the annual Pat Lowther Memorial Award.

8. KIDNAPPED: In 1985, the kidnapping of restaurateurs Jimmy and Lily Ming from their Strathcona home shocked the city. The kidnappers demanded $700,000 in ransom, even after the Mings, parents of two small children, were strangled, dismembered, and left in garbage bags along the Squamish Highway. The family operated the Yangtse Kitchen on Robson Street. Asian gangs were blamed, but the murders were never solved.

9. THE BILLIONAIRE'S DAUGHTER: Derek James was a traffic controller at Vancouver International Airport; his wife Jean Ann was a former flight attendant with Canadian Pacific Airlines. They were close friends with Shinji Wakabayashi, an executive with Japan Airlines, and his wife Gladys Wakabayashi, the third child of Taiwanese billionaire Y.S. Miao. The Jameses split up in 1990. Jean suspected that Derek was sleeping with the much younger Gladys. On June 24, 1992, Jane went to the Wakabayashis' Shaughnessy home and slit Gladys's throat with a box cutter. Police suspected Jean, but there was no forensic evidence linking her to the murder. It took another 16 years and a Mr. Big sting until Jean, 69, was convicted of first-degree murder.

10. THE HEAD IN THE DITCH: Doug Guyatt was cleaning up the front yard of his Colwood home one afternoon in June 1992 when he found his wife's severed head in a bag in the ditch. Her long, silver-grey hair had been shorn from her head. Shannon, a 34-year-old computer programmer, had been missing for 11 days. A police investigation found that Shannon had filed for divorce, and detectives believed that her husband had murdered her so he could collect on a life insurance policy and pay off the mortgage on their home. The rest of her body was never found and Guyatt died in prison in 2014.

3 FAILED TERROR PLOTS WITH TIES TO B.C. — AND 5 THAT SUCCEEDED

1. INDIAN MINISTER PLAYS DEAD, SURVIVES SHOOTING, 1986: Malkiat Singh Sidhu was one of several Indian politicians murdered by militants in 1991 amid the country's long-running conflict with Sikh separatists—but if a cohort of Canadian extremists had their way, he would have been assassinated five years earlier on B.C. soil.

Sidhu was visiting the province for a family wedding in May 1986 when four armed men forced his car to stop on a remote gravel road on Vancouver Island. They smashed the vehicle with hammers and shot at him five times, wounding the Punjabi planning minister on the arm and chest.

Sidhu played dead, but survived. The perpetrators —one of whom, Jaspal Singh Atwal, would later pose for an infamous photo with Sophie Gregoire Trudeau—were all caught and jailed for the despicable crime.

2. MILLENNIUM BOMBER NABBED ON FERRY, 1999: Before the 9/11 attacks changed the course of history, there were the so-called Millennium attacks—a series of plots that were to be executed on or around New Year's Day, 2000. While the attacks were either bungled by the perpetrators or foiled by authorities, the intentions behind them were nonetheless chilling.

Among them was the planned bombing of Los Angeles International Airport, to be carried out by al-Qaeda terrorist Ahmed Ressam. He loaded a rented Chrysler sedan with explosives and boarded a ferry from Victoria, B.C. to Port Angeles, Wash., only to be caught by a customs agent on arrival.

His fellow al-Qaeda members who tried to blow up a U.S. warship in Yemen fared no better—they overloaded the boat they were using to carrying their explosives and sank before they could trigger the blast.

3. 'FOILED' CANADA DAY BOMBING AT THE B.C. LEGISLATURE, 2013: You can't fairly discuss this "foiled" "terror plot" without the generous use of quotation marks—because it probably never would have happened were it not for some overzealous Mounties. Indeed, while John Nuttall and Amanda Korody did set what they believed to be active pressure cooker bombs at the B.C. legislature on Canada Day 2013, the attempt was, according to B.C. Supreme Court Justice Catherine Bruce, "truly a case where the RCMP manufactured the crime."

A jury found the couple guilty on terrorism charges, but Bruce overturned their convictions, finding Nuttall and Korody mentally incapable of seeing the plot through on their own. Undercover police, posing as Muslims, provided them with training, equipment, and a lot of really questionable moral support.

4. NUDE PARADING RADICALS TERRORIZE B.C., 1961: Back in the mid-1900s, the Sons of Freedom, a fanatical sect of Doukhobors, made sensational headlines for parading around naked and burning their own clothes and money. (When they said they were anti-materialism, they meant it.)

Unfortunately, not everything they did was so harmlessly amusing. Some liked to spread their message with TNT.

For decades, members of the Sons of Freedom waged what the papers described as a "war against society in B.C." By 1961, they were blamed for hundreds of acts of violence, including the bombing or burning of 176 homes, 55 schools, eight churches, and four post offices—not to mention dozens of power poles and railway tracks. (Of course, the government hardly helped the situation by seizing their children in the 1950s and placing them in a residential school.)

Members were also suspected of planting a timed bomb on a Canadian Pacific Railway train in 1924, killing nine people on board, though investigators were never able to secure charges.

5. THE BOMBING OF CANADIAN PACIFIC FLIGHT 21, 1965: There is some reasonable debate about what constitutes a terrorist act, and it's certainly possible the term doesn't apply to the deadly blast that downed Canadian Pacific Flight 21—because the perpetrator was never identified, and the motive remains a mystery decades later.

There is no question, however, that it was one of the worst mass murders in modern Canadian history.

The four-engine plane departed on a flight from Vancouver to Whitehorse on July 8, 1965, with 52 men, women and children on board. But the journey only lasted a few hundred kilometres before an explosion, believed to have been triggered by a bomb in the restroom, tore a hole in the back of the aircraft.

According to one newspaper report, officials heard "three staccato cries of 'May Day' ... just before the plane vanished from radar screens." Some passengers were sucked outside as the cabin depressurized, and sent plummeting to their deaths. Everyone else was killed when the plane crashed into the brush.

Four passengers were identified as potential suspects, but no one was ever charged.

6. NOTORIOUS AIR INDIA BOMBINGS, 1985: Most British Columbians are familiar with the terrible fate of Air India Flight 182. At the time of this writing, it remains the worst terror attack in Canadian history.

All 329 passengers and crew died when the Boeing 747, which was bound for Mumbai, exploded in the air and plunged into the Atlantic Ocean. Only 132 of the bodies were found—the majority were lost at sea.

And the shocking death toll would have been much higher if a second bomb, which was intended for another Air India flight, hadn't detonated early at New Tokyo International Airport, killing two baggage handlers.

Both bombs were built in B.C. and began their journeys stowed away in luggage on connecting flights out of Vancouver. One airline employee recalled an anxious man dropping off a suitcase at baggage check, but the mysterious figure never boarded, and was never identified.

A photo of the Air India Boeing 747 that was destroyed in a terror attack in 1985, taken two weeks before the fated flight.

Tragically, though the cold-blooded attacks were unquestionably a coordinated effort, only one person was ever held responsible by Canada's justice system: bomb-maker Inderjit Singh Reyat, a Sikh extremist from Vancouver Island who refused to implicate anyone else in the crime. And even Reyat was never convicted of murder, only manslaughter and some lesser charges.

Two other suspects, prominent Sikh businessman Ripudaman Singh Malik and mill worker Ajaib Singh Bagri, were acquitted at trial for lack of evidence. At least the proceedings led to additional charges of perjury against Reyat, who lied over and over on the witness stand.

7. SUBSTATION BOMBING BY THE SQUAMISH FIVE, 1982: They injured innocent people, supported themselves through thievery, and arguably did real harm to the environmental movement—but the eco-terrorists known as the Squamish Five still had their fans. (It doesn't hurt that two of them were punk rockers.)

In 1982, the group detonated a bomb at a BC Hydro substation, causing a whopping $5 million in damages. Their intention, according to a communique claiming responsibility for the blast, was to slow "a wave of industrial development planned for Vancouver Island."

"In the last two hundred years industrial civilization has been raping and mutilating the Earth and exterminating other species at an ever increasing rate," they wrote, a message that likely rang true to some non-terrorists as well.

Later that year, members would make headlines again by firebombing a chain of porno shops they believed were selling snuff films. All five were eventually caught and jailed, but one of them, Ann Hansen, managed one last act of defiance before being hauled off to prison—she hurled a tomato at the judge who handed down her life sentence.

8. BOMBINGS OF NATURAL GAS PIPELINES, 2008-09: The series of bomb blasts that targeted Encana pipelines in northeastern B.C. back in 2008 and 2009 were preceded by a warning letter fired off to local media. "We will no longer negotiate with terrorists which you are as you keep endangering our families with crazy expansion of deadly gas well in our home lands," it said, somewhat ironically.

What followed were six bombings around Tomslake, a sleepy hamlet near the Alberta border. None of the explosions actually managed to rupture a pipeline, though one did level a metering shed.

It didn't take long for authorities to identify a suspect. Wiebo Ludwig, the leader of a crazed Christian commune located a half hour's drive away, was already a known eco-terrorist, having been convicted years earlier in similar pipeline bombings. He was also, by some accounts, quite an asshole. According to an *Edmonton Journal* article, the former pastor once lambasted his own 90-year-old mother for failing to properly submit to her husband's authority. After he was finished ranting, he refused to give her a hug, saying he would "sooner hug a prostitute."

"I think you need to hear that," he told her. "We're not in agreement."

Police eventually arrested Ludwig, but never found sufficient evidence to charge him or anyone else in the bombings—despite a $1 million reward put up by Encana.

3 TIMES 'SEVERED FEET' APPEARED ON B.C. BEACHES BUT TURNED OUT TO BE DISGUSTING PRANKS

The mysterious feet that began washing up along the B.C. and Washington coasts back in 2007 captured the public's imagination in a way few stories do, and the intrigue only grew as shoe after shoe turned up on the shore filled with human flesh and bone. For a time, some even speculated there might be a serial killer at work in the Salish Sea.

There wasn't. And while the actual explanation was fascinating in its own way, it was mostly just sad. According to the official theory, the owners of the feet likely died in the water by accident or suicide, and each foot disarticulated naturally over time. The buoyancy of the deceased's footwear did the work of carrying the remains to the shoreline, where they could best ruin the evening of a dog walker or a pair of lovebirds holding hands.

In the end, the only actual sickos involved were the pranksters who decided to replicate the macabre scenes for what was, one can only assume, their own amusement.

1. THE ANIMAL PAW: Five actual feet had washed ashore by the time the first hoax made headlines in 2008. The "foot" in question was found by a woman strolling along the beach in Campbell River on June 18, and the seemingly grim discovery was quickly reported to police.

Coroners later determined someone had, for whatever reason, decided to insert a "skeleton-ized animal paw" into a sock, and place that sock into a shoe along with some seaweed. As a result of the ruse and the subsequent police resources it wasted, authorities would later hesitate to confirm an actual washed-up foot was human until they could get DNA confirmation.

2. TWO FOR ONE: It wasn't until a few years later that the next hoax would turn up to fool the public and annoy law enforcement. And this time, the perpetrator doubled down. Not one, but two shoes containing what was initially believed to be human remains were discovered roughly one hour apart in the sleepy Victoria suburb of Oak Bay on September 5, 2011.

Despite first impressions, police were quick to form an alternative theory: that the shoes had been stuffed with raw meat by another obnoxious mischief-maker. The timing of the hoax, which took place during back-to-school week, led authorities to suspect this one might have been the work of local teens.

3. CHILD'S PLAY: Perhaps the most ill-advised of the hoaxes was the one discovered on August 30, 2012 at Victoria's scenic Clover Point, involving no fewer than five child-sized sneakers—three of which were stuffed with meat and bones. Only one tiny shoe turned up initially, but that was enough to put local police on alert. Officers closed down the beach for their investigation, which turned up two more shoes that day, and another pair the following day.

Needless to say, authorities were not amused. Testing determined the shoes contained some kind of poultry—possibly chicken drumsticks—and police held a stern news conference to express their displeasure. They also decided to lay the children's shoes out on a table, leading one reporter to note the disgusting smell of "rotting meat and seaweed" wafting from the evidence.

DEVILS AMONG US: 5 SERIAL KILLERS WHO HAUNTED B.C.

1. THE BEAST OF BRITISH COLUMBIA: To date, Clifford Robert Olson Jr. remains the most notorious child killer in Canadian history. Between November 1980 and July 1981, the brutish sociopath extinguished the life from 11 children and teenagers. Some he raped. Some he bludgeoned. Some he strangled. And though he would later try to portray himself as remorseful, his attempts always rang chillingly hollow.

Just take his interview with journalist Peter Worthington. "Words can't express how badly I feel for the families of these kids," he claimed before abruptly changing the subject. "Say, how do you think the Blue Jays will do tonight?"

Olson was 40 years old when he claimed his first victim, but his cruel streak emerged decades earlier. He bullied his fellow students as a boy, and, like many budding serial killers, was known to torment housepets. He dropped out of school after the eighth grade and was a full-blown outlaw by his late teens, stealing, bilking, and burglarizing at every opportunity. Yet he was completely inept when it came to covering his own tracks. He was constantly in and out of prison, spending only four years of his adult life as a free man.

As fate would have it, his release from the Matsqui Institution in July 1980 lasted longer than most, with devastating results. The murders he committed over his eight-month reign of terror targeted boys and girls alike. The oldest was 18. The youngest was only nine. Olson notoriously managed to kill four of his victims even after the RCMP had identified him as a suspect, and he was poised to strike yet again when officers finally moved in to arrest him on a remote dirt road on Vancouver Island. He had driven there with two young women whose lives were surely hanging in the balance.

Sadly, Olson found ways to continue satisfying his sadistic impulses long after he was locked away. He relished his ability to upset people from behind bars. There was his controversial plea deal, which forced the government to fork over $100,000 in exchange for the locations of the bodies. Or his headline-making parole applications, which he submitted despite having no chance of release. Worst of all were the ghoulish letters he sent his victims' families, which would describe the murders in detail. They ended only after corrections staff began screening his mail.

He finally died on September 30, 2011 at the age of 71, giving Canadians across the country a rare cause to celebrate cancer.

2. THE BOOZING BARBER: Gilbert Paul Jordan shared many of the common traits of a serial killer. He led a life of crime that began at a young age. He was a sexual predator who targeted vulnerable women. He showed a chilling lack of remorse.

What set him apart were his methods. As one judge put it, Jordan "did not use a weapon, such as a gun or a knife … alcohol was his deadly instrument of choice." He would use hard liquor, including vodka and rum, to incapacitate women and rape them, and his devious behaviour resulted in at least eight deaths between 1965 and 1987.

Jordan would meet his victims at dive bars and take them to a seedy hotel or the Slocan Barbershop he operated in East Vancouver. There, he would pressure them to continue binge drinking until they were passed out. "Down the hatch, hurry. Twenty bucks if you drink it right down," a police officer overheard him saying one night. "You need another drink. I'll give you 50 bucks if you can take it."

Some of the women who survived encounters with Jordan said he shoved the bottle into their mouths when they refused to keep going. Tragically, his crimes flew under the radar for far too long.

It's possible police were caught off guard; Jordan is said to be the first person in Canada caught using alcohol as a deadly weapon. But advocates argue the justice system's failure to stop Gilbert Paul James for so many years can also be explained, in part, by the demographics of the victims. They were Indigenous, and many were alcoholics or sex workers. Their deaths did not arouse much suspicion, and were deemed accidental, even though two of them, Mary Johns and Patricia Andrew, had enough alcohol in their blood to kill them twice over.

In the end, Jordan was only convicted on one count of manslaughter. The victim, Vanessa Lee Buckner, had a blood alcohol content of .91, more than 11 times the legal driving limit.

3. THE PIG FARMER: To some, Robert "Willie" Pickton was a quiet and reserved farmer in Port Coquitlam. Others knew him for throwing wild, drug-fueled raves in the "Piggy Palace," a converted building on a rural property he shared with his brother. But dozens of women learned his true nature—that of a cold-blooded killer who stalked Vancouver's Downtown Eastside—just in time to carry his dark secret to their graves.

After he was finally captured in 2002, Pickton confessed to a staggering 49 murders. Speaking to an undercover agent who was posing as his cellmate, he even lamented never reaching an "even 50," as he put it, as if human lives were nothing more than points to be tallied. The true death toll from his years of unchecked cruelty could be much lower—serial killers have a tendency to lie and exaggerate—but Pickton was ultimately charged with slaughtering 27 women.

Wherever the truth lies, one of the many tragedies of the case is that some of his victims may have been spared if not for the failings of police. Pickton popped up on investigators' radar several times between 1997 and 1999. The first, and most chilling, was when a woman survived an attack on the brothers' farm by slashing Pickton's jugular with a kitchen knife.

Like many of his other targets, she was a sex worker in the Downtown Eastside who accepted an invitation to his property one fateful evening in March 1997. She told police they had sex, and shortly after Pickton crept up behind her and placed a handcuff on her wrist. Sensing the extreme danger she was in, she fought back, and by the time the melee was over they were both being treated in hospital for knife wounds.

Pickton was charged with several criminal counts, including attempted murder, but they were stayed the following year because police said the victim was a drug user and unable to properly testify in court. Blood-stained clothes seized off Pickton's person happened to contain the DNA of two missing women, but they weren't tested until years later.

In 1998, a tipster also told police he believed Pickton was responsible for some of the disappearances in the DTES, and that the farmer had, according to a report, "claimed he could dispose of a body by putting it through a grinder and feeding the remains to his pigs." The year after that, another sex worker in New Westminster was threatened and Pickton was identified as a suspect—yet it would be three more years before he was finally formally accused in the murders.

In a report that admitted many investigative failures, the Vancouver Police Department noted the missing women unit it initially put together to solve the cases lacked resources, training, and strong leadership. Police denied they gave the disappearances low priority because the women were sex workers, but admitted it took them far too long to conclude they were dealing with a serial killer. They also laid significant blame at the hands of Coquitlam RCMP, who held jurisdictional authority but "essentially abandoned" the case in 1999.

In the end, Pickton was brought to justice thanks to what police themselves admit was a lucky break. A former employee of the farm reported seeing illegal guns at the property, leading to a search that turned up items belonging to two of the missing women, including an inhaler. In Pickton's view, the only thing that ended his streak was that he'd become "sloppy."

4. THE PREDATOR: The people of Malawi are so famously kind, the country is sometimes called "The Warm Heart of Africa." Charles Eli Kembo, who came to Canada in 1989 claiming refugee status, was quite an exception. Between December 2002 and July 2005, the manipulative con man murdered four people in Metro Vancouver: his wife, Margaret Kembo; his best friend, Arden Samuel; his girlfriend, Sui Yin Ma; and his stepdaughter, Rita Leung.

Prosecutors argued Kembo killed them for financial reasons, even though he stood to gain shockingly little for the cost of a human life. Every victim was described as being "low net worth," yet Kembo managed to profit after their disappearances by selling off their things or opening credit cards in their names. In his stepdaughter's case, he signed up for GST cheques and a student loan.

The crimes were also bizarrely brazen. One wonders how long Kembo thought he'd fly under the police radar as the people around him dropped like flies, with two of their bodies haphazardly cast into the Fraser River and one abandoned in a public park. Only Ms. Kembo, his first victim, was apparently disposed of with any care. Her remains have never been found.

But what we know from the other killings suggests Kembo likely had other motivations beyond money. He mutilated Samuel's genitals during his murder, and had sex with Leung during hers. He tried to argue the sex with his stepdaughter was consensual, though Justice Sunni Stromberg-Stein found the claim both "despicable" and "patently untrue."

"You disparaged the name of this young woman who still has friends and family in this community with your blatant lies," Stromberg-Stein said during sentencing. The judge, who eventually gave Kembo life in prison, said the brutal killings were the result of escalating criminal behaviour that began "the moment (he) set foot in Canada carrying a false passport."

His arrival certainly did kick off a marathon of theft and fraud. Over the years Kembo made refugee claims under at least three other names and defrauded the welfare system under 22. By the time he was arrested for murder, police said he was maintaining as many as 50 aliases for various illicit purposes. He applied that same aptitude for lies and manipulation in his personal relationships, yielding charm as a weapon, drawing people in and using them until he needed them no more.

"You are a predator," Stromberg-Stein told Kembo. "You preyed on innocent vulnerable people, conning those closest to you, exploiting those who made the mistake of trusting you."

The newspapers never gave Kembo a snappy serial killer nickname, but "predator" seems to sum him up pretty well. Even after being locked up, Kembo managed one last swindle. He wrote a teen novel called "The Trinity of Superkidds" (sic) and managed to get it listed for sale on Amazon—using an alias, of course.

5. THE COUNTRY BOY: When police pulled Cody Legebokoff over in November 2010, they found blood all over him—on his chin, his shirt, his shorts, his shoes. The 20-year-old tried to explain it away as the messy byproduct of deer hunting. He was, after all, a country boy, and country boys hunt.

"That's what we do for fun," he told the officers.

But it was not deer blood. And Legebokoff, despite having a fairly typical upbringing in the small northern community of Fort St. James, was not a normal country boy. He was, and remains at the time of this printing, Canada's youngest serial killer.

On that fateful November evening, he had driven Loren Donn Leslie, a compassionate 15-year-old girl who was legally blind, into the woods to stab her with a Leatherman multi-tool and bludgeon her with a pipe wrench. She was the last of his four victims, and represented a break in the pattern; his other targets were all adult women, all mothers, and all sex workers.

Concrete motives for the killings didn't come out at trial because Legebokoff feigned innocence. But for whatever reason, over a period of just 14 months, those three women and one girl became the focus of his deadly rage. As judge Glen Parrett noted, "the injuries caused in each case were massive and disfiguring, the object of each attack appearing to be aimed at not simply killing the victims but degrading and destroying them."

And though Legebokoff's lawyers tried and tried to humanize him on the stand, to draw out something resembling remorse, they were chasing rainbows. All the killer revealed in his testimony and interviews with police, according to judge Parrett, was a "complete void."

"The tone and manner and his constant reference to the body of Loren Leslie as 'it' gives us a glimpse of his attitude towards his targets and the extent to which he lacks, on any level, empathy or remorse," Parrett said. "He should never be allowed to walk among us again."

Legebokoff grew up like a regular country boy—playing sports, making friends and going fishing with his caring family—but beneath that facade lurked a monster.

10 HAUNTING MISSING PERSONS CASES FROM B.C.

1. MICHAEL DUNAHEE, 1991: This was the disappearance that sparked panic in parents across B.C. Little Michael Dunahee was four years old when he vanished from an elementary school playground in Victoria. He was playing just a few metres from his parents, but there were no witnesses to what happened to him. The disappearance sparked a massive police investigation, and tens of thousands of tips from the public, but there still have been no solid leads. The family had one little moment of hope in 2013, when a young man came forward who bore an uncanny resemblance to composite drawings of what Michael might look like today. But alas, DNA testing proved he was not the missing child.

2. THE JACK FAMILY, 1989: Ronald and Doreen Jack and their two children, nine-year-old Russell and four-year-old Ryan, disappeared after leaving their home in Prince George, bound for a logging camp where they'd been offered jobs. They never reached their destination. Their last contact with anyone was on August 2, 1989, when Ronald called his mother from the Burns Lake area. Police still believe there are people out there who hold clues about what happened to the Jacks—in 2018, Mounties made a public plea for an anonymous tipster who'd passed information on to investigators to come forward and reveal what they know.

3. LINDSEY NICHOLLS, 1993: Lindsey Nicholls was 14 years old and had just moved into a temporary foster home in the Comox Valley when she went missing in the summer of 1993. On the morning of her disappearance, she'd argued with her foster mother and left the house, saying she was going to meet friends in Courtenay. She was never seen again. Police believe Lindsey may have run away to Vancouver, but she left everything she owned, including treasured belongings, in her room at the foster home. More than two decades after her disappearance, police still haven't uncovered any leads about what might have happened to the teenager.

Lindsey Nicholls disappeared in 1994 and hasn't been seen since.

4. DENNIS CROOK, 1985: Somehow, more than three decades into their investigation, police keep finding new clues about what happened to 35-year-old Dennis Crook. The U.K.-born Victoria man's friends reported him missing after he failed to show up for work, but his vehicle was still parked outside his home. In 2018, some new pieces of evidence appeared—investigators finally obtained a photograph of Crook, and a long-lost sister provided a DNA sample in case there might be a match with an unidentified body. Police also discovered Crook had owned a sailboat called the Beverly Ann, which had been moored Oak Bay for many years. The whereabouts of that boat are also unknown. Could it be the key to finding Dennis Crook?

5. ROBERTA FERGUSON, 1988: Roberta Ferguson was camping with friends in Cultus Lake when she went missing. Right around sundown, she set out from the campsite on foot; her friends believed she was heading home to Surrey. A witness spotted the 19-year-old shortly after that. Ominously, the young woman from the Dunvegan Cree First Nation was speaking to a man inside a red sports car. When her family reported her missing, the RCMP told them to wait 24 hours to file a report. Ferguson was never seen again, and her family believes she was murdered.

6. JOANNE MARIE PEDERSON, 1983: Sadly, Joanne Marie Pederson's case is another example of a missing girl or woman who was last seen in the company of an unknown man. Little Joanne Marie was just 10 and using the pay phone outside the Penny Pincher convenience store in Chilliwack when a witness spotted her on a winter day in 1983. She was calling to ask her parents to pick her up; she'd been locked out of the house. But the witness said an unidentified man was standing in the phone booth with the little girl. When Joanne's parents arrived, the girl was gone.

7. EDNA BETTE-JEAN MASTERS, 1960: In 2013, more than half a century after 21-month-old Edna Bette-Jean Masters disappeared, the RCMP reopened their missing person investigation, hoping that public attention might spark someone's memory of what happened. Little Bette-Jean, as she was known, was playing at a friend's house in the Red Lake area, west of Kamloops, when she went missing. A couple was seen leaving the area in a rust-coloured Chevrolet, but investigators never managed to identify or speak with them. Despite an extensive search using an airplane, a police dog, and team of volunteers, no traces have ever been found of the small girl with curly blonde hair.

8. LAWRENCE WELLINGTON ALLARD, 1975: The family says Lawrence Allard's mother first reported him missing in 1975—she claimed her 35-year-old son had been abducted by two men who broke into her Kamloops home and left in a black Cadillac. But after more than 40 years, Mounties have not acknowledged the family's version of events. Police maintain that Allard's mother didn't report him missing for two years after he disappeared, a stance that has left the family frustrated and angry. Allard's niece recently offered up a private reward for anyone who can provide more information about what happened.

9. CARMEN ROBINSON, 1973: For a time, police thought 17-year-old Carmen Robinson might have been a victim of the notorious serial killer Ted Bundy, but investigators have never found any evidence that Bundy visited Vancouver Island, where Robinson lived and was last seen. She was also briefly thought to be the victim of another serial killer, Clifford Olson—he told police that he knew where the teenager was buried. Investigators even agreed to fly Olson from the Kingston Penitentiary in Ontario to Victoria, but when he pointed out the supposed burial spot, there was no evidence of a body. Though the tall blonde girl's good looks prompted police to suspect Robinson was attacked and killed by someone with a sexual motive, all investigators really know about her disappearance is that she was last seen stepping off a bus near her home in View Royal on December 8, 1973.

10. GEORGE DAVIS, 2004: The last time anyone saw 40-year-old George Davis, he was driving his 1981 Chrysler Lebaron to get cigarettes in his hometown of Creston. His family was immediately concerned about his disappearance—Davis has a condition similar to epilepsy, and needed to take medication to control his seizures. Unfortunately, he'd left his pills at home. Davis was never seen again, and his car has never been found.

BONUS: 1 PERSON WHO WAS FOUND SAFE AFTER 52 YEARS

LUCY JOHNSON, 1961: The RCMP immediately suspected foul play when Lucy Johnson's husband Marvin reported her missing in 1965. For good reason, too—Marvin had apparently waited four years to call in the disappearance. Police dug up the family's yard in Surrey in an attempt to find Lucy's body, but their search was fruitless. Marvin would die long before the mystery was solved, and her two children spent nearly 52 years wondering what had become of their mother.

And then, in 2013, Surrey Mounties featured Lucy Johnson in an ongoing series about missing people, and her daughter put out a public plea for help. Pretty quickly, a tip rolled in from Whitehorse, Yukon: Lucy Johnson was alive and well at 77 years old, with a whole new family. Sadly, she revealed that she'd left because Marvin was abusive. She'd tried to take her kids with her when she fled, but he would not allow it.

8 REMARKABLE B.C. PRISON BREAKS

1. THE NOTORIOUS TRAIN ROBBER: Bill Miner was a true Wild West legend. William A. Pinkerton of the notorious detective agency once called him "one of the most remarkable single-handed stage and train robbers who ever operated in the Far West." Miner is widely credited with being the first criminal to use the phrase "Hands up!" in a stick-up, and robbed trains up and down the West Coast of North America.

He was the architect of B.C.'s first ever train robbery in 1904, when he and two sidekicks got away with $10,000 in gold near Mission. Two short years later, Miner would pull off the province's last ever train robbery, this time on a mail car east of Kamloops. That landed him in New Westminster's B.C. Penitentiary, but not for very long—he escaped from a work gang on August 8, 1907 in the company of three other inmates by digging under a fence. Miner made it south to the U.S., where he continued to rob banks and trains before dying in prison in 1913.

2. THE SPONTANEOUS ESCAPE: Forget any preconceptions about meticulously planned prison breaks—William Ellis's escape from the B.C. Pen on July 7, 1910 was more of a fluke than anything else. Ellis was serving three years for break and enter when he saw another inmate, Joseph Nalee, making a run out the open front gate. The story is that Ellis was only trying to see how far Nalee would make it, but when he realized no one was watching him, he decided to keep on going. Ellis only enjoyed six days of freedom before Vancouver police found him hiding in the bushes along the CPR tracks on the city's east side and put him back behind bars, according to a report in the *Vancouver Daily World*.

3. THE DISAPPEARING ACT: Wo Sing was serving two years for burglary at the B.C. Pen when he escaped the prison on April 30, 1928. He was working as domestic help in the acting warden's home at the time, and the *Vancouver Sun* reported that "the prisoner was garbed in civilian attire and wore a grey overcoat when he escaped." A guard was suspended because of the prison break, but Sing was never found. Perhaps benefiting from the racism of those trying to hunt him down, it was reported that the fugitive likely managed to blend in with other Chinese-Canadians in Vancouver's Chinatown or at a work camp in the Interior.

4. THE CHATTY CONVICT: One Sunday evening at the end of May 1973, reporter Dave Stockand of the *Vancouver Sun* received an unusual phone call from 27-year-old John Emitte McCann, prisoner number 3384 at the B.C. Pen. McCann, a convicted robber, had scaled the prison's fences to freedom on May 19, and said he wanted to "set the record straight" about certain aspects of the escape. Stockand agreed to meet up with the escapee, and McCann insisted the prison break was actually a form of protest on behalf of all inmates at the Pen, which he described as overstaffed and under-resourced. "It just doesn't make sense. They are not progressing, they are regressing."

Mind you, of course, McCann already had a record for escaping—a prison guard was beaten with an iron bar during one break from Oakalla Prison in 1967. And in the days before he'd surprised Stockand with that phone call, he'd used his newfound freedom to rob Vancouver's Eldorado Motor Hotel and a Toronto Dominion Bank on Nanaimo Street. McCann was re-arrested in early June, and returned to his cell.

5. THE 13: It was New Year's Day 1988, when 13 inmates made a break from Oakalla Prison in Burnaby. All of the escapees were being held in an underground concrete isolation unit after a destructive riot, according to newspaper reports at the time. They managed their breakout after one prisoner overpowered a guard using a makeshift knife and stole his keys. On the outside, the inmates took off in groups, stealing cars to make their getaways. Three escaped

The view of a jail cell at Oakalla Prison taken in the 1940s.

prisoners carjacked a young couple outside a pub on Kingsway. "They pulled me out of the car," 21-year-old Colleen Cockerly told the *Vancouver Sun*. "My husband Kevin put up a bit of a fight and got punched in the face."

All 13 were eventually recaptured, but their exploit had a lasting impact. Though Oakalla had seen many escapes in the past, this was the biggest ever, and it helped draw attention to the horrid conditions inside the prison. A commission of inquiry was struck up, and recommended the institution be shuttered. It was closed for good in 1991.

6. PLUCKED FROM THE PRISON GROUNDS: It was Canada's first ever prison escape by helicopter. It took just 137 seconds for Robert Lee Ford and David Thomas to break out of the Kent Institution on June 18, 1990, according to the *Vancouver Sun*. The two men—Ford was a convicted murderer and Thomas an armed robber—had the help of a masked accomplice, who hijacked the chopper and forced its pilot to land on the grounds of the Fraser Valley prison. The helicopter touched down in the midst of a lockdown, and so the two inmates had to make a mad dash for their ride as the hijacker fired at the prison guards, hitting one in the knee. It was an escape worthy of a Hollywood movie, but freedom didn't last long for Ford and Thomas. They were arrested two days later at a campsite on Echo Island in Harrison Lake.

7. FATAL CONSEQUENCES: It was a horrific episode that highlighted an epidemic of overcrowding in B.C.'s prisons. On May 3, 1994, convicted killer Michael Roberts and robber Timothy Cronin simply walked away from the minimum-security Ferndale Institution in Mission. The escape itself wasn't remarkable—there was only a waist-high fence around the facility—but what happened next was.

After the pair placed dummies in their beds and fled the prison, they made their way south to Washington state. Just three days after the escape, they met up with a man named Elijio Cantu in Seattle and demanded he give them his car, according to the *Seattle Times*. When Cantu refused to help, they stabbed and strangled him to death and stole the vehicle. They were later arrested in Oregon after an attempted robbery. A Corrections Canada investigation would eventually confirm the obvious: that Cronin and Roberts should never have been placed in a minimum-security facility in the first place.

8. THE DESPERATE JAIL GUARD: More than a decade after his daring escape, the whereabouts of Omid Tahvili are still a mystery. The North Shore gangster was awaiting trial for masterminding the abduction and torture of a Surrey man when he made his getaway from North Fraser Pretrial Centre on November 14, 2008. Tahvili had taken advantage of a guard named Edwin Ticne, who was struggling with a gambling addiction and a crumbling marriage. Tahvili offered Ticne $50,000 if he'd help with the escape, promising to meet at a nearby gas station once he was out to pay out the bribe. According to the *North Shore News*, Tahvili was dressed in a contract cleaner's golf shirt, a baseball cap and sunglasses when Ticne led him through the security doors and out of the jail. Unfortunately for Ticne, Tahvili never appeared at the planned meeting place, and Ticne was sentenced to three years in prison for his role in the escape.

(Opposite) Joe Fortes appears in his swimming costume, sometime between 1915 and 1920.

PEOPLE

BIF NAKED'S LIST OF TREMENDOUS AND BRILLIANT B.C. WOMEN

Bif Naked is a celebrated and notorious performer in music, TV, film, and dance, a memoirist and poet, and a tireless advocate and humanitarian. She was orphaned in India, emancipated by punk rock, and empowered by surviving breast cancer, kidney failure, heart surgery, divorce, and working as a woman in the entertainment industry for 25 years.

1. JEAN SWANSON: Jean Swanson is a hero of mine. She is an activist, not just some politician. She is a member of the Order of Canada, and her book *Poor-Bashing* remains one of the most important reads of my life. Jean's devotion to the community, to social justice and to the environment as she fearlessly fights for others is an example of what the rest of us could be doing to work toward a fair and just city, country and planet.

2. AMBER DAWN: Amber Dawn is a writer like no other. Not that I've ever met, anyway. And once you've met Amber Dawn, like me, every part of you will be on fire. Especially your mind! She is a memoirist, a poet, an activist, a survivor, and an icon. She is a living flame from a sweet, smoking candle. Her work keeps growing and glowing, and we are happy to lick her glorious flames.

3. LESLIE VARLEY: Leslie is a Nisga'a woman and a leader—and a survivor. Her work both informs and inspires understanding. Formerly, as director of the Aboriginal Health Program at Provincial Health Services Authority, she helped develop a program providing Indigenous cultural safety training that would grow positive partnerships and develop awareness between service providers and Indigenous people. Her vision continues as the executive director of the B.C. Association of Aboriginal Friendship Centres. She encourages and uplifts everyone in the community and encourages a thriving and healing world view.

4. JAIPREET KAUR: Jaipreet is a Kundalini yoga and meditation teacher, and one of the greatest sources of pure joy on the planet. She has been travelling to India for most of her life and now is dedicated to leading others on retreats there, and to the heart of compassion. She takes her students by the hand and walks with them on their journey to wisdom, courage, balance, and surrender. There is no better teacher, not just for yoga but for how to live. I know her students will agree with me, and we are always blessed to be in her presence.

5. SHAHRZAD RAFATI: Shahrzad is a legend and a force of nature. As the founder and CEO of BroadbandTV Corp., she has brought her dreams to the global digital market and carved her own path to success. She also co-founded Chopra Yoga, with Dr. Deepak Chopra himself. Prime Minister Justin Trudeau appointed Shahrzad to represent Canada on the G20 Business Women Leaders Task Force, praising her for being a proven leader with a remarkable success story. Not only has she revolutionized an industry and inspired with her commitment to equity, award-winning Shahrzad Rafati is considered one of the most creative people in business in the world.

6. DR. SHARON GURM: Naturopathic physician Dr. Sharon Gurm is the founder and medical director of Port Moody Health Integrative Medicine & Cancer Care, a multidisciplinary and collaborative healthcare centre. Not only is she a visionary and distinguished speaker, her eloquence and grace carry her as she floats from advising patients to caring for her family, to being a runner and yogi. She makes being a beautiful genius look easy!

7. IRENE LANZINGER: It's not easy being a woman in the world, and even harder to be a woman in the workforce. Irene Lanzinger has spent decades fighting for fairness for women, for workers, and for everybody. When I met Irene, she was president of the B.C. Federation of Labour, and she was the first woman to ever hold the position. She inspired more women to enter leadership roles, including me, and she continues to motivate and encourage us.

8. GENESA GREENING: Being on the City of Vancouver's women's advisory committee was a position I volunteered for, and the greatest thing that came from it was meeting Genesa Greening. At the time, she was still a director at Vancouver's Union Gospel Mission, and I learned much from her compassionate example about serving the most vulnerable and underserved communities.

Genesa's parents were pastors and her values mirrored mine as we both had a faith-based upbringing. Today, as the CEO and president of the B.C. Women's Hospital Foundation and as a mom, Genesa Greening was named one of Canada's Most Powerful Women by the Women's Executive Network. I say this is also due to the power of love.

9. GLORIA LATHAM: For almost 25 years, Semperviva Yoga has been recognized as a leading world-class yoga studio and international teacher training college. One of the biggest reasons is its co-founder and director, Gloria Latham. She has become one of the most celebrated yoga and meditation teachers, not only in Vancouver, but internationally, through her many workshops, retreats, and online presence. Her classes are transformational and inspire meaning and joy. She facilitates happiness and spiritual growth in the hearts and minds of everyone who meets her.

10. MEBRAT BEYENE: For over 20 years, Mebrat has worked in social justice, worked closely with women-serving organizations, and in the nonprofit sector as the executive director for WISH Drop-in Centre, a safe place in Vancouver's Downtown Eastside for self-identified women and street-based sex trade workers over 19. Mebrat's dedication to improving the lives of women involved in the street-based sex trade and her compassionate and respectful leadership has inspired me, and everyone she fearlessly works on behalf of. She is a positive and wonderful role model for all of us. Also of note is her glorious singing voice!

FRED LEE'S LIST OF 10 BRITISH COLUMBIANS I'D LOVE TO HAVE A DRINK WITH

Social butterfly and "Man About Town" Fred Lee shares all of Vancouver's A-list happenings, red carpet parties, must-attend galas and fabulous fundraisers in his weekly social column for The Province *newspaper. He also writes a monthly society page in* Vancouver Magazine.

1. JIMMY PATTISON: An opportunity to sit down with one of Canada's most successful entrepreneurs, not to mention wealthiest—priceless!

2. MICHAEL BUBLÉ: From Vancouver's BaBalu Lounge to international fame, no doubt B.C.'s favourite crooner has a few good stories to share of his rise to stardom.

3. KIM CATTRALL: Imagine the tell-all from the *Sex and the City* siren about her three on-screen BFFs after several rounds of Cosmos.

4. DOUGLAS COUPLAND: A fascinating experiment to understand the creative genius behind the reclusive pop artist and author and to learn how he interprets the world.

5. MARGARET TRUDEAU: The walls at 24 Sussex can't talk. But Maggie can, on being married to Canada's 15th prime minister and then giving birth to the country's 23rd.

6. SETH ROGEN: Just imagining a lot of shits and giggles and instructions to mind the gap from the funnyman and voice of TransLink while sharing his journey from the halls of Point Grey Secondary to the hills of Hollywood.

7. TREVOR LINDEN: What's life like after hockey for Captain Canuck?

8. CHIP WILSON: What were you thinking? That's where we'd begin with the outspoken Lululemon mogul and creator of the Little Black Stretchy Pants.

9. BOB RENNIE: Will Vanhattan's bubble finally burst? Mr. Condo King is the next best thing to a real estate crystal ball.

10. CHRISTY CLARK: No doubt the former premier has a few choice words on B.C.'s always colourful politics. (Off the record, of course.)

10 STORIES THAT WILL MAKE YOU WISH YOU'D KNOWN JOE FORTES

Seraphim Joseph Fortes, or "Old Black Joe" as he was sometimes known, was so much more than the namesake of an upscale restaurant in downtown Vancouver. Born in Trinidad and Tobago in 1863, Fortes sailed to B.C. aboard the Robert Kerr after spending his young adulthood in England. He spent nearly four decades in Vancouver, where he became the fledgling city's first lifeguard and one of its most beloved citizens.

After his death in 1922, *The Province* newspaper published a glowing obituary, proclaiming, "He was able to say that he gave more than value in service for all that he has received, and he has died a creditor of the community." The Vancouver Historical Society formally recognized Fortes as the "Citizen of the Century" in 1986. Here are a few reasons why that was entirely appropriate.

1. HE SAVED A MOTHER AND SON FROM THE GREAT FIRE OF 1886: Not too long after Fortes had settled in Vancouver, the new city was almost completely destroyed. When the Great Vancouver Fire swept through the downtown peninsula on June 13, 1886, Fortes was working as a porter at the Sunnyside Hotel at Carrall and Water. Showing early signs of the heroism that would come to define him, Fortes helped a mother and her young son flee the burning hotel and find refuge on his old ship, the Robert Kerr, still anchored out in Burrard Inlet.

Not only that, but Fortes and the hotel's proprietor were both "badly scorched" as they rushed to retrieve most of the guests' luggage from their rooms, according to the newspapers. The fearless duo was nearly caught in the flames, but saved themselves and the luggage by pushing out into the inlet on a small boat.

2. HE DIDN'T SUFFER RACIST FOOLS: Fortes was one of Vancouver's earliest black residents, and as the story goes, he didn't tolerate the racist notions of some of his fellow citizens. In a tale recorded in the "At Street Corners" column of *The Province* newspaper, a longtime resident recounted meeting Fortes back when he was bartending at the Bodega saloon on Carrall Street. From the beginning, Fortes was a "very straight, honourable man," the old-timer recalled, but he once "saw Joe treat a Yankee captain that insulted him in the right way."

Fortes was always polite and attentive during busy times at the Bodega, but on this particular night, "Joe was having all he could do to attend to customers when this Yankee captain called out, 'When are you going to attend to me, you damned n——r?'" Fortes ignored him, but the bigot repeated the slur. "Joe finished what he was doing without turning a hair. Then he walked through the swinging door that led to the billiard room and came out again in front of the bar. 'Now I'll attend to you sir,' he said. 'I'll have you to know that I'm a British subject, and that's a better man than you are.'

"And he took him by the collar, walked him to the door, pushed him out into the street and told him that if he came back he would get something he would not like."

3. HE ONCE TALKED A MAN OUT OF SUICIDE: Like the story above, this is pure hearsay, but considering everything else we know about Fortes, it's entirely believable. The anecdote was reported in *The Province* in 1926, four years after Fortes' death, when supporters were trying to raise funds for a lasting memorial to the beloved lifeguard.

As a "well-known citizen" told the newspaper, it was a cold, wet night when a local man was feeling down on his luck. "He was not well and he was broke. The whole world looked gloomy. He went down to English Bay with the intention of ending his sufferings. There he met Joe, and the old [man] seemed to sense what was the matter." As the citizen remembered it, Fortes insisted the man come inside his home for something warm to eat, then gave him a "five-spot" and a little something extra.

"He gave him just what he was most in need of, a little encouragement and homely advice. He kept the young fellow there all night, and the next morning managed to get him a job." According to the paper, that young man would go on to become a prosperous member of the community.

4. HE TAUGHT HUNDREDS OF CHILDREN TO SWIM: As far as we can tell, nobody has ever tried to put an exact number on how many children learned to swim under Fortes' instruction. Before his arrival in Vancouver, or so the legend goes, swimming wasn't really an activity that the locals indulged in. But he helped turn the beach at English Bay into hub of joyous and safe splashing every summer. As one writer for the *Vancouver Sun* wrote in 1914, "The youngsters adore Joe, and Joe idolizes the kiddies. He fathers the whole bunch, no matter how many there are, and on sunny days at the bay, warns one, plays with a crowd of others, while all the while keeping his weather eye open on the bathers, some of whom might be too venturesome and get into deep water."

And it wasn't just kids he taught. Another newspaper columnist recounted watching Fortes patiently supervising a new arrival from the Prairies who stood more than 6 feet tall as the big galoot tried to learn how to float.

5. HE WAS AN IMPRESSIVE SWIMMER LONG BEFORE ARRIVING IN B.C.: Fortes' parents, a well-to-do Trinidadian farmer and a Spanish woman, wanted him to follow in the family trade or find a religious vocation, but the young man was drawn to the sea from the beginning. He sailed away to Liverpool as a teenager to find his fortune. It was in England that he honed his swimming skills, and before he bored of Dear Old Blighty, he'd won a three-mile race across the River Mersey, earned a gold medal in lifesaving, and toured through France with the Liverpool Good Templars exhibition swimming team.

6. HE SAVED AT LEAST 29 PEOPLE FROM DROWNING: Few people believe that Fortes saved the lives of just 29 people during his decades in Vancouver, but that's the official number. Many of his contemporaries reckoned it was more than 100. Among his rescues were J.C. McCook, a newly appointed American consul on his way to take up his post in Dawson City, and John Hugo Ross, who would later die in the sinking of the Titanic.

The *Vancouver Daily World* recounted one September 1919 rescue that showed just how determined Fortes was to save every life he could. Two Chinese fisherman were stranded on a shoal far offshore in rough waters, and they were unable to make their way to dry land. Fortes and a policeman tried reaching them in a patrol boat, but they were tossed about on the waves for more than a hour before they had to head back to shore and regroup. "Then, despite the protestations of many of the hundreds of watchers, the officer and Joe Fortes put out in a rowboat … and despite the strenuous work necessary to get in touch with the fishermen, succeeded in getting them aboard the small craft."

7. HE DID IT ALL OUT OF KINDNESS: For many years, Fortes received no material reward for taking on his self-appointed role as guardian of English Bay and patient instructor of children. By all reports, he patrolled the beach out of love of the ocean and compassion for his neighbours. At first, he lived in a tidy little tent by the beach during the summers, but later moved into a small cottage at the end of Bidwell Street, where he could survey the shoreline from his porch.

It was in 1900 that the city finally put Fortes on the payroll, and within days he had proved his worth, saving the life of a five-year-old boy who'd been knocked into the water by two dogs playing near the shoreline. One night the same summer, after he'd retired to his cottage, Fortes jumped into the water fully clothed to save a couple whose boat had capsized in the dark. Those are just two of several daring rescues recounted in the newspapers that year.

8. HE INSPIRED FIERCE DEFENDERS: After Fortes' first summer as a paid employee of the city, one of the few Vancouverites yet to be charmed by the lifeguard wrote in to *The Province* to object to the public expense. The displeased "Ratepayer" said he failed to see a need for taxes to support a lifesaving professional at any seaside, anywhere. That one letter prompted a flood of outrage that filled the newspaper's editorial pages.

As one enraged correspondent wrote, Fortes "has more than paid for the few dollars he has received this summer while employed as swimming instructor … by saving quite a number of lives which are to-day to his credit on the records of the city." Furthermore, the letter continued, "The amount of Fortes' wages that 'Ratepayer' pays, if the truth were known, would not buy him a five cent glass of pop each year."

(The above-mentioned "Ratepayer" would make his exact objections to Fortes clear in a follow-up letter to the paper, writing "I would not allow a coloured man or any other man to learn my girls how to swim.")

9. HE PROTECTED A VICTIM OF DOMESTIC ABUSE: Being a lifeguard during Vancouver's frontier days could sometimes be a dangerous job. Fortes once found himself at the business end of a gun after he came to the aid of a battered woman. The culprit, according to *The Province*, was one Fred Klein, "an old acquaintance of the police court."

A drunken Klein returned to his home at English Bay one afternoon in the fall of 1900, only to find that his live-in girlfriend was also inebriated. "He proceeded to sober her up by pouring pails of water over her, following this treatment by a thorough pummelling. Ever the defender of those who needed defending, Fortes came to her rescue. Klein drove him off with a rifle."

10. HE HAD THE BIGGEST FUNERAL VANCOUVER HAD EVER SEEN: Fortes died on February 4, 1922 at the age of 58, after suffering from pneumonia and a stroke. On the day he was laid to rest, schools across the city observed a moment of silence for the man who had meant so much to Vancouver's children. Thousands of people were turned away from the service at Holy Rosary Cathedral, and an estimated 10,000 lined the streets to salute the funeral procession as it made its way to Mountain View Cemetery. Fortes' hearse towed the rowboat he'd used in his many rescues, and the little vessel was filled with flowers.

During the service, Father William O'Boyle described Fortes as a "living example of broadminded, Christian brotherly love" and said "He gave his best and was indeed God's image carved in ebony." The *Vancouver Daily World* marked the sombre occasion with a front page spread, declaring "Servant—Friend—Protector."

A water fountain still stands as tribute to Fortes near English Bay, bearing the simple message: "Little children loved him."

11 LESSER-KNOWN FACTS ABOUT TERRY FOX

1. HE WAS ON RICK HANSEN'S WHEELCHAIR BASKET-BALL TEAM: Back in 1977, years before the Marathon of Hope, Rick Hansen recruited Terry Fox to join him on the Vancouver Cable Cars wheelchair basketball team. They became good friends, and helped the Cable Cars win the national championships together in 1978 and again in 1979.

Hansen later credited Terry with helping to inspire his own incredible journey, the Man in Motion World Tour.

2. THERE ARE SCHOOLS, HIGHWAYS, AND EVEN A MOUNTAIN NAMED AFTER HIM: Driving on the Trans Canada Highway just outside Thunder Bay, Ont., you will pass a white post marking the fateful spot where Terry was forced to cut his journey short. It sits on an 83-kilometre stretch that was dubbed the Terry Fox Courage Highway in his honour—and that's just one of 15 highways and roads named after him across the country.

There are also 14 schools, including Terry Fox Secondary in his hometown of Coquitlam and Terry Fox Elementary in Abbotsford.

Last, but certainly not least, on the B.C. side of the Rocky Mountains towers a 2,639-metre peak called Mount Terry Fox—an appropriately-sized monument to an incredible young man.

3. HE RAN AN ASTOUNDING DISTANCE: Even though he never completed his Marathon of Hope, Terry still managed to run 5,373 kilometres in 143 days, averaging nearly one full marathon per day—an absolutely herculean effort. For context, that's farther than the distance from L.A. to New York. Measured vertically, it's about 600 times as tall as Everest, and would reach about 1/70th of the way to the *moon*.

4. HE HELPED INSPIRE A BETTER PROSTHETIC: It's hard to imagine running a marathon every day for months, but it's nearly impossible to fathom how much more difficult it was because of Terry's prosthetic leg, which was fairly rudimentary by today's standards. It was heavier than modern prosthetics, weighing about four kilograms (for comparison, the Flex-Foot Cheetah used by Oscar Pistorius weighs 512 grams), and was actually designed mostly for walking. Fox said the pain of running sometimes became so great, he would cry to himself on the road.

But during the Marathon of Hope, he met with Dr. Guy Martel to discuss the challenges of running on a prosthetic. Though it wouldn't be completed until years after Terry's death, Dr. Martel and his team eventually developed a superior leg that would have eliminated the need for Terry's hop-skip method of running.

5. EVERYDAY PEOPLE HELPED KEEP HIM RUNNING: One benefit of Terry's rudimentary prosthetic was that it was fairly easy to fix when it broke. There were at least two instances where regular people stepped up to help, first in Newmarket, Ont., where a mechanic repaired Terry's artificial leg using parts from the rear suspension of a 1978 Chevy Malibu, and again in Sault Ste. Marie, Ont., where a welder rushed out to offer his services by mending a snapped spring.

6. HE REQUESTED 26 PAIRS OF SHOES FROM ADIDAS: Given that Terry Fox set out on the Marathon of Hope as an unknown—and one who had spent most of his money on university—he had to ask for a little help. He successfully convinced Adidas to provide the shoes necessary to run across the entire country by sending a heartfelt request to the CEO, which closed with: "The people in cancer clinics all over the world need people who believe in miracles. I'm not a dreamer, and I'm not saying that this will initiate the definitive answer or cure to cancer, but I believe in miracles. I have to."

He wore through nine left shoes on his journey, but only ever needed one right one for his prosthetic.

7. HE TOOK A PRINCIPLED STAND AGAINST ENDORSEMENTS: Though Terry needed a handful of sponsorships to make his dream possible, he was very wary of muddying his message—he even reportedly fretted about the distinctive and identifiable stripes on his free Adidas shoes. So much did he care about the purity of his cause that he rejected every endorsement deal offered after his run made him a household name.

"I've been told I can get rich out of this run," he said in August 1980. "But I've decided I'm not for that. That would ruin it. I have only one objective and that is all to do with cancer research."

8. ROD STEWART DEDICATED A SONG TO HIM: British rocker Rod Stewart was so inspired by the Marathon of Hope that he dedicated the song "Never Give Up on a Dream" to Terry. While the tune might not be considered one of Stewart's best, there's an undeniable poignancy to the lyrics that remains powerful decades after its release:

"Inspiring all to never lose / It'll take a long, long time before they fill your shoes / It'll take somebody, somebody who's a lot like you / Who never gave up on a dream."

9. HE BEAT OUT WAYNE GRETZKY AND MICHAEL JORDAN: In 1990, eight years after Terry died, TSN named him Athlete of the Decade. Air Jordan and The Great One were among the other contenders, but their incredible talents couldn't touch the impact of Terry Fox's legacy.

10. CANADA ISN'T THE ONLY COUNTRY INSPIRED BY TERRY FOR: Sure, there are more than 9,000 Terry Fox Runs held in communities across Canada every year, but to say his inspirational story has transcended our borders would be an understatement. The first international Terry Fox Runs began just one year after his death, and they have since taken place in 36 countries, including Bahrain, Indonesia, South Korea, and Cuba.

11. MORE THAN $750 MILLION HAS BEEN RAISED IN HIS NAME: Terry Fox was lying on a stretcher with a crowd of microphones in his face when he announced his lung cancer diagnosis to the world. Overcome with emotion, he still managed to sound hopeful: "All I can say is if there's any way that I can get out there again and finish it, I will."

He never had that chance. But he lived long enough to realize his goal of raising $24 million for cancer research—$1 for every Canadian citizen at the time.

If only he could have seen how much further it would go.

Rick Hansen heads for Princeton on May 15, 1987 during his Man in Motion World Tour.

10 B.C. MEMORIES I'LL CARRY WITH ME FOREVER, BY RICK HANSEN

Rick Hansen, C.C., O.B.C., six-time Paralympic medalist, is a Canadian icon best known as the "Man In Motion" for undertaking an epic 26-month, 40,000-kilometre journey around the world in his wheelchair. He is the founder of the Rick Hansen Foundation, an organization committed to creating a world without barriers for people with disabilities.

1. TERRY FOX'S MARATHON OF HOPE: (April 12 – September 1, 1980)
My dear friend Terry Fox's Marathon of Hope was a powerful moment in time. It was the beginning of a Canadian and global movement to raise awareness and funds for cancer research. His legacy and fighting spirit live on as an annual tradition in Terry Fox runs held internationally around the world.

2. LAUNCH OF THE MAN IN MOTION WORLD TOUR: (March 21, 1985)
When I departed from Oakridge Centre on the start of my Man In Motion World Tour, I left with two dreams: of a world without barriers for people with disabilities and a cure for paralysis after spinal cord injury. I could have never predicted that it was the beginning of my life-long journey to create a world that is healthy and inclusive for all.

3. EXPO 86: (May 2 – October 13, 1986)
Expo 86 helped Vancouver grow into an international city, proving it was not only capable of hosting the world but also of working together to overcome the segmentation of diversity to achieve big dreams. With the leadership of Jimmy Pattison and my father-in-law, Patrick Reid, Expo 86 also became my final inspiration to commit to the launch of my Man In Motion World Tour.

4. END OF THE MAN IN MOTION WORLD TOUR: (May 22, 1987)
The tour lasted two years, two months and two days, and spanned 40,072 kilometres across 34 countries. In the end, it raised $26 million, awakened Canada and the world to the potential of people with disabilities, and marked an ultramarathon for social change. The homecoming banner that greeted me read, "The End is Just the Beginning," and it truly was. The impact of the tour was far greater than I could have ever imagined, and it continues to inspire me to believe that my best work is in front, not behind me.

5. THE 1994 COMMONWEALTH GAMES: (August 18 – 28, 1994)
The XV Commonwealth Games held in Victoria marked the first demonstration para-sport events in the games' history, and it has had a lasting legacy on accessibility and inclusion for athletes with a disability. Since 2002, the Commonwealth Games now integrates athletes with a disability in their sports program, which means there is just one class of athletes, and they all have full medal status.

6. 82ND GREY CUP: (November 27, 1994)
As a BC Lions football fan, and also as Honorary Chair of the 1994 Grey Cup, it was a spectacular moment to watch our hometown heroes hoist the Grey Cup at BC Place.

7. OPENING OF BLUSSON SPINAL CORD CENTRE: (November 18, 2008)
The opening of the Blusson Spinal Cord Centre marked a personal milestone in making progress toward one of my dreams of finding cures for paralysis after spinal cord injury (SCI). The fully accessible facility is now a world leader in integrated SCI research and care, and also home to the Rick Hansen Institute, which brings together a global network of collaborators to accelerate progress and life-enhancing solutions for those with SCI.

8. 2010 WINTER OLYMPIC GAMES: (FEBRUARY 12 – 28, 2010)
The 2010 Winter Olympics and Paralympic Games represented two events inside one games, celebrating one class of people. It was a humbling experience to be one of the final torchbearers to bring the Olympic Flame into BC Place during the opening ceremonies. There is nothing like the power of sport to unite humanity, and I certainly felt the pride and joy of hosting the world in my hometown and country.

9. THE MEN'S GOLD MEDAL HOCKEY GAME: (FEBRUARY 26, 2010)
I can almost hear the entire country erupt with joy again as I think back on that legendary moment, with just 24.4 seconds on the clock, when Sidney Crosby scored the winning goal in overtime during the men's gold medal hockey game at the 2010 Winter Olympics. The feeling was electric. As a sports fan, being part of that collective celebration left an indelible memory.

10. 2010 WINTER PARALYMPIC GAMES: (MARCH 12 – 21, 2010)
Nowhere in the definition of an athlete does it say you have to use your legs. It was a privilege to be a speaker at the opening ceremonies of the 2010 Paralympic Winter Games, where I watched my fellow Canadians welcome and celebrate Paralympic hopefuls from around the world for their ability as athletes.

10 TIMES KIM CAMPBELL WAS DELIGHTFULLY CANDID ONTWITTER

As it happens, the first and only woman to serve as Canadian prime minister is also the first and only prime minister born and raised in British Columbia. And now that she's in her 70s, Kim Campbell is still making history. For instance, she is, to the best of our knowledge, the first and only prime minister to call a sitting U.S. president a "motherf**cker" on Twitter.

Campbell's frank and unfiltered style endeared her to Canadians across the country for a very brief period back in 1993. Though the honeymoon period was short-lived, these wonderfully candid tweets show she hasn't watered down her approach to public life.

Kim Campbell is not afraid to speak her mind on social media.

1. ON PRESIDENT DONALD TRUMP: *"He really IS a motherf**ker!"*
This now-deleted tweet was inspired by U.S. Democratic Representative Rashida Tlaib, who enraged Donald Trump supporters by promising to "impeach the motherfucker" shortly after taking office. Even though Campbell added two asterisks to keep things safe for work, she took some flak for the tweet and eventually removed it.

2. ON THE HEALING POWER OF CHEESE: *"Oh Wow! This is the BEST NEWS EVER!"*
Here Campbell was referring to a *Huffington Post* article about how preservatives in cheese might help fight cancer—news that is, in our opinion, worthy of the hyperbole.

3. ON SCANDAL SHOWRUNNER SHONDA RHIMES: *"I admire her very much. Her tv shows have created a diverse and inclusive landscape of competence, stature and power!"*
This tweet heaping effusive praise on Rhimes, who also created *Grey's Anatomy* and *How to Get Away With Murder*, joining the national board of Planned Parenthood is a reminder of how Campbell put the progressive in Progressive Conservative.

4. ON EMASCULATING PAUL RYAN: *"Naughty but funny!"*
One month before the 2016 U.S. election, a photo starting making the rounds showing Mike Pence and Paul Ryan shaking hands with the caption, "LEAKED PHOTO: Mike Pence grabbing a pussy." Campbell didn't come up with the joke, but she certainly appreciated it.

5. ON THE VALUE OF ORGASMS: *"Oh drat! It's about vibrators! I thought as a child of the 60's, I might be worth a bundle! :)"*
Ushering in a new era of sex-positivity and candor among former prime ministers, this is Campbell riffing on a New York Post headline that read, "Women's orgasms are literally worth billions."

6. ON SARAH PALIN RE-ENTERING PUBLIC SERVICE: *"Gag me with a spoon!"*
Palin's name was floated as a potential ambassador to Canada back in February 2017. Campbell was not entirely on board with the idea.

7. ON THE BEST WAY TO RESPOND TO INTERNET TROLLS: *"I assure you if I WERE a stripper, I would NOT be cheap!"*
The best way to wither a troll is to enjoy yourself, as Campbell demonstrated while replying to a bonehead who called her a "cheap stripper."

8. ON MIXING DIRTY JOKES WITH INSIDE BASEBALL:
"A certain young lawyer named Rex,
Had diminutive organs of sex,
When charged with exposure
He said, with composure,
'De minimis non curat lex!'"

This dirty limerick was around for at least a couple decades before Campbell, who practised law prior to entering politics, decided to share it on Twitter in April 2018. The latin phrase in the punchline refers to the legal principle that judges shouldn't concern themselves with, as Duhaime's Law Dictionary puts it, "extremely minor transgressions."

9. ON FELLOW STATESPERSON BORIS JOHNSON: *"He is a pusillanimous vandal of historic proportions - a despicable destroyer of the creations of his betters! In short a frabjous ass!"*
Months after Johnson expressed his support for Brexit, describing the day of the vote as "Britain's Independence Day," Campbell dropped enough $5 words on the former London mayor to buy him a haircut.

10. ON OPPOSITION TO MODERNIZING O CANADA: *"Really obtuse! If we sang, 'in daughters all command' would that include men? Why is 'male' the default in 2016?"*
Campbell apparently didn't appreciate Andrew Coyne's column in the *National Post* that made the slightly tortured argument that because "all thy sons" is now interpreted as inclusive of all Canadians, keeping it in the anthem is "not a contradiction of the principle of the equality of the sexes … it is a reminder of its triumph."

THE MONEYBAGS BRIGADE: A LIST OF B.C.'S 9 RICHEST PEOPLE

If B.C. stands for "bring cash," these folks should be just fine. Here's the estimated net worth of all British Columbians on *Canadian Business Magazine*'s 2018 ranking of the 100 richest people in Canada.

1. JIMMY PATTISON: $6.41 BILLION: If it's possible to describe a billionaire as beloved, Pattison would be a good candidate for the term. The man behind the Overwaitea Foods grocery empire helped turn both Expo 86 and the 2010 Olympics into reality, thereby stamping his name on two of B.C.'s most defining events in modern history.

2. THE GAGLARDI FAMILY: $3.92 BILLION: Bob and Tom, the Gaglardi father-and-son team, have a huge portfolio of businesses, including hotels, the Moxies restaurant chain and the Dallas Stars of the NHL.

3. THE AQUILINI FAMILY: $3.3 BILLION: Everybody in Vancouver knows who the Aquilinis are—they're the family that owns the most reliably frustrating aspect of the city, the Vancouver Canucks. They're also working with the Gaglardis to build a new ski resort in Squamish, which would cement their status as the first family of winter sports in B.C.

4. THE LALJI FAMILY: $3.07 BILLION: The most high profile moment for this family was likely when their names were listed in the Panama Papers—the infamous leaked documents detailing how the world's wealthiest people had parked their assets in offshore entities. Back at home, the best known pieces of their portfolio include Park Royal Shopping Centre in West Vancouver and the Fairmont Hotel Vancouver.

5. CHIP WILSON: $2.92 BILLION: Love him or hate him, Chip Wilson is probably B.C.'s most famous billionaire. The founder of Lululemon has a knack for saying and doing things that piss people off, and that's likely why he was eventually forced out of his own company.

6. BRANDT LOUIE: $2.11 BILLION: Brandt Louie carries on the family legacy started by his grandfather, Hok Yat Louie, as CEO of the H. Y. Louie Company, best known for the massive drug and department store chain London Drugs.

7. HASSAN KHOSROWSHAHI: $1.16 BILLION: You could say Hassan Khosrowshahi rebuilt his family's lost empire after fleeing Iran in 1981, but that would be a bit of an understatement. Since his arrival in Canada, Khosrowshahi is responsible for creating the electronics superstore Future Shop, and now invests in real estate development, licensing rights and pharmaceuticals.

8. CALEB AND TOM CHAN: $1.07 BILLION: At first glance, these Vancouver brothers don't seem like household names. But they are, and you probably didn't even realize it—they're actually the Chans responsible for the state-of-the-art Chan Centre for the Performing Arts at UBC. Their company specializes in building housing developments, including condo towers and planned golf course communities.

9. U. GARY CHARLWOOD: $1.03 BILLION: The U is for Uwe. German-born Charlwood has made his money by scooping up ownership stakes in a bunch of companies with hundreds of franchises, including Uniglobe Travel and Century 21 Canada.

10 OUTRAGEOUS STORIES ABOUT B.C. BILLIONAIRE CHIP WILSON

The founder of Lululemon introduced Vancouver's unique yoga-yuppie lifestyle to the world. He also gives generously to charity and is responsible for securing a permanent place for the beloved A-maze-ing Laughter sculpture at English Bay. Still, he's probably best known for his many public relations gaffes and his knack for ticking people off.

1. 'FABRICO CANADA': Before there was Lululemon, there was Westbeach, the surf and snowboard line that was Wilson's first foray into the fashion world. It was also where he first began to bristle against the rules of the game, lashing out when federal officials made it clear in 1994 that his clothing needed to have bilingual labels. He pledged to use only garbled French—maybe "Fabrico Canada" instead of "Fabrique au Canada"—and told *The Canadian Press* "We'll make it so bad that it's going to be a joke."

2. OPEN CONCEPT SEEMED LIKE A GOOD IDEA: Wilson's vision for the Lululemon offices in the early days was the perfect distillation of West Coast egalitarianism—an open concept design space with the big boss right in the centre of it all. But as he told the *Financial Post* in 2005, all the chatter and general activity got really annoying really quickly. When a reporter visited the space, she discovered that Wilson had banned all talking between the peak working hours of 9 a.m. and 1 p.m. "This has really increased everyone's productivity," Wilson told her.

3. 2010 TROLLING: After Lululemon lost its long-shot bid to be the official clothier of the 2010 Winter Games, Wilson threw an Olympic-sized tantrum. With just months to go before the flame arrived in Vancouver, Lululemon introduced a new line of sweatshirts, T-shirts and toques under the banner "Cool Sporting Event That Takes Place in British Columbia Between 2009 & 2011 Edition." The Olympic organizing committee accused Wilson of poor sportsmanship, but hoodies bearing the slogan became one of the brand's big sellers.

4. THE POSE-OFF: Wilson has a knack for making his customers the target of his, uh, unique sense of humour. In 2002, his company placed an ad in *Yoga Journal* advertising the "Lululemon Athletica Invitational Yoga Pose-Off," outraging dedicated yogis, who flooded the magazine with angry letters, complaining that competition was completely antithetical to the spirit of the practice. But the whole thing was an April Fools' joke—Wilson said he was trying to poke fun at yoga enthusiasts who take themselves too seriously. He later explained in a letter to the magazine: "I believe that healthy yogis are ones who can laugh at what we did."

5. SOME THOUGHTS ON THE PILL : For someone without ovaries, Wilson sure has a lot of opinions on birth control. In a 2009 blog post, he linked it to both high divorce rates and breast cancer, writing that the latter "was due to the number of cigarette-smoking Power Women who were on the pill … and taking on the stress previously left to men in the working world." He doubled down on those claims in his 2018 book, *Little Black Stretchy Pants*, adding that both the pill and "three-martini lunches" helped contribute to the rising prevalence of breast cancer.

6. IF IT FEELS LIKE SEAWEED…: For a time, one of the most popular Lululemon lines was made with a fabric called VitaSea, said to contain seaweed that would "release marine amino acids, minerals and vitamins into the skin." But in 2007, *The New York Times* had the fabric tested in a lab, and reported there was no evidence of any actual seaweed content. Wilson pushed back, telling the *Times*, "If you actually put it on and wear it, it is different from cotton.... That's my only test of it," but Lululemon was ultimately forced to remove any claims of health benefits from the labelling for the line. He still hasn't gotten over the controversy. In his 2018 book, Wilson said he believed the story was a lie manufactured by a short-seller who made a "back room payoff to the writer."

7. BLAMING BIG BODIES: Wilson's most famous gaffe is probably the one that led to him stepping down as chairman of Lululemon's board in 2013. When customers complained that the fabric on their yoga pants was pilling, he told a host of Bloomberg TV the problem was that "some women's bodies just don't work for it."

But this wasn't the first time Wilson had shared his thoughts on larger women wearing Lululemon gear. In 2005, he told the *Sherbrooke Record* that he didn't sell any plus-sized clothing because the extra fabric was too expensive. He said he charged extra for bigger sizes, he worried about human rights complaints, because he believed plus-sized people are extra sensitive. "It's a money loser, for sure."

8. UNSOLICITED ADVICE: Even after he left Lululemon for good in 2015, Wilson still had plenty of opinions about how the company should be run. He even started a website, elevatelululemon.com, to offer his thoughts on how his baby was performing. In 2017, he took things a step further, buying up ad space in the bus shelter outside Lululemon's Vancouver headquarters. The ad was insistent: "LULULEMON BUY UNDER ARMOUR NOW!" Alas, his advice was not taken.

9. SOME THOUGHTS ON PUNCTUALITY: Whatever feelings Wilson might have had about *The New York Times* after the VitaSea exposé, they apparently didn't affect his willingness to sit down with the paper for a feature story in 2016. But the longer format gave him plenty of opportunities to stick his foot in his mouth, and he did not disappoint.

Wilson kicked off a breakfast interview with reporter Katherine Rosman by lecturing her about arriving 15 minutes late, condescendingly telling his entourage of young female employees, "Now we know that when we have breakfast with Katie, we don't really have to be there when we say we will be there." He went on to describe her sense of punctuality, bizarrely, as "Jewish Standard Time." Unfortunately for Wilson, Rosman later witnessed him missing an appointment entirely, simply because "the time [got] away from us."

10. A REALLY BIG DOCK: Wilson has a bit of a history with ticking off his neighbours. In 2013, he angered Kitsilano residents by spending $7,000 for a graffiti mural along the seawall behind his mansion. The problem was that he didn't have a permit for the art, and he was later forced to paint over it. Someone—who knows who, really?—painted this message in its place: "The City of Vancouver: Consistently opposing the arts."

Two years later, Wilson pulled one of his classic pranks on the neighbourhood, putting up a fake development proposal sign outlining plans to build an 8,000-square-foot floating helicopter dock in English Bay. That turned out to be an early April Fool's joke.

His plan for water access to his property on the Sunshine Coast, however, was not. In 2017, in spite of vocal opposition from local residents who wanted to preserve their quiet waterfront idyll, Wilson began construction on a gigantic 4,800-square-foot dock at Middlepoint. The dock would be nearly the length of a football field, with space for two 50-foot yachts.

11 CROTCHETY QUOTES FROM LEGENDARY NEWSPAPERWOMAN 'MA' MURRAY

Decades after her death, Margaret "Ma" Murray remains a legend in the B.C. journalism indus-try, her legacy sustained by the community newspaper awards that bear her name. But as the years go on, there are fewer and fewer people who remember what made her famous in the first place—namely, her acid tongue, which she unleashed readily and with relish as the editor of the *Bridge River-Lillooet News*.

Born in rural Kansas and reportedly only educated up to the third grade, Murray's spelling wasn't always perfect and she occasionally bent the truth, but her opinions, which one could charitably call unvarnished, nevertheless earned her fans across Canada and the U.S.

Keeping in mind she was a humourist at heart, here are 11 memorably cantankerous quotes from ma.

1. ON TV NEWS: "Television is all right for people who are sick or can't get out of the house, but my God, anyone who can sit and watch that all night long has something wrong with their head." *The Canadian Press, March 14, 1970*

2. ON STUDENT JOURNALISTS: Murray once called The Ubyssey, a student newspaper at the University of B.C., "unwholesome and pointless craperoni" for its decision to publish lewd pictures in a symbolic gesture against censorship in 1968. The editor, Murray added, was "narrow-minded and pigeonheaded." *Vancouver Sun, October 4, 1982*

3. ON PIERRE ELLIOTT TRUDEAU: The former prime minister was a "half-assed socialist when he got that job," according to Murray. "I was a delegate at that convention and I never voted for him. I told him, I said, 'I don't think you have got enough experience.'" *Vancouver Sun, April 11, 1978*

4. ON PREMIER W.A.C. BENNETT: Speaking to a gathering of young Catholics, Murray once described Bennett as "a little dictator and the next thing to a gangster" who had been governing so long "he thinks he's ruling by Divine Right." *Richmond Review, March 10, 1965*

5. ON BEING 83 YEARS OLD: "My knees have no reflexes anymore. But my tongue hasn't been harmed any." *The Calgary Herald, April 22, 1970*

6. ON THE WOMEN'S LIB MOVEMENT: "Beats me what all the fuss is about," Murray said. "Eve was created when God found Adam wasn't worth a damn without her. When he created Eve, He put a lot of new gadgets in her, including a brain." *The Canadian Press, February 19, 1976*

7. ON MAKEUP: "This country uses $70 million worth of cosmetics a year. We used to rub some cream off the top of the milk on our faces and that did a pretty good job." *Squamish Times, December 8, 1971*

8. ON ELECTRICITY: "It's high time the electrical industry did something to head off boredom and the waste of excess leisure time which electricity has given people," she said. "If we give our women and our youth another 60 years of 'nothing to do' … they'll all turn out to be complete morons." *Calgary Herald, June 27, 1966*

9. ON UNIONIZED LABOUR: "They cheat on their work and they're the darnedest (sic) bunch of lotus eaters you ever saw." *The Canadian Press, February 19, 1976*

10. ON FIRST AID: Appearing before a convention of the Industrial First Aid Attendants, Murray declared that "once upon a time, we were all first aiders … if you couldn't set a bone, you'd try it first on a dog or a calf." *Vancouver Sun, September 26, 1966*

11. ON RELUCTANCE TO REPLACE THE UNION JACK WITH A CANADIAN FLAG: "Are Canadians so damned thin-skinned that they want to hang onto the old country's apron strings, or are Canadians so steeped in imperialism or so cowardly of this fallacy of the mother country that they are never going to be weaned?" *The Canadian Press, May 10, 1965*

(Opposite) Humpback whale.

FLORA AND FAUNA

NO REALLY, YOU SHOULDN'T HAVE: 7 INVASIVE SPECIES WE'RE ALL STUCK WITH NOW

1. KNOTWEEDS (PLANT):
How they arrived: These monsters, dubbed the "thugs of the invasive plant world" by the *Campbell River Mirror*, are native to Asia and were originally brought into B.C. for decorative purposes.

Where they're found: So far? Knotweeds have spread to the Lower Mainland, Vancouver Island, Sunshine Coast, Haida Gwaii, Nechako, Cariboo, Thompson-Okanagan, and Kootenay regions.

Why they suck: Knotweeds are considered some of the worst invasive species in the world. That's because they grow quickly and are capable of forcing their way right through asphalt, building foundations, retaining walls—you get the idea. Homeowners unlucky enough to encounter the scourge can see their properties devalued, and knotweed can also damage bridge abutments and other vital infrastructure.

2. GIANT HOGWEED (PLANT):
How it arrived: This highly competitive and fast-growing plant, whose toxic sap can blind you, made its way from Asia to North America as a garden ornamental.

Where it's found: Giant hogweed has been seen in the Lower Mainland, Fraser Valley, Gulf Islands and parts of Vancouver Island.

Why it sucks: The toxins in giant hogweed sap can cause blisters, welts and burns that leave behind purple scars. And as previously mentioned, if you value your vision, never let it get in your eyes.

3. BALSAM WOOLLY ADELGID (INSECT):
How they arrived: This Christmas tree-destroying insect was transported from Europe to North America by accident. Oops!

Where they're found: Balsam wooly adelgids infestations have been observed in the province's coastal forest areas, including Vancouver Island and the Fraser Valley, and around Rossland.

Why they suck: The insects feed on the stems and branches of true firs, injecting them with toxic saliva and stunting their growth or killing them—and the females, who reproduce asexually, can drop up to 10,000 babies in their lifespan.

4. APPLE MAGGOT (INSECT):
How they arrived: It's unclear, but inside an apple is a reasonable guess. They're indigenous to eastern North America.

Where they're found: These disgusting maggotsare already found throughout the Lower Mainland, Vancouver Island, the Gulf Islands, and Prince George. As of this writing, B.C.'s Southern Interior is the only major fruit growing region in North America that's free of the pest—but let's see how long that lasts.

Why they suck: Female maggots lay eggs underneath the apple's skin, and the larvae tunnel throughout the juicy fruit until it's rotten and decayed. Let's put it this way: if you bit into an infested apple, you would know.

5. GOLDFISH (FISH):

How they arrived: Goldfish, which are native to East Asia, are said to be the first foreign fish species introduced in North America. P.T. Barnum took credit for their arrival in the 1850s, but by some accounts goldfish had already been around for well over 100 years by that point.

Where they're found: There are self-sustaining goldfish populations throughout much of the southern half of B.C. Why? Because too many pet owners decide, for presumably compassionate reasons, to set them free without actually considering the consequences.

Why they suck: Goldfish compete with native fish species for food—and in some cases turn native fish species *into* food. They're also known to disturb sediment, which can harm underwater plants.

6. DEATH CAP MUSHROOMS (FUNGUS):

How they arrived: These poisonous mushrooms, which are native to Europe, are believed to have been carried into the province decades ago on the roots of imported trees.

Where they're found: Death cap mushrooms have been recorded primarily in Vancouver and Victoria, where they grow under a variety of trees, including hazelnut, hornbeam, beech, linden, sweet chestnut, and oak. They've also been found elsewhere in the Lower Mainland and Vancouver Island, and in the Fraser Valley and on Galiano Island.

Why they suck: As the name suggests, death cap mushrooms can kill you—and they're particularly dangerous because they can easily be mistaken for edible puffballs or Asian paddy straw mushrooms, depending on how young or old they are. People who accidentally chow down on death caps usually begin feeling nauseated and start vomiting within 12 hours, and after a few days can experience seizures, comas, and, in unfortunate cases, death.

7. EASTERN GREY SQUIRRELS (MAMMAL):

How they arrived: The bushy-tailed squirrels, which are native to eastern North America, were actually delivered to Stanley Park sometime around 1914, reportedly as a gift. Unfortunately, the gifter did specify there were no take-backs.

Where they're found: Since arriving in Vancouver, the squirrels have made their way throughout the Lower Mainland, into the Okanagan, and even across the water to Vancouver Island. According to the B.C. government, their spread was likely aided, in some instances, by the squirrels hitchhiking onto vehicles.

Why they suck: They can displace the province's native squirrels, who are smaller, and eat native birds' eggs and nestlings. They're also known to do a number on people's homes, digging up lawns, chewing on wire, and nesting inside attics and roofs.

Sources: The B.C. Inter-Ministry Invasive Species Working Group, Invasive Species Council of BC

10 FAMOUS TREES: A LIST THAT COULD ONLY BE WRITTEN IN B.C.

1. BIG LONELY DOUG, PORT RENFREW AREA: It's an apt nickname for this 70-metre tall tree. Doug is Canada's second largest Douglas fir, and it stands all alone in the middle of a Vancouver Island clearcut, thanks to a logger named Dennis Cronin, who noticed its massive size and marked it to be saved from the cutting crews in 2011. There are estimates the lumber logged from Doug would have earned a $50,000 payday. Its trunk has a diameter of four metres, and its canopy stretches a whopping 18 metres from side to side. It's not clear exactly how old Doug is, but growth rings from the stumps nearby suggest it may have been growing here for a millennium. The tree is the subject of Harley Rustad's 2018 book *Big Lonely Doug: The Story Of One Of Canada's Last Great Trees*.

2. RED CREEK FIR, PORT RENFREW AREA: Just 20 kilometres metres away from Big Lonely Doug is the biggest known Douglas fir on the entire planet. This giant is 74 metres tall, with a trunk diameter of more than four metres. The Red Creek Fir is estimated to be between 750 and 1,000 years old.

3. LADY CYNTHIA, LADYSMITH: Unless you have a problem with pink, this is probably the prettiest tree on this list (though some might argue it's technically a bush.) Lady Cynthia is rhododendron that's been growing in this small Vancouver Island town for more than 115 years, though it reportedly sprouted its first leaves in Scotland before taking the long sea voyage to B.C. When it's in bloom, its branches are festooned with more than 4,000 bright pink flowers, and the local chamber of commerce is hoping to cash in on the rosy glory, inviting tourists to drop by and soak in the majesty.

4. KIIDK'YAAS, A.K.A. THE GOLDEN SPRUCE, HAIDA GWAII: This famous tree, alas, is no more, thanks to a confusing and ill-conceived act of protest against the logging industry—the full story is laid out in John Vaillant's 2006 book *The Golden Spruce: A True Story of Myth, Madness and Greed*. The giant Sitka spruce had a genetic mutation that meant its needles were yellow instead of the usual green. Haida mythology holds that Kiidk'yaas was once a mischievous young boy who was turned into a tree after causing a storm to wreck his village.

The sacred tree was felled in 1997 by an unemployed forest engineer named Grant Hadwin, who wrote a manifesto blaming the act of destruction on his "rage and hatred towards university trained professionals and their extremist supporters." Hadwin was arrested and charged, but he disappeared under mysterious circumstances before he could stand trial. The last signs of him were a broken kayak and some belongings that were found on Mary Island.

5. THE GNARLIEST TREE IN CANADA, PORT RENFREW AREA: This bumpy, lumpy cedar stands in a forest that members of the Pacheedaht First Nation know as T'l'oqwxwat. Some movie fans prefer the nickname Avatar Grove. This tree is named for the absolutely mammoth knot near its base, and it's not far from Big Lonely Doug and the Red Creek Fir.

6. ELAHO GIANT, SQUAMISH AREA: Sadly, this is another tree that has been lost to history. This ancient Douglas fir was likely more than 1,000 years old, with one of the thickest trunks on record. Like the other Douglas firs on this list, the Giant owed much of its longevity to its thick bark, which protected it from periodic forest fires. But in recent years, as the climate warms, wildfires in B.C. have become hotter and more intense, and when flames rushed through the Elaho Valley in 2015, the Giant was toast—despite the best efforts of firefighters.

7. STANLEY PARK HOLLOW TREE, VANCOUVER: It's a stretch to call it a tree these days, but the Hollow Tree is still one of the most famous landmarks in Stanley Park. Once upon a time, it was a Western Red Cedar that lived for somewhere between 600 and 800 years. When it died more than a century ago, it left a huge hollow stump, with space inside to fit several

At birth, cougar cubs weigh about half a kilogram. They have blue eyes for the first year of their life and tawny brown coats with black spots, which helps keep them safe from predators.

tourists at a time. The stump was badly damaged in the windstorm of 2006, and the Vancouver park board considered letting the tree fall and rot. But this is Vancouver, and the public demanded the stump be saved. Now, it's held upright by a hidden metal frame.

8. THE CARMANAH GIANT, CARMANAH WALBRAN PROVINCIAL PARK: This is it—the tallest tree in Canada, at 95 metres high. It's also believed to be the tallest Sitka spruce in the world. The Giant is estimated to be about 400 years old, and it likely managed to grow so tall because it's sheltered from the wind inside a deep ravine. For anyone who loves big, old trees, Vancouver Island's Carmanah Valley is filled with some of the largest specimens in the country, including a few cedars that have stood for a millennium.

9. SAN JUAN SPRUCE, NEAR PORT RENFREW: The area around Port Renfrew is also a pretty major hotspot for significant trees. And while the Carmanah Giant may be the world's tallest Sitka spruce, its San Juan cousin is the biggest Sitka by volume—about 333 cubic metres of lumber. It's also a bit funny looking. There's a secondary trunk growing out of its side, and that offshoot has grown for so long that it's a pretty massive tree in its own right.

10. EUGENIA PLACE OAK, VANCOUVER: Its branches probably reach higher than any other tree in the Lower Mainland, but that's only because it's cheating. On its own, this pin oak isn't especially tall at all, but it just happens to be growing at the top of a 19-storey condo tower overlooking English Bay. The first tree was planted in the middle of a giant circular terrace after the building was completed in 1987. The tree died after the drought of 2015, and there was no choice but to replace it—the building permit for the development stipulated that the owners had to have a rooftop tree. Hoisting a new tree up that high wasn't cheap; the final replacement bill was estimated at $554,000.

PAULA WILD'S LIST OF 10 THINGS YOU DIDN'T KNOW ABOUT B.C.'S APEX PREDATORS

Paula Wild is the author of seven books including The Cougar: Beautiful, Wild and Dangerous *and* Return of the Wolf: Conflict & Coexistence.

COUGARS

1. Although most cats don't like water, cougars are excellent swimmers. One wearing a GPS collar was tracked swimming 6.5 kilometres from downtown Nanaimo to Gabriola Island.

2. Cougars move through communities more often than most people realize. And a surprising number of cougars find their way into downtown Victoria. In 1992, a four-year-old, 60-kilogram healthy male was tranquilized and removed from the underground parking garage of the Fairmont Empress Hotel.

3. Vancouver Island has the highest density of cougars worldwide. It also has the highest rate of cougar attacks on humans.

4. Cougars communicate with each other by making high-pitched chirping sounds that humans often mistake for birds. When in heat, females sometimes let out blood-curdling screams that sound like a woman being murdered.

5. Cougars have been observed jumping 5.5 metres straight up from a standstill and 18.5 metres down from a tree.

Wolves will eat any type of meat from a mouse to a moose. Those living along the BC coast also eat a lot of fish and seafood such as seals and clams.

WOLVES

1. The tip of a wolf's nose is a complex landscape of ridges and creases that creates a pattern as distinct as a human fingerprint. Each nostril moves independently, allowing wolves to determine the direction a particular scent is coming from.

Scientists know that wolves can smell prey from a distance of 2.5 kilometres. Some speculate that, under certain conditions, they may be able to detect prey 100 kilometres away.

2. Wolves are the marathon runners of the animal kingdom and can trot 8 kilometres per hour all night long in search of prey. When closing in for a kill, they can run up to 60 kilometres per hour for a short distance.

3. Wolves lead a feast and famine existence and can go up to two weeks without eating. When they do chow down, they gorge and can gain as much as 10 kilograms in one feeding.

4. Each wolf has a distinct howl and wolves in different regions howl in their own dialect. To the human ear, a wolf howl often sounds sad and lonely, but to a wolf it can mean anything from "Where are you?" to "I'm looking for a mate" or "Hey, we're all together and everything's cool!"

5. As carnivores, wolves will eat anything from a mouse to a moose. While most wolves depend on ungulates for their sustenance, some eat a lot of fish. In fact, some wolves on B.C.'s coastal islands primarily eat salmon, seals, and shellfish, as well as mink and other marine-related animals, and may seldom—if ever—see a deer.

10 FACTS ABOUT THE WHALES AND DOLPHINS OF B.C.

1. THE FORGOTTEN KILLER WHALES: Most British Columbians know about the northern and southern resident killer whale populations, which feed on salmon, and the transient or Bigg's killer whales, which eat mammals like porpoises and seals. But there's another orca population in B.C.—the offshore killer whales who spend their time in groups of up to 100 animals. Scientists don't know a lot about these elusive animals, but they do have a pretty good idea of what they eat: sharks.

2. THE DISTINCTIVE SOUNDS OF HUMPBACK WHALES: The plaintive song of a humpback whale is all about sex. The males sing their deep, almost mournful songs during winter breeding season in the tropics to attract females, and their tunes are specific to their chosen pickup area. Not only that, but the humpback whale songs in every mating area seems to evolve from year to year.

3. THE JETSETTING GREY WHALES: These guys are the frequent fliers of B.C.'s underwater world. Grey whales have one of the longest migrations of any mammal on the planet, travelling up to 20,000 kilometres every year from their breeding grounds in Mexico to their summer hangouts in the Arctic and then back again.

4. THE ENORMOUS BLUE WHALES: The blue isn't just the biggest mammal on Earth—it's the biggest animal that's ever existed. Just one blue whale tongue can weigh as much as an elephant. The heaviest blue ever recorded weighed 173 tonnes—that's about twice the estimated weight of the biggest known dinosaur, the *Argentinosaurus huinculensis*.

5. THE SPEEDY FIN WHALES: The naturalist Roy Chapman Andrews described the fin as "the greyhound of the sea." These whales can swim in bursts of up to 45 kilometres an hour—significantly faster than the average speed of a modern cruise ship. And yet, fin whales are the species most likely to be killed by ship strike, and scientists haven't been able to explain why.

6. THE BRAINY SPERM WHALES: They may not compare with blue whales in overall size, but sperm whales have the biggest brains of any animal, at about eight kilograms—roughly five times the weight of a human's. Those giant brains sit inside disproportionately huge heads that measure about one-third of a whale's total length.

7. THE NOISY HARBOUR PORPOISES: This is the smallest cetacean that lives in B.C. waters. They also live in coastal waters across the northern hemisphere, and in the Maritimes and New England, some fishermen call them "puffing pigs" for the distinct snorting sound they make when they come up for air.

8. THE CROSS-BREEDING DALL'S PORPOISES: Visitors to B.C. who've never heard of these little black-and-white cuties sometimes mistake them for baby killer whales, but they're missing the distinctive white eyepatches of orcas. Female Dall's porpoises have been known to crossbreed with harbour porpoises in B.C., even though the species rarely interact. When they're born, the babies tend to prefer hanging out with the more social Dall's.

9. THE GREGARIOUS PACIFIC WHITE-SIDED DOLPHINS: Oh man, these guys just can't stand to be alone. In the Salish Sea, you can often see them in groups of a couple hundred, but sometimes even that isn't enough socializing for them. This is the one cetacean species that is frequently found hanging out with other species—including killer whales, sea lions, porpoises, humpbacks, and other dolphin species.

10. THE OVER-HUNTED MINKE WHALES: Minkes are the second smallest baleen whales, with a maximum length of just 9 metres—their cousins the blues grow to three times that length. For a time, that meant minkes were overlooked by commercial whalers, but by the mid-20th century, most other species had been decimated and minkes became the new target. Fleets from Japan, Norway, and Iceland still hunt minkes today.

5 DISTURBING STORIES ABOUT B.C.'S MOST BELOVED WILDLIFE

1. KILLER WHALE INFANTICIDE: Few animals in B.C. are more beloved than these big, intelligent, black and white cetaceans. They're playful and curious, and they demonstrate strong family bonds that make them seem almost human. But the fact is they're still animals, and that's never more clear than when you're talking about the mammal-eating transient killer whales, which have been known to toss seals in the air in a gruesome game of ping pong before slaughtering them.

In the winter of 2016, scientists witnessed some transient orca behaviour that left them horrified. While observing a group of transients, they watched as a large male whale held a calf under the water until it drowned. The researchers believe the male orca was hoping to mate with the calf's mother, and that he killed her baby to force her into a fertile state.

2. THE MOOSE THAT STOMPED A COP: Most Canadians know never to mess with a moose, but in this case, the poor Mountie was only trying to help. According CBC, it was a Thursday in Prince George, and an RCMP officer was parked at the side of the road in his cruiser when he noticed two moose crossing at an intersection. Another vehicle was heading straight for the animals. Perhaps forgetting that a moose usually wins out in any battle with a moving vehicle, the cop put his cruiser into drive and tried to block the second car.

But instead of seizing the opportunity to mosey on out of town, one of the moose fixated on the cruiser, rammed the front grill, smashed the windshield, and then jumped straight onto the roof and started stomping. One of its hoofs shattered the driver's side window and bashed the Mountie's shoulder. Luckily, the cop escaped with just a few bruises.

3. A SEA OTTER'S MACABRE DELIGHTS: Nothing cuter than these fluffy little guys, right? The way they float on their backs holding hands is too adorable! But the sexual appetites of some sea otters are far from sweet. Take the story a longtime Nootka Island lighthouse keeper told the *Vancouver Sun* a few years back about an otter her family nicknamed "Whiskers." Whiskers was friendlier than you might expect for a wild animal, and enjoyed playing fetch with the assistant lightkeeper's son. But Whiskers also liked teasing the local dogs. One day, the sea otter apparently managed to lure one of the dogs into the water—and then drowned him. When the keeper's family investigated the commotion, they found Whiskers humping the carcass while the other neighbourhood dogs barked wildly from the shore.

4. BLACK BEAR CANNIBALISM: As the time for hibernation draws close every fall, it's not unusual for B.C.'s bears to get a bit aggressive. After all, they need to eat up if they want to pack on enough pounds to make it through the winter. But in September 2018, an advisor with the Cheslatta Carrier Nation near Burns Lake was doing a helicopter flyover over an area burned by wildfire when he saw some black bear behaviour that "sent chills down my bones," he told CBC. At the centre of the frightening scene, one bear was bent over the carcass of another, feasting on the meat. According to conservation officers, bear cannibalism isn't unheard of, but it's still rare to see.

5. THE MARMOTS THAT (MIGHT HAVE) CAUSED A PLANE CRASH: OK, this one is just a theory, and the experts say there's not a lot of evidence to support it, but it's too eerie to ignore. The idea was raised after a small plane crashed in Vernon in 2012, killing the two people inside. The twin-engine Piper had been based at Kelowna International Airport, which was overrun with marmots. Other pilots who fly out of there speculated that marmots might have chewed up some vital components in the plane, causing it to crash. One local flying club member estimated to a CBC reporter that 80 per cent of aircraft at the facility had been damaged by marmots. On the other hand, the Transportation Safety Board, a fairly reliable source on these matters, described that scenario as pretty unlikely.

10 TIMES EXOTIC ANIMALS RAN WILD IN B.C.

1. THE CAIMAN THAT FELL OUT OF A WINDOW: This was "a very lucky caiman," in the words of an animal protection officer. Despite plunging three storeys from the window of a Kitsilano apartment in 2006, the 1.5-metre reptile walked away with only one injury—a dislocated toe. It turns out the beast, which resembles a small alligator, was part of the apartment tenant's beloved menagerie of exotic lizards, snakes, turtles, and toads—all kept well fed and clean inside one small Vancouver home.

2. A WALLABY ON THE LAM: Gracie the wallaby had two exciting days of adventure after she somehow escaped from her Langley home in the winter of 2017. How exactly the small Australian marsupial spent those days is still a mystery, but she was captured after she surprised a local resident enjoying a morning cup of coffee on their backyard deck. Police used a fishing net to catch her, then carried Gracie home in a dog crate.

3. A GENTLE SIBERIAN TIGER LOST IN THE WILD: This remarkably tame big cat was being transferred from its home at a former petting zoo near Fort St. John when the truck it was travelling in got into a crash on the Alaska Highway in 2006. The massive tiger was dazed and wandering near the highway when conservation officers finally tracked it down. They were ready to shoot it with a tranquilizer gun before the owner arrived and told them that wouldn't be necessary. Instead, the owner patted the beast on the head, tied a rope around its neck, and walked it calmly into an enclosure usually reserved for problem bears.

4. THE MYSTERIOUS WANDERING CHEETAH: We're still waiting to hear the full story on the cheetah with the bright orange collar that was spotted wandering along a highway north-east of Creston one day in 2015. It's likely it was a cat named Annie Rose, the former resident of an Alberta zoo with an unsettling habit of stalking children. Luckily, no kids were harmed in the escape—as far as we know—but we don't know anything about how it got away from its enclosure in Creston or how it was recaptured. The cheetah's owners, a local couple who own a pair, were later charged with possessing an alien species without a permit, but the charges would eventually be stayed. The cheetahs were later transferred to Ontario, after B.C. officials denied the owners a permit to keep them.

5. A CAPUCHIN MONKEY ESCAPE ARTIST: This itty bitty primate made his escape from an animal sanctuary in Lake Cowichan and never looked back. Despite a search that lasted more than a week in 2018, conservation officers just couldn't track the monkey through the dense forest in the area, and said the springtime bounty in the woods would offer plenty of food for a clever little creature. The capuchin had been a resident of a private facility called the Primate Estate, and it wasn't the first escapee—neighbours have complained in the past about stampeding miniature ponies in their yards, larger primates stealing cat food, and a tiger on the lam.

6. A VERY UNFORTUNATE SERVAL CAT : This exotic beast had a history of escaping its home in Sooke. It went missing for several weeks over the summer of 2014 before being trapped and returned to its owners. Sadly, it escaped again that winter and was struck and killed by a pickup truck.

7. GYPSY, THE ROVING BALL PYTHON: The first time Delta Police saw Gypsy, a two-metre long snake, it was snoozing with its owner on the ground outside a local Walmart in the summer of 2018. Ten days later, officers learned Gypsy was missing, last seen in a farmer's field in Ladner. Nine days later, the non-venomous snake appeared near the bridge to Westham Island. But after that, the trail went cold.

8. THE WATER BUFFALO THAT SURPRISED A SCHOOL: It was the principal that spotted the huge Asian bovine touring the playground of a Langley Christian elementary school in 2018. The bull water buffalo checked out the swings before charging off to visit nearby middle and high schools—plus a church. The ungulate was a new arrival at a local farm, but apparently wasn't a fan of the rigid order of its new herd, and simply wandered out the front gate. An animal control officer had to use her car to corral the beast and bring it home.

9. THE INFAMOUS SURREY PEACOCKS: This isn't a story about just one bird—or even a handful of birds. For at least a decade, the Surrey neighbourhood of Sullivan Heights has been home to a feral flock of peafowl, estimated at as many as 150 birds. It's likely the colourful creatures got loose when a hobby farmer abandoned them in 2006. What exactly to do about the peacocks has been a matter of some dispute. The neighbourhood has been sharply divided for years between those who feed the birds and protect them, and those who want them gone. In 2018, city council approved a plan to relocate them to a rescue centre, but peacock fans vowed to fight that until the bitter end.

10. THE GREAT ELEPHANT HUNT: The year was 1926, and the Sells Floto Circus had arrived by rail to perform in the city of Cranbrook. It was a major event for the small community, but things went sideways as the circus animals were being unloaded from the train. Something—maybe smoke from a nearby wildfire—spooked the elephants as they were stepping out. All 14 giants skedaddled out of there as fast as they could, stampeding out of the railway yard and into town.

They stomped through the streets, frightening everyone in sight, and then ran out into the countryside. All railway crews in the area were warned to be on the lookout for elephants on the tracks. By the next morning, only half the pachyderms were safely back with the circus company. Another three were later found in an orchard, happily munching on apples. One died of pneumonia (and gunshot wounds) but the rest were eventually recaptured. A male elephant named Charlie Ed became a local legend after he evaded apprehension for six weeks. He finally wandered back into town just in time to miss the first snow.

6 DINOSAURS (AND DINOSAUR-LIKE CREATURES) THAT ROAMED B.C.

1. AMBLYDACTYLUS: Dam-building and dinosaur discoveries seem to go hand-in-hand in B.C. While the W.A.C. Bennett Dam was under construction in the 60s, dinosaur footprints were found along the bed of the Peace River. When construction began on a second dam over the river in 1975, a group of geologists set off on an expedition to look for more. They described their discoveries in a 1979 paper, evoking a "rich assemblage of dinosaur footprint tracks."

That included at least two Amblydactylus species, one of them never seen before and named *A. kortmeyeri* in honour of Carl Kortmeyer, the man who found it. This genus of dinosaurs is known only from their footprints, but some theorize they may have been duck-billed and herbivorous, resembling the better-known hadrosaurs.

2. COLUMBOSAURIPUS: Up until 2002, there were only two reports of fossilized dinosaur bones being discovered in B.C., according to palaeontologist Richard McCrea. For decades, only preserved footprints had been found for the vast majority of dinosaurs thought to have lived here.

That includes *Columbosauripus ungulatus*, which was first documented in the Peace River region in 1932. The birdlike, three-clawed imprint suggests a bipedal meat eater that lived in the province's northeast during the Cretaceous period.

3. HADROSAURS: Finally, some bones! B.C.'s first major concentration of dinosaur fossils was discovered near Tumbler Ridge in 2002, and included the bones of these duck-billed veg-etarians, according to McCrea. The most complete fossilized hadrosaur skeleton was found in 2009, but it was missing its head. Researchers suspected a hungry tyrannosaurus may have been responsible for that—more on those guys in a bit.

4. ANKYLOSAURS: Among the more than 200 skeletal elements uncovered near Tumbler Ridge in the early aughts were the remains of these armoured beasts with their distinctive club-like tails from the Cretaceous period. Fossilized ankylosaur tracks have been found in B.C. as far back as the 1930s, and continue to be found in large numbers today.

5. ELASMOSAURUS: Mike Trask and his 12-year-old daughter Heather were the ones to make this lucky find one day in 1988. They were wandering along the Puntledge River, west of Comox, searching for fossils, when it happened. According to the Courtenay Museum and Palaeontology Centre, Mike was kneeling on the ground to examine something when Heather noticed a group of solid masses rising from the exposed shale nearby. She and her dad did a little digging, and were shocked to discover an arrangement of fossilized bones.

This would turn out to be the first elasmosaur recorded in B.C. Not technically dinosaurs, these water-dwelling plesiosaurs lived in North America about 80.5 million years ago. They could grow to be more than 10 metres long.

6. TYRANNOSAURS: This is the big one. It's a relatively new discovery, but one of the most exciting finds ever made in B.C. Vacationing chiropractor Rick Lambert spotted the fossil near Tumbler Ridge in 2017—not only did it belong to a fearsome tyrannosaurus, but it was also the first dinosaur skull found in the region, according to *The Canadian Press*. The exact species isn't yet known.

Hundreds of tyrannosaur teeth have also been found during excavations near Tumbler Ridge, including in areas where other, less fearsome, dinosaurs have been found without their heads.

(Opposite) A hiker is seen on the North Coast Trail, which runs 59.5 kilometres at the northern tip of Vancouver Island.

THE GREAT OUTDOORS

STEPHEN HUI'S 10 LONG B.C. HIKES WORTHY OF YOUR BUCKET LIST

Stephen Hui is the author of 105 Hikes In and Around Southwestern British Columbia. *He's currently researching his second hiking guidebook. Find out more at 105hikes.com.*

1. GREAT DIVIDE TRAIL: (1,130 kilometres, Rocky Mountains)
Once you've ticked off the rest of the hikes on this list, you'll be primed to backpack all or part of the Canadian counterpart of the Continental Divide Trail in the United States. On its way from Waterton Lakes National Park to Kakwa Provincial Park, the GDT criss-crosses the British Columbia–Alberta border and provides an incredibly scenic thru-hiking challenge.

2. EAST BEACH TRAIL: (80 kilometres, Haida Gwaii)
Running from Tlell to Tow Hill via Rose Spit and North Beach, this remote route covers a whole lot of coastline. Enjoy six days of magical beach walking and solitude in Naikoon Provincial Park on Graham Island.

3. SUNSHINE COAST TRAIL: (178 kilometres, Powell River)
Traversing the Upper Sunshine Coast from Sarah Point to Saltery Bay, the SCT comes with more than a dozen huts for shelter and a few mountains to sweat up and over. It's truly a long walk in the woods—one that visits old-growth groves, clear-cuts, and everything in between. Make sure to pack enough toilet paper. (I didn't.)

4. HESQUIAT TRAIL: (46 kilometres, Hesquiat Peninsula Provincial Park)
Certainly, the West Coast Trail and Nootka Trail are on many more tick lists. Set off on this lesser known seaside trek from Escalante Point to Boat Basin for a wilder backpacking experience between Nootka and Clayoquot sounds.

5. STEIN HERITAGE TRAIL: (90 kilometres, Stein Valley Nlaka'pamux Heritage Park)
Environmentalists, outdoor recreationists, and First Nations fought for 20 years to spare the Stein River watershed from the logger's axe, winning the park's protection in 1995. The classic traverse from headwaters to river mouth leads through alpine tundra and old-growth forest, and past ancient pictographs and glacial landforms.

6. NORTH COAST TRAIL: (59.5 kilometres, Cape Scott Provincial Park)
Don't expect this rugged trail at the northern tip of Vancouver Island to be an easy walk on the beach. Fortunately, in between tiring cable car crossings and steep rope sections, you'll be wowed by stunning beaches and sightings of black bears and grey whales.

7. CHILKOOT TRAIL: (53 kilometres, Chilkoot Pass)
Beginning in Dyea, Alaska, and ending in Bennett, B.C., this historic trail was blazed by Tlingit traders long before being overrun by Klondike gold prospectors in the 1890s. Considered the "poor man's route" back in the day, passage over Chilkoot Pass is now limited to a maximum of 50 hikers per day.

8. HUDSON'S BAY COMPANY (1849) HERITAGE TRAIL: (74 kilometres, Hope to Tulameen)
Travelled by Indigenous peoples, fur trade brigades, gold miners, and cattle ranchers, the HBC Trail has a storied past. Crossing the Cascade Mountains, this footpath and its 10 campsites beckon backpackers seeking a six-day hike into history.

9. VANCOUVER ISLAND TRAIL: (770 kilometres, Victoria to Cape Scott)
Formerly called the Vancouver Island Spine Trail, this long-distance path (80 per cent complete as of 2018) heads inland to start, traverses Strathcona Provincial Park, and follows the coast north of Port McNeill. Hikers will need two months or more to finish the job.

10. HOWE SOUND CREST TRAIL: (29 kilometres, Cypress Provincial Park)
Noted for its ruggedness, this trophy hike sets off from Cypress Bowl, goes between the Lions (also known as the Twin Sisters), and descends to Deeks Lake before ending south of Porteau Cove. Don't even think about trying to do the whole thing in one day.

10 BEAUTIFUL B.C. BEACHES

As recommended by Destination British Columbia.

1. AGATE BEACH, NORTHERN HAIDA GWAII: Nearly 100 kilometres long, this remote beach is a great spot for beachcombing and spotting wildlife.

2. LONG BEACH, PACIFIC RIM NATIONAL PARK RESERVE: As the name suggests, this is the longest stretch of beach on the west coast of Vancouver Island. It's popular with surfers, and a fun place to check out the sea life inside tide pools on the rocks.

3. CHRISTINA LAKE, WEST KOOTENAY: Christina Lake is a great place to get out the motorboat and waterskis. There's also plenty of space for picnics in the shade, and good opportunities for biking nearby.

4. SW̓IW̓S PROVINCIAL PARK, OSOYOOS: If warm water is your thing, this is the place. The campground is hugely popular in the summer though, so if you want to stay the night you'll have to reserve early.

5. SHUSWAP LAKE, SHUSWAP: During the summer, the beaches at Shuswap Lake come alive at night when all the houseboats dock and partiers spill out onto the sand.

6. SAN JOSEF BAY, NORTHWESTERN VANCOUVER ISLAND: For anyone seeking that secluded castaway experience, the beach at San Josef Bay is only accessible by foot, boat or helicopter, which means it's often completely empty.

7. WRECK BEACH, VANCOUVER: You don't have to be naked to enjoy Vancouver's famous nude beach, but it helps. At the far edge of the University of British Columbia's main campus, Wreck Beach feels like it's a world away from the city.

8. KALAMALKA LAKE, VERNON: The swimming is great, but Kalamalka Lake is really all about the Instagram opportunities. The crystal-clear water turns a beautiful blue-green colour when it heats up.

9. RATHTREVOR BEACH, PARKSVILLE: This beach is nearly two kilometres long, with great access to campgrounds, hiking trails, and nature programs. If you're into bird watching, it also happens to be a great spot to tick some species off your list.

10. TRIBUNE BAY, HORNBY ISLAND: If you're looking for a white sand beach but can't afford a Caribbean vacation, this is the spot. The water is shallow and reasonably warm for the West Coast, so if you squint your eyes it's almost like you're in the tropics.

BOW-WOW! DARCY MATHESON'S LIST OF 10 EXTREMELY SCENIC AND DOG-FRIENDLY B.C. BEACHES

Darcy Matheson is Vancouver editor for Daily Hive *and a contributor at* Modern Dog *magazine. She's also the author of* Greening Your Pet Care: Reduce Your Animal's Environmental Paw-Print *and the proud dog mama of two very naughty terriers, Murphy Brown and Seymour.*

British Columbia is an embarrassment of riches when it comes to scenic places to hang out by the water. Tree-lined glacier-fed lakes? Check. Urban seawalls overlooking the Pacific Ocean? Check. Kilometres of sandy river shorelines with unobstructed mountain vistas? Check. Thankfully, there are some amazing beaches that are also dog friendly, where Fido is welcome to run and swim to his heart's content.

1. KITS DOG BEACH/HADDEN PARK, VANCOUVER: A favourite of Vancouver locals, Hadden Park is just around the corner from famed Kitsilano Beach. The sheltered beach takes in views of Stanley Park and downtown Vancouver and is perfect for letting Fido take a dip and socialize with other urban pooches. Grab a coffee at nearby Granville Island, pull up a log, and watch kayaks, paddle boarders, and yachts cruise by. Hundreds of happy pooches pack this park on weekends.

2. BUNTZEN LAKE, ANMORE : Here's a fun fact about Buntzen Lake: it's so stunning it actually used to be called Lake Beautiful before it was renamed after the Buntzen Powerhouse hydroelectric station in 1905. This nearly five-kilometre-long lake east of Vancouver has a fenced-off swimming area completely dedicated to dogs, so you don't need to worry about Fido bugging, or being bugged by, kids and swimmers. The forested lake is surrounded by a wealth of leash-optional hikes. If you're feeling like a big adventure, check out Diez Vistas (it literally translates to 10 views), which crosses the summits surrounding the lake and ends with a dip in the lake with your dog.

3. AMBLESIDE PARK, WEST VANCOUVER: Taking in views of Stanley Park and the Lions Gate Bridge connecting Vancouver to the North Shore, this park is packed with 3.5 hectares of beach, grassy areas, and trails that are all dog-friendly. There's ample space for swimming and exploring and playing fetch, and a waterfront paved seawalk to stroll with your pup, too.

4. CANINE COVE IN LOST LAKE PARK, WHISTLER: An easy walk from Whistler Village on the scenic Valley Trail, Lost Lake is a secluded tree-lined gem nestled in the forest. Canine Cove is a 10-metre or so beach on the northeast side of the lake where you and your dog can swim together. It also has stunning vistas of the Whistler Valley mountains. The lake is surrounded by nearly 100 kilometres of hiking and biking trails of varying difficulties, so you can easily spend the day exploring with your pooch.

5. RATHTREVOR BEACH, PARKSVILLE: No chilly dogs here! One of the warmest ocean beaches in the entire country, Rathtrevor Beach is sandy and spans a full two kilometres on the shores of the Strait of Georgia. Though much of the beach is off-limits to dogs to protect the migratory bird population, there is a dog-friendly area outside of the provincial park. With lots of tide pools to jump in, Fido gets extra space to stretch his legs at low tide, when the beach is expanded by a full kilometre. It's flanked by well-maintained walking trails in the provincial park, which is packed with old-growth Douglas firs. Stay long enough and you can catch one of the stunning sunsets this eastern Vancouver Island beach is famous for.

6. DALLAS ROAD, VICTORIA: Sitting right on the Pacific Ocean, the beach below Victoria's Dallas Road is dog-friendly and absolutely breathtaking. With gorgeous views out to the Strait of Juan de Fuca and the Olympic Mountains, it's definitely chilly for human swimming, but just perfect for dogs.

7. SPANISH BANKS DOG BEACH, VANCOUVER: Arguably the most stunning beach in all of Vancouver, a large stretch on the west end of Spanish Banks Beach is designated off-leash and is a dog's paradise. The bowl-shaped beach cove is perfect for a game of fetch, or throwing down a blanket and having a picnic, or suntanning. At low tide the beach extends far into the water and creates tide pools perfect for splashing in. There are also wooded off-leash trails in the nearby UBC Endowment Lands if you feel like more exercise, and a seawall walk extending past nearby Jericho Beach.

8. MCDONALD BEACH PARK, RICHMOND: A freshwater doggie oasis just a skip away from Vancouver International Airport, this 10-hectare beach park lies on the north arm of the mighty Fraser River. With a network of wooded trails to explore and a large grassy field to roam, the showpiece of this park is the huge swath of dog-friendly sandy beach stretching along the waterfront, where dogs can paddle to their hearts' content. From the beach, you can check out the log boom movement and working boats.

9. SUNSET BEACH DOG BEACH, VANCOUVER: As its name suggests, this downtown Vancouver beach takes in stunning sunset views. Sitting at the mouth of False Creek, the small dog-friendly beach is just off the seawall, which at 28 kilometres is the world's longest uninterrupted waterfront path.

10. COSENS BAY BEACH, OKANAGAN VALLEY: Part of the rugged 3,218 hectare Kalamalka Lake Provincial Park, the eastern end of Cosens Bay is completely secluded and its glacier-fed waters are the most turquoise you'll see outside of the Caribbean Sea. The grassland park is dotted with groves of Douglas fir and ponderosa pine. With 432 varieties of vascular plants identified in the park, it's a peaceful place to enjoy nature with your four-legged friend by your side.

THE TOP 7 WAYS TO DIE WHILE SNOWMOBILING IN B.C.

Whether they're skiing, snowboarding, snowshoeing, tobogganing, ice climbing, or snow-mobiling, people love taking advantage of B.C.'s pristine mountains during the winter—but make no mistake: there's danger in those hills.

An average of 23 people die annually taking part in those six activities alone, according to coroners' statistics. But the most common way to perish, hands down, is on a snowmobile.

Here are the most common ways to die riding one.

1. GETTING CAUGHT IN AN AVALANCHE: 6.89 deaths annually

2. CRASHING INTO A TREE: 1 death annually

3. ROLLING YOUR SNOWMOBILE: 0.78 deaths annually

4. FALLING OFF SOMETHING HIGH: 0.67 deaths annually

5. CRASHING INTO ANOTHER SNOWMOBILE: 0.56 deaths annually

6. GETTING THROWN OFF YOUR SNOWMOBILE: 0.44 deaths annually

7. CRASHING INTO ANOTHER KIND OF "FIXED OBJECT": 0.33 deaths annually

Statistics taken from The BC Coroners Service's "Winter Activity Deaths in British Columbia" report, covering nine winters from 2007/08 to 2015/16.

10 DEVASTATING B.C. NATURAL DISASTERS

1. CASCADIA EARTHQUAKE, 1700: This was the original Big One, a quake on the night of January 26, 1700 caused by a 1,000-kilometre undersea thrust fault rupture that stretched all the way from Vancouver Island to northern California. The megathrust triggered landslides and a massive tsunami, which destroyed an entire Huu-ay-aht village and killed everyone who lived there, according to Natural Resources Canada. It collapsed homes belonging to the Cowichan peoples, and the shaking was so violent and lasted so long that people became physically ill.

It's not known exactly how many people were killed by the earthquake and tsunami, but the oral histories of the Indigenous peoples on Vancouver Island suggest several thousands died. The tidal wave also inflicted damage as far away as Japan, and recent thinking suggests the tremors might have also set off the next disaster on this list.

2. TSEAX CONE ERUPTION, 1700s: The Tseax Cone volcano sits at the heart of the Nass Valley in northwestern B.C. It doesn't look like much today—just a squat, dumpy hill crowned by a spiral of trees—but sometime in the 1700s, it caused one of the worst natural disasters in recorded Canadian history. The volcano's eruption spread lava over close to 40 square kilometres of the valley, damming Crater Creek and the Tseax River, and pushing the Nass River out of its bed.

Much worse, though, was the human toll. The Nisga'a villages of Lax Ksiluux and Wii Lax K'abit were completely destroyed by lava, and an estimated 2,000 people died.

3. SPENCES BRIDGE LANDSLIDE, 1905: "Just after three o'clock, there was a rumble from the mountainside and three minutes later it was all over," a journalist with *The San Francisco Call* reported after Arthur Seat mountain gave way on August 13, 1905. The debris buried the Nlaka'pamux village of Spences Bridge and dammed the Thompson River, creating a wave that crested at somewhere between 3 and 4.5 metres high. Eighteen people died, including the nonagenarian Chief Lillooet, and three Nlaka'pamux fishermen who were catching salmon just below the slide.

4. ROGERS PASS AVALANCHE, 1910: It remains the worst avalanche disaster in recorded Canadian history. Just before the deadly slide came down on March 4, 1910, a crew of workers was sent to clear snow that an earlier avalanche had sent spilling onto the CPR mainline through Rogers Pass. Almost all of them were caught when the next disaster hit, and 62 men were killed. The victims included recent immigrants from Japan, Ireland, Scotland, Sweden, Poland, and Denmark, as well as longtime Canadian residents, but only some of the dead seemed to matter—the *Ottawa Citizen* ran an article headlined "Complete list of the Whites who perished."

5. FRASER RIVER FLOOD, 1948: The Fraser Valley had seen extensive flooding in the past, but by the time the spring of 1948 rolled around, the area was home to scores of farms, growing suburbs, industrial operations, two transcontinental rail lines, and the Trans-Canada Highway. All that development made the impact of the rising floodwaters that June so much more destructive. The Fraser peaked at 7.6 metres at Mission on June 10 after the rapid melting of heavy snowpack in a severe hot spell. More than a dozen diking systems were breached and about 22,000 hectares of land was flooded. Ten people were killed, 16,000 were evacuated, 1,500 were left homeless and 2,300 homes were destroyed or damaged. Altogether, the flooding caused $20 million in damages, or about $235 million in 2019 dollars.

6. TYPHOON FREDA, 1962: When the remains of Typhoon Freda smashed into B.C. on October 12, 1962, the electricity went out almost immediately across the Lower Mainland as falling trees crashed into the power lines, according to BC Hydro. The storm's winds were violent, blowing at speeds of up to 145 kilometres per hour, and knocking down an estimated 3,000 trees in Stanley Park. "This is the worst storm to hit Vancouver in the life of our city," Mayor Tom Alsbury told CBC. Seven people died in the storm, and the equivalent of $683 million in 2019 dollars in damage had to be repaired.

7. THE TSUNAMI OF 1964: It was just about dinner time on March 27, 1964, when the earthquake struck Alaska. The shock waves were felt up and down the coast, but for B.C., the real damage wouldn't come until hours later, when tidal waves began striking communities. Prince Rupert felt it first, about three hours after the quake. Then, shortly after midnight, waves as high as 2.4 metres began pounding Port Alberni, the *Vancouver Sun* reported. Homes and businesses in the inland logging town were lifted off their foundations by the wave and sent floating in the Somass River. Thankfully, no one died—the 139 casualties of the quake were all in the U.S—but Port Alberni was left with about $5 million in damages to the town and $10 million to its biggest employer, MacMillan, Bloedel and Powell River.

8. THE HOPE SLIDE, 1965: Nearly 50 million tonnes of dirt, rock, and debris were sent tumbling from the slopes of Johnson Peak at dawn on January 9, 1965. It's not clear what exactly triggered the slide, but an earlier avalanche in the same area had cut off a handful of vehicles travelling along the Hope-Princeton highway at that early hour. They were waiting for clearing crews to arrive when the second slide came tumbling down on top of them. Four people were killed, the *Hope Standard* reported, but two of the bodies were never recovered.

9. M CREEK DISASTER, 1981: Three straight days of rain had poured into the creeks along the North Shore mountains before it was simply too much water for M Creek to hold, according to the *Vancouver Sun*. In the early hours of October 28, 1981, the creek's banks collapsed, sending a torrent of debris against the M Creek bridge on Highway 99, just north of Lions Bay. The slide knocked out one of the bridge's columns, then another, taking out 20 metres of roadway in all. In the predawn darkness, cars kept spilling over the edge of the washed-out highway, until nine lives were lost. The incident earned the road the nickname "Highway of Death," courtesy of *The Province* newspaper.

10. THE WILDFIRES OF 2017 AND 2018: More of B.C. burned in these two summers than in all of the previous 25 years combined—upwards of 2.57 million hectares, or more than twice the size of Haida Gwaii. The summer of 2017 carried the greatest human toll, with roughly 65,000 people forced out of their homes by fire and 500 buildings destroyed, including about 230 homes. The entire city of Williams Lake had to be evacuated as massive fires ripped through community after community in the Cariboo and south-central B.C. At the time, it was the worst wildfire season in recorded history, smashing records for just about every metric.

But then 2018 rolled around, and an even bigger area of the province was consumed by flames. This time, the fires hit much more lightly populated areas of the province, including in the north. Nonetheless, some communities were devastated, including the Tahltan First Nation community of Telegraph Creek. And yet, despite all the damage and heartache of those two summers, there was a silver lining: not a single life was lost.

(Opposite) The Vancouver Grizzlies' Mike Bibby gets around the LA Clippers' Darrick Martin during a 1999 game in Vancouver.

SPORTS

ASHLEIGH McIVOR'S 10 FAVOURITE B.C. SKI RUNS

Ashleigh McIvor is a retired Canadian ski cross Olympic gold medallist and world champion from Whistler. She now works as a broadcaster, model and public speaker.

1. PEAK TO CREEK, WHISTLER MOUNTAIN: Take the Peak chairlift to Whistler Mountain's highest point (2,182 metres) and spend a moment enjoying the breathtaking scenery—before this 11-kilometre ski run takes your breath away for other reasons! The massive Inukshuk makes for a great photo opp, and you'll get views of the vibrant, teal-coloured Cheakamus Lake (when it's not frozen), the magnificent Black Tusk, and the entire Tantalus Range. I love Peak to Creek—North America's longest ski run—for its uninterrupted fall-line pitch. It's literally the fastest, most direct way to get from the top of the mountain to the bottom. And who wouldn't love a run that finishes at Dusty's?

2. RIDGE RUNNER, BLACKCOMB MOUNTAIN: Hop off the new Crystal chairlift on Blackcomb Mountain and ride the Ridge all the way down. This nice, wide run is quite commonly the groomers' choice "run of the day," so you can expect smooth corduroy snaking its way all over knolls, rollers, through gullies and even some off-camber side-hilling. Such varied terrain makes for natural intervals—with sections of the most demanding terrain you'll find on a blue run anywhere in the world. But do not be afraid, for there is always another flat, cruisy section within reach.

3. OCTOPUS'S GARDEN, POWDER KING: Did you know that Powder King gets 41 feet of snow in a winter? After it was announced that ski cross would be added to the Olympic Program for 2010, Canada formed a national team. One of our first training camps was on this run. And we got to sneak a few pow laps with the snowboard cross athletes who were also in town between training runs.

4. BEARPAW HELI-SKIING: Picture perfectly spaced trees, sustained steep, fall-line skiing with the deepest pow you've ever skied—it feels bottomless, and you won't lay eyes on a track. Throw a few pillows* in and you've got yourself a recipe for a top-10 B.C. ski run.

*pillows: skier-lingo for massive puffs of powder on top of boulders or rugged terrain, that you can just bounce down from one to the next as they explode under your skis!

5. SURPRISE, BIG WHITE: This fave is borrowed from my former teammate, 2018 ski cross Olympic champion Kelsey Serwa—a Big White girl through and through. Surprise is a steep black diamond run that's amazing on a day with good visibility, but beware: I've been up there in a complete whiteout before and it is hard to get your bearings! That's just par for the course if you're a powder hound like I am.

6. SUNCATCHER, SUN PEAKS: And I had to consult my hero—Canadian skiing icon Nancy Greene Raine—for the name of this one. It's a nice steep run that's accessible from the base via one lovely quad chair. And it has a beautiful and inviting ski cross track on it, built by another hero of mine, Jeff Ihaksi—the 2010 Olympic course builder.

7. MOORE PARK, SNOWWATER HELISKIING: Another name I had to consult a friend for! This is his response: "What fortuitous timing; we were actually ripping those lines yesterday—Moore Park is the run. Steep 40+ degree east aspects, 1,600 vertical. Lots of changes since you were here. Still just 12 guests but a ton more infrastructure and a rally track for driver training." I still remember how good those turns felt.

8. BACKSIDE BOWL, WHITEWATER: This is a double black diamond run, so please ensure that you are well-prepared and understand the risks associated with venturing into challenging terrain like this if you feel compelled to check it out. I got to ski here with some freeride mountain bike legends back in the day: Richie Schley, Smiley Nesbitt, and local Nelson shredder Robbie Bourdon. Not to mention, Retallack Cat Skiing is very close by and it has way too many amazing runs to even try to pick just one.

9. SHRED ZONE, SASQUATCH MOUNTAIN RESORT (PREVIOUSLY KNOWN AS HEMLOCK VALLEY): Just weeks before our race in the Vancouver Olympics, we had a top-secret training camp in the inland Coast Mountains. The ace up our sleeves was that the Olympic course designer and builder I just mentioned, Jeff Ihaksi, had built us a training course with the exact same start we would be racing out of in the Olympics. It was a set of 10-plus features—bumps, jumps, step-ups, step-downs, and two massive Aztec-style mounds of snow to get up and over. It was incredibly tricky to get through swiftly. The opportunity to practice this mock start section for several days before race day at Cypress allowed me to go into my race with so much more confidence than my competitors who were just laying eyes—and skis—on it for the first time.

10. ASHLEIGH McIVOR'S GOLD, CYPRESS: Last but not least, my Olympic race run. Our race course meandered its way down this steep slope, so our speed was controlled enough to make the biggest jumps on the ski cross circuit seem manageable. But the best part of this run is the insanely beautiful views down to the city, as well as up magnificent Howe Sound. That scenery was what kept me calm and in the zone—a crucial component to my Olympic success.

KAT JAYME'S LIST OF 10 REASONS TO BRING BACK THE VANCOUVER GRIZZLIES

Kat Jayme is an award-winning writer and director of the Grizzlies documentary Finding Big Country.

In 1995, Vancouver was buzzing with excitement over the NBA's expansion to the Great White North. At last, the city's first and only NBA team had arrived.

After the Vancouver Grizzlies won their first two games, fans were on Cloud 9, believing they had a championship team in the making. Unfortunately, those dreams were quickly crushed. The Grizzlies lost the next 19 games straight, then another 23 straight that same season. And it didn't get better from there. During their time in Vancouver, the Grizzlies lost 359 games, never won more than 23 games per season, and never qualified for the NBA playoffs. And after six seasons, the team was sold to a Chicago billionaire who relocated the Grizzlies to Memphis, Tennessee.

It's been 17 years since the team left town, yet the memories of the Grizzlies are forever etched into the minds of Vancouverites who grew up in the city in the 90s. And despite their horrible track record, fans still yearn for the day when the NBA will return back to Vancouver. Here are just 10 reasons why we need to #BRINGBACKTHEGRIZZ.

1. THE GRIZZLIES WERE NEVER GIVEN A FAIR SHOT: In 1989, the NBA expanded to create the Orlando Magic, who quickly became a powerhouse after getting the number one draft pick two years in a row. Overnight, the Magic became playoff contenders with Shaquille O'Neal and Penny Hardaway. Because of the Magic's success, the NBA slapped a bunch of rules on the next expansion teams, the Vancouver Grizzlies and the Toronto Raptors, which made it harder for the teams to succeed right away. As a result, the Grizzlies were not allowed a top draft pick their first three seasons, and also had a lower salary cap for their first two seasons.

2. SUPER GRIZZ AND HIS BAZOOKA: Hands down, the Grizzlies had one of the league's best, funniest, and most entertaining mascots. Super Grizz was loved by all. If you were to talk to anyone who grew up with the Grizzlies, one of their best memories would be of Super Grizz jumping and somersaulting in the air and dunking during the halftime show. He also had a bazooka and slingshot that he'd use to throw free T-shirts into the stands. He was awesome.

3. WE NEED ANOTHER CANADIAN TEAM TO CHEER FOR AND REPRESENT #WETHEWEST: The Toronto Raptors joined the NBA the same year Vancouver did. Like Vancouver, they struggled their first few years, but the Raptors stuck it out and are now playoff contenders. They are the only team representing Canada. We definitely need another.

4. OUR FIRST RUN WAS TAINTED BY A BAD TRADE: The Grizzlies are infamous for their head-scratching draft picks, but in 1999 they seemed to have picked the right guy: Steve Francis, an explosive point guard from Maryland. The only problem was he absolutely did not want to play for Vancouver. The Grizzlies drafted him anyway, and Francis instantly demanded a trade. The team conceded and traded him to the Houston Rockets in what was the biggest sports deal in history at that time. Francis ended up being named rookie of the year. In Houston, he was a three-time NBA all-star and became a great showman and performer—just what the Grizzlies desperately needed.

5. THEY'RE PART OF VANCOUVER HISTORY: Despite representing our city for years, the Grizzlies don't get much love. You won't even find a banner honouring them at Rogers Arena. Sure, they weren't the best team in the league, but the Grizzlies are still a huge part of our sports history. And despite their record, they truly had a lot of hope and potential. Vancouver even had our own Big Three: Bryant "Big Country" Reeves, Shareef Abdur-Rahim and Mike Bibby.

6. OUR DOLLAR IS UP! : One of the main reasons the Grizzlies left town was because of our low Canadian dollar. We were earning in Canadian and having to pay players in American. Not only has that improved, Vancouver has also changed significantly since the Grizzlies left town. We are a world-class city that has a major basketball following.

7. WE NEED A TEAM FOR THE NEXT GENERATION OF VANCOUVERITE BALLERS: The Grizzlies inspired a generation of Vancouverites to dream that one day they would play for their home team in the NBA.

8. EVEN DAVID STERN AGREES: David Stern, the former NBA commissioner, once said in an interview that his only regret during his time in the NBA was relocating the Grizzlies to Memphis. We totally agree!

9. THEY SHOULD HAVE NEVER LEFT IN THE FIRST PLACE: As an expansion team, we all knew it was going to be tough. Coaches, players, and even the fans knew the road wasn't going to be easy. Fans were even told the Grizzlies were going to need a "10-year plan." And they were right. The Grizzlies were sold after six years and on their 10th year, they finally made it to the playoffs in Memphis. That should have been us.

10. THERE ARE NO GRIZZLIES IN TENNESSEE : Enough said.

10 MEMORABLE MOMENTS FROM THE 2010 VANCOUVER OLYMPICS

1. ALEXANDRE BILODEAU WINS CANADA'S FIRST HOME GOLD: After two runs as Olympic hosts and no gold to show for it in either Montreal or Calgary, Canadians were understandably pretty nervous that the drought would continue in 2010. Thankfully, Bilodeau broke the unlucky streak just two days into the Games with a gold in men's moguls, and everyone could breathe easy again. Team Canada would go on to blow everyone's expectations out of the water, bringing home a record-setting 14 golds.

2. GEORGIAN LUGER NODAR KUMARITASHVILI DIES IN TRAINING: The 2010 Games got off to a tragic start. Kumaritashvili, a 21-year-old from Georgia, was training for his Olympic debut when he lost control on the last turn of the Whistler course. He was thrust over the side of the track and crashed into a steel support pole at more than 140 kilometres an hour. Medics tried to save the young athlete, but he died in hospital.

3. K.D. LANG COVERS HALLELUJAH : Yeah, Leonard Cohen's secular hymn is probably one of the most covered songs on Earth, but lang's version was special. The iconic Canadian chanteuse's magical performance during the opening ceremonies captivated the crowd—apparently, Cohen had turned down an invitation to sing at the Games, saying there was no need with lang there to do his song justice.

4. THE OLYMPIC CAULDRON MALFUNCTIONS: Despite some memorable performances, the opening ceremonies did not go off without a hitch. The Olympic cauldron was designed with four columns that were supposed to rise out of the ground as the torchbearers each lit one arm. But one of the pillars failed, leaving speed skater Catriona Le May Doan standing awkwardly with nothing to do.

5. STEPHEN COLBERT LIGHTENS THINGS UP: The beloved American comedian brought *The Colbert Report* and his blustering conservative caricature to Vancouver for the Games—which he dubbed the "Vancouverage of the Quadrennial Cold Weather Athletic Competition." Huge crowds of fans flocked to his tapings, and despite merciless mocking of Canadians during his episodes, he also took back earlier comments calling us "syrup suckers" and "ice holes."

6. HELICOPTERS DROP SNOW ON CYPRESS: February 2010 was an unseasonably warm month, and by the time the Games arrived, there was almost no snow on the slopes of Cypress Mountain, the venue for freestyle skiing and snowboarding. The show must go on, so organizers were forced to airlift and truck in snow from higher elevations.

7. THE WORLD FALLS IN LOVE WITH VIRTUE AND MOIR: It's hard to remember a time before Tessa Virtue and Scott Moir were Canada's sweethearts. But the ice dancers were virtually unknown outside figure skating circles before 2010, when their obvious chemistry and flawless performances captured the hearts of TV viewers around the world. It helped that they broke a ton of records, too—they were the first North Americans to win gold in ice dancing, the youngest ice dancing team to win an Olympic title, the first to win on home ice, and the first to take home gold in their Olympic debut.

8. JON MONTGOMERY CHUGS A PITCHER OF BEER: Montgomery cemented his status as a Canadian sports hero when he chugged a pitcher of beer on live TV while celebrating his gold medal skeleton win on the streets of Whistler. He was instantly beloved. Contrast that with the response to the gold-medal-winning women's hockey players, who were photographed smoking cigars and drinking on the ice. The team had to apologize after organizers expressed their disapproval.

9. JOANNIE ROCHETTE PULLS OFF AN EMOTIONAL WIN: Figure skater Rochette was on the ice, practising for her short program, when she learned that her mother had died of a heart attack shortly after landing in Vancouver to watch her daughter compete. Nonetheless, Rochette went on to skate just two days later, pulling off a poignant performance and then bursting into tears as the crowd gave her a standing ovation. The routine would help earn her a bronze medal.

10. VANCOUVER EXPLODES INTO A MASSIVE STREET PARTY: You couldn't have scripted a better ending for the Games. The gold medal men's hockey game was the final event of the Olympics, and the Canadians were facing off against their perpetual American rivals. Vancouverites and visitors crowded into sports bars and living rooms across the city for the morning puck-drop, and were on the edge of their seats until Sidney Crosby scored the game-winning goal for Canada in overtime. As soon as the game was decided, everyone spilled into the streets for a celebration fueled by pure joy (and plenty of beer).

DANIEL WAGNER'S LIST OF 10 DEVASTATING MOMENTS THAT DEFINE BEING A VANCOUVER CANUCKS FAN

Daniel Wagner is a Vancouver-based hockey writer. He's the co-founder and editor of "Pass it to Bulis," the official Canucks blog of the Vancouver Courier.

It's a quintessential part of living in British Columbia: complaining about the Vancouver Canucks or, at the very least, listening to everyone around you complain about the Vancouver Canucks. The 50-year history of the Canucks is chock-full of heartbreaking moments, to the point that "broken" is the default state of every Canucks fan's heart.

Without a constant sense of impending doom, are you even a Canucks fan? Here are just a few of the moments that have left fans always expecting the worst.

1. CANUCKS LOSE A HALL OF FAMER TO A SPIN OF THE WHEEL: The Canucks' first loss came before they even played a game in the NHL. The Buffalo Sabres entered the NHL the same year as the Canucks, so the league literally spun a wheel to decide who would get the first overall pick in the 1970 Entry Draft and the prize of future Hall of Famer Gilbert Perreault.

The wheel had numbers around the outside: even for the Canucks, odd for the Sabres. When the wheel stopped, NHL president Clarence Campbell announced the Canucks had won, but as the Canucks celebrated, Sabres coach Punch Imlach calmly pointed out that the wheel had landed on "11," which is, according to my math, an odd number. The Sabres got Perreault, who went on to tally 1,326 points in Buffalo while wearing the number 11.

The Canucks settled for defenceman Dale Tallon at second overall, who suffered by comparison to Perreault and played just three seasons in Vancouver.

2. THE TERRIBLE TENURE OF BILL LAFORGE: Bill LaForge was a highly-touted junior coach when the Canucks hired him in 1984. Unfortunately, he treated the adults on the Canucks just like the teenagers he coached in junior, even forcing the team to sing a "fight song" in the locker room after victories. It's a good thing they didn't win much: the Canucks went 4-14-2 under LaForge, including a 13-2 loss to the Philadelphia Flyers, before he was fired.

All-Star forward Darcy Rota got the worst of LaForge's amateur antics. He was coming off spinal fusion surgery when LaForge subjected him to "The Gauntlet," a drill unheard of in professional hockey. As he skated down the boards with his teammates pummelling him, Rota re-injured his neck, causing him to immediately retire at the age of 31.

3. THE CANUCKS TRADE CAM NEELY: Every NHL team wants to draft a player like Cam Neely, who was the prototypical power forward: a terrifying combination of size and skill that could put you through the glass as easily as he put the puck in the net. The Canucks were the lucky team that actually drafted Neely, but, after three seasons in Vancouver, they traded him and a first-round pick to the Boston Bruins for Barry Pederson.

Pederson was decent with the Canucks, but Neely became a beast in Boston, with three 50-goal seasons, including 50 goals in just 49 games in 1993-94. Neely was elected to the Hockey Hall of Fame in 2005; Pederson, to the best of my knowledge, has not been elected to anything.

The first-round pick in the trade became All-Star defenceman Glen Wesley, who had a 20-year NHL career.

4. NATHAN LAFAYETTE HITS THE POST: It's 1994. The Canucks, led by Trevor Linden, Pavel Bure, and Kirk McLean, have forced Game 7 in the Stanley Cup Final against the New York Rangers. Down by one in the third period, Canucks rookie Nathan Lafayette gets a glorious chance to tie the game and force overtime when Geoff Courtnall sets him up with a wide-open net.

Clank! The puck hits the post and skitters away. That post is the closest the Canucks get to the Stanley Cup, which is hoisted a few minutes later by the captain of the Rangers, Mark Messier.

A riot ensues.

5. MARK MESSIER. JUST … MARK MESSIER: It didn't seem devastating when the Canucks signed Mark Messier in 1997, even if fans were still sore at his dirty tactics and Cup-clinching goal in 1994. Surely the six-time Stanley Cup champion would put the Canucks over the top, right? Instead, disaster.

On the ice, the aging centre was a shadow of his former self and the Canucks missed the playoffs in all three of his years with the team. Off the ice, he was somehow even worse.

Messier demanded to wear number 11, which had been unofficially retired for 25 years in honour of Wayne Maki, an original Canuck who had passed away from brain cancer. Messier also took the captaincy from Trevor Linden, but provided little of his much-ballyhooed lead-ership to his new teammates, siding with coach/manager Mike Keenan as he traded away beloved players like Linden, Gino Odjick, and Kirk McLean.

To this day, Messier is the most hated Canuck of all time.

6. NICKLAS LIDSTROM'S CENTRE ICE SLAPPER: Markus Naslund, Todd Bertuzzi, and Bren-dan Morrison formed the West Coast Express, one of the most feared forward lines of the early 2000's, but they never made it out of the second round of the playoffs. One devastating moment illustrates why.

The 2001-02 Canucks were underdogs in their first-round series against the top-seeded De-troit Red Wings, but shocked the league by winning the first two games in Detroit. They had all the momentum as the series moved to Vancouver for Game 3.

That's when Red Wings defenceman Nicklas Lidstrom sent an innocent-looking shot from centre ice towards the Vancouver net. Goaltender Dan Cloutier reached out to catch the puck … and whiffed completely. The brutal long-distance goal killed the Canucks' momen-tum: the Red Wings won four straight to take the series, then went on to win the Stanley Cup.

7. 'WE CHOKED': Heading into the final game of the 2002-03 season, Markus Naslund led the NHL in points, on pace to win the first Art Ross Trophy in franchise history, while the Canucks were also just ahead of the Colorado Avalanche for first in the Northwest Division. The Canucks were looking for an easy win over a lousy Los Angeles Kings squad and a point or two for Naslund.

Instead, the Kings shut out Naslund and the Canucks. Meanwhile, in Colorado, Peter Forsberg had a three-point night to overtake Naslund for the Art Ross and push the Avalanche past the Canucks for the Northwest Division title. Naslund tried to rally the despondent Canucks crowd with his post-game speech, but two words overshadowed the rest: "We choked."

A few weeks later, the Canucks choked again, giving up a 3-1 series lead to the Minnesota Wild in the second round of the playoffs. Cloutier allowed four goals on just 16 shots in the deciding Game 7.

8. TIM THOMAS SHUTS OUT THE CANUCKS: It's 2011. The Canucks are a team of destiny, dominating the regular season to an insane degree, then slaying the dragon that was the Chicago Blackhawks in the playoffs. Canucks fans gather in the streets of Vancouver to watch the Stanley Cup Final, with hope briefly replacing the sense of impending doom.

The doom, even if they didn't sense it, never went away. Bruins goaltender Tim Thomas has one of the greatest playoff performances in NHL history, holding the high-scoring Canucks to just eight goals in seven games. In the Vancouver streets, fans watch with growing despair and frustration as Thomas shuts out the Canucks 4-0 in the deciding Game 7.

A riot ensues.

9. DUNCAN KEITH ELBOWS DANIEL SEDIN IN THE FACE: The Canucks bounced back from their 2011 disappointment by winning their second straight Presidents' Trophy. While not quite as dominant as the year before, the Canucks were still the favourite for the Stanley Cup. At least, they were until the Blackhawks' Duncan Keith intentionally elbowed Daniel Sedin in the face, giving the Canucks' leading goal scorer a concussion when he didn't even have the puck.

The NHL suspended Keith for five games; Daniel missed 12 games, including the first three games of the playoffs. The Canucks lost all three of those games en route to a 4-1 series win by the eventual Stanley Cup winners, the Los Angeles Kings.

10. ROBERTO LUONGO SITS ON AN OUTDOOR BENCH: At the close of the 2012-13 season, the Canucks had the champagne problem of two great goaltenders: Roberto Luongo and Cory Schneider. While most fans expected Luongo to get traded, Canucks general manager Mike Gillis moved Schneider at the 2013 draft to solidify Luongo as the starter in Vancouver for years to come.

The next season, the Canucks hosted the Heritage Classic, a marquee outdoor game. Luongo, who had been looking forward to the game all season, was stunned when head coach John Tortorella gave backup goaltender Eddie Lack the start. Luongo sat on the bench in his custom-designed retro goalie gear as fans chanted his name and booed Lack.

The snub was the last straw and, two days later, Gillis acquiesced to Luongo's trade demand and sent him to the Florida Panthers. Thanks to an inane coaching decision, the Canucks went from two great goaltenders to none in less than a year.

The Fernie Swastikas were just one of three Canadian teams to use the swastika before its unfortunate association with Nazi atrocities.

10 DEFUNCT B.C. SPORTS TEAMS

1. VANCOUVER GRIZZLIES, NATIONAL BASKETBALL ASSOCIATION (1995-2001): For six sweet seasons, Vancouver got to feel what it's like to be an NBA town. An NBA town with a losing team, sure, but it was something. The pain of saying goodbye as the Grizzlies moved on to Memphis still lingers today.

2. VANCOUVER ROYAL CANADIANS, UNITED SOCCER ASSOCIATION (1967): Let's just say it took a while to convince North Americans that soccer is fun to watch. The USA league was created by flying in teams from soccer-mad Europe and South America, slapping new names on them, and then assigning them American and Canadian cities to represent. The league lasted one season. Vancouver's team, a.k.a. England's Sunderland A.F.C., placed fifth out of six teams in their division. Oh well.

3. FERNIE SWASTIKAS, WOMEN'S HOCKEY (1922-1926):
Obviously, the team's name and its swastika-emblazoned uniforms look pretty bad in hindsight, but please remember this was pre-Second World War, when the swastika was still seen as an ancient symbol of good fortune. There were actually three Canadian hockey teams called the Swastikas in those days. The Fernie team was pretty remarkable, beating out big-city teams from Calgary and Vancouver to win the 1923 Alpine Cup for women's hockey.

4. VANCOUVER GRIFFINS, NATIONAL WOMEN'S HOCKEY LEAGUE (2000-2003):
Thankfully, women's hockey didn't end in Canada when the 1920s did. The NWHL was short-lived, sadly, but it was a professional league and it gave rising amateur stars from the Olympics a place to earn some money playing the game. The Griffins were lucky enough to have the U.S. team captain wearing the big "C" for two seasons, and placed first in the Western Division in the 2001-2002 season.

5. VANCOUVER VOODOO, ROLLER HOCKEY INTERNATIONAL (1993-1996): Yeah, you probably could have guessed that professional inline hockey was a 90s thing. And unlike some of the other teams on this list, the Voodoo were actually pretty successful and featured some future and former NHL stars moonlighting during the summer off-season. Though Vancouver never won a conference championship or the all-important "Murphy Cup," they did win their division every year they played.

6. VANCOUVER MILLIONAIRES, PACIFIC COAST HOCKEY ASSOCIATION AND WESTERN CANADA HOCKEY LEAGUE (1911-1926): Ah, the favourite piece of trivia for every defensive Vancouver hockey fan. Yes, the city has won a Stanley Cup before—who cares if the year was 1915 and the team wasn't the Canucks? The Millionaires played on Canada's first artificial ice surface at the Denman Arena, which later burned to the ground. The team became the Maroons in 1922, and played until the Western Canada Hockey League disbanded in 1926.

7. VICTORIA STEELERS, PACIFIC FOOTBALL LEAGUE AND CONTINENTAL FOOTBALL LEAGUE (1966-1967): Mid-century Victoria's dream of a major league team just didn't pan out. After just one season of semi-professional football in the Pacific Football League, the Steelers went pro in the short-lived Continental Football League. The team was 4-8 in the 1967 season, but they relocated to Spokane the next year. The league broke up in 1969 after just five seasons.

8. VANCOUVER RAVENS, NATIONAL LACROSSE LEAGUE (2002-2004): They had a great logo featuring a hunky black bird with big, beefy pecs, but the Ravens struggled to maintain an enthusiastic fanbase, and folded after just three seasons in the NLL. In the end, the team had more than $1 million in debts, and the club missed payroll in the spring of 2004. They only managed to make it as long as they did thanks to some bridge financing.

9. VANCOUVER BLAZERS, WORLD HOCKEY ASSOCIATION (1973-1975): The Canucks had only been in the NHL for three years when Vancouver got its second big league professional hockey team. The Blazers actually had to share the ice at Pacific Coliseum with the Canucks. But this city just wasn't big enough for the both of them, and after two seasons, the Blazers moved on to Calgary to become the Cowboys in 1975.

10. VANCOUVER ASAHI, BASEBALL (1914-1941): The first half of the 20th century was a troubled time to be an Asian-Canadian in Vancouver, but the Asahi and their patented "brain ball" style of play were a rightful source of pride for the city's Japanese community. The team won the Pacific Northwest Championship five years running starting in 1937, but sadly their time at the top was cut short by racist government policy. In 1942, the team was disbanded when the players were shipped off to internment camps with their families.

(Opposite) B.C. agreed to protect 6.4 million hectares of the Great Bear Rainforest—home to the gorgeous Kermode bear—from logging amid pressure from activists.

PROGRESS

ROD MICKLEBURGH'S LIST OF 10 KEY MOMENTS IN THE HISTORY OF THE B.C. LABOUR MOVEMENT

Rod Mickleburgh's long journalism career included time as a labour reporter for both the Vancouver Sun *and* Province *and many years with the* Globe and Mail. *His most recent book,* On the Line: A History of the British Columbia Labour Movement, *was published in 2018.*

A group of longshoremen stand on the dock of the Moodyville sawmill in 1889.

1. FIRST WORKERS, FIRST STRIKE: In 1849, the Hudson's Bay Company imported a group of workers from Scotland to mine the HBC's fledgling coal deposit at Fort Rupert, near present-day Port Hardy. They were the first non-Indigenous industrial workers in what would soon be the province of British Columbia. Dissatisfied almost immediately by their working conditions, they went on strike. Several were thrown in the brig. That long-ago confrontation launched a pattern of worker resistance and repression by authorities that has rocked B.C. for more than 150 years.

2. AN INDIGENOUS UNION: You won't find this in many history books, but until late into the 19th century, the wheels of B.C.'s early industry were turned mostly by Indigenous workers. In the first coal mines and sawmills, in the woods and on the farms, on the docks and in the fish canneries, and particularly on the water catching salmon, labour was provided in large measure by Indigenous peoples.

As racism and employer preferences gradually began to sideline them, they retained a special niche on the Vancouver waterfront, loading and unloading lumber. In 1906, Squamish and Tsleil-Waututh stevedores formed a union and joined the radical Industrial Workers of the World, which accepted workers of all races. The local was known by everyone as the Bows and Arrows. It continued to exist in various forms until the 1930s.

3. GENERAL STRIKE: In 1918, prominent union leader and organizer Ginger Goodwin, fleeing a dubious summons to report for military duty, was shot dead by a special constable in the woods near Cumberland. On the day of his funeral, enraged trade unionists in Vancouver walked off the job for 24 hours, the first general strike in B.C. and Canadian history. This so incensed the business community they corralled a large number of returned veterans, who charged into the Labour Temple at 411 Dunsmuir, ransacked its offices and forced union official Victor Midgely out onto a window ledge to avoid a beating. The strike continued, undeterred.

4. WORKER PROTECTION: Fiery Socialist James W. Hawthornthwaite, elected to the provincial legislature by the coal miners of Nanaimo in 1901, managed to convince enough MLAs to pass Canada's first Workmen's Compensation Act the next year. Covering many, though not all, industries, it provided compensation for injured workers, a desperately needed breakthrough in a resource-based province with such a grim toll of workplace calamities. But the act had many loopholes. In 1917, the legislature passed a more comprehensive act that did the trick, giving virtually every injured B.C. worker the security of a guaranteed pay cheque. That principle is still in place today.

5. WOMEN SHATTER WORKPLACE BARRIERS: The Second World War transformed Canada. One of the major changes brought large numbers of women into the industrial workforce for the first time. With a million men overseas, their labour was critical to the country's war effort. In B.C., they worked in the woods, sawmills, manufacturing plants, aircraft factories and, in particular, West Coast shipyards, helping churn out warships for the Canadian and British Navies. This province had the highest percentage of women shipyard workers in the country, and all were in well-paying union jobs. Although most had to give up their jobs at the end of the war, there was no turning back. Women would no longer be a workplace anomaly.

6. LEGAL RIGHTS AT LAST: For 70 years, B.C. workers had been joining unions and striking to try and improve wages and working conditions. Almost always, they failed. Companies would refuse to recognize their unions, hire strikebreakers at will, blacklist those who went on strike and rely on the state to intervene on their side. Unions couldn't win.

Finally, in 1944, forced to action by the need to keep wartime workers happy, the federal government issued a landmark order-in-council with the captivating name of PC 1003, making bargaining and union recognition compulsory for the first time. B.C. soon passed a similar law. With legal rights at last, union organizing took off. By 1958, 53.9 per cent of B.C. workers belonged to a union.

7. RECONCILIATION: For years, the message in labour's well-known anthem, Solidarity Forever, was more sung than real. Deep, longstanding divisions between craft and industrial unions perpetuated rival organizations and feuds that never seemed to heal, limiting labour effectiveness. That came to an end in November 1956, with the founding convention of a united B.C. Federation of Labour. Craft and industrial union delegates sat together for the first time. By the 1960s, the Fed's third incarnation was the most militant labour organization in Canada.

8. AN END TO UNION JAILINGS: Once they were forced to recognize and bargain with unions, employers discovered a new weapon to thwart labour aspirations—the ex parte court injunction. Merely on application to the B.C. Supreme Court, a company could obtain an injunction banning virtually any union picketing or action that proved effective. In the heat of battle, not all were obeyed. Union leaders going to prison became increasingly familiar. The NDP government of Dave Barrett put a stop to it. In 1973, it enacted the most progressive labour code in North America. The code removed the courts' jurisdiction over labour relations and handed it to a powerful new Labour Relations Board, where it has remained ever since.

9. OPERATION SOLIDARITY: Through the summer and into the late fall of 1983, the B.C. labour movement spearheaded by far the most concerted, broad-based and spirited anti-government protest movement in the province's history. Under the banner of Operation Solidarity, waves of trade unionists, social activists and community groups who joined in fought back against an unprecedented assault by the Social Credit government on basic union and social rights long taken for granted. The movement brought B.C. to the verge of a province-wide general strike. In the end, the government NDP backed down on the anti-union bills, but left intact measures that abolished the Human Rights Commission, wiped out tenant rights and eroded many other social programs. Despite the unhappy conclusion, there had never been anything quite like Operation Solidarity.

10. A BOLD AND BREATHTAKING DECISION: On June 8, 2007, the Supreme Court of Canada released the most significant declaration of union rights ever issued by Canada's top court. Nearly five years after the Gordon Campbell Liberal government unilaterally stripped the Hospital Employees Union of their well-established protections against contracting out, the SCC struck down the Liberals' action. According to the court's stunning decision, meaningful collective bargaining was a union right guaranteed by the Canadian Charter of Rights and Freedom. The provincial government had violated the Charter. In 2016, on the same principle, the SCC quashed once and for all similar legislation against B.C. teachers. The irony of a legal system that had presided over union repression for so many decades emerging as labour's strongest protector was delicious.

DAVID SUZUKI'S LIST OF 10 ENVIRONMENTAL GAINS IN B.C.

Award-winning geneticist and broadcaster David Suzuki became familiar to audiences around the world as host of CBC TV's The Nature of Things *beginning in 1979. He's written or co-authored more than 50 books, and is the founder of the David Suzuki Foundation, which aims to conserve and protect the natural environment and help create a sustainable Canada.*

British Columbia is a wonderful place, with rich and varied cultures, spectacular wilderness, a wide range of ecosystems, and vibrant cities and towns. Anything we can do to protect the lands, air, and waters that we depend on for health, wellbeing, economic opportunity, and so much more, is good. Ultimately, though, we must get beyond the individual gains that can be eroded or overturned to looking at the big picture.

1. CARBON TAX: B.C. became a leader in climate solutions when it implemented North America's first broad-based carbon tax in 2008. It wasn't easy. It became a contentious election issue and faced opposition from unlikely sources. But once adopted, it proved that reducing greenhouse gas emissions could go hand-in-hand with economic prosperity. From its inception to 2015, provincial real GDP grew more than 17 per cent, while net emissions declined by 4.7 per cent.

Unfortunately, the tax was frozen in 2012 at $30 per tonne of emissions, far too low to have the needed effect. It is now rising again, to $50 a tonne by 2021. It's a start, and perhaps helped the federal government realize that carbon pricing is necessary and enjoys public support where it has been implemented.

2. AGRICULTURAL LAND RESERVE: B.C.'s NDP government established the Agricultural Land Reserve in 1973 to protect the province's fertile farmlands. Farming is prioritized and non-agricultural uses are restricted on its 4.6 million hectares. It was an important step, but the amount of land it covers should be expanded. Instead, it has been chipped away under successive governments in the face of development pressures.

3. PROVINCIAL PROTECTED AREAS: Decades of conflict pitted forestry, mining, and other industries against environmentalists and Indigenous peoples, eventually leading the B.C. government to more than double the amount of recognized protected areas since the early 1990s. By 2019, protected lands and waters covered 15.4 per cent of B.C.'s land base and 3.2 per cent of its marine areas, with a goal to reach 17 per cent of terrestrial areas and inland water and 10 per cent of coastal and marine areas by 2020. From Clayoquot Sound to the Great Bear Rainforest to the Stein Valley to the Tatshenshini, more of what makes B.C. spectacular is being set aside—although logging and development are not prohibited in provincial parks.

4. GWAII HAANAS NATIONAL MARINE CONSERVATION AREA: The co-governance agreement between the Haida Nation and Government of Canada to expand the jurisdiction of Gwaii Haanas to a 3,500-square-kilometre underwater protected habitat was based on the Haida understanding that land isn't separate from its surroundings, that ocean and forest are interlinked. This was an important agreement because of its profound ecological insight.

5. CANCELLING OF ENBRIDGE'S NORTHERN GATEWAY PIPELINE: We have coastal First Nations to thank for their unified opposition to this bitumen pipeline because of the threat to their culture and way of life. It was not about money, even though many Indigenous communities are desperate for community economic development and were offered large sums to let the pipeline through. Opposition from a broad range of people in B.C. and beyond helped strengthen the position of First Nations. The 2014 Supreme Court decision in Tsilhqot'in Nation v. British Columbia established the rights of Indigenous groups over their territories, opening the way for Indigenous perspectives and jurisdiction in the face of increasing development pressures.

6. HUMPBACK WHALE RECOVERY: While populations of some whales, such as the southern resident orcas, are declining, humpbacks in B.C. waters have gone from near extinction in the mid-1990s to an estimated 3,000 to 5,000 now. Their comeback is a bit of a mystery. A 1965 whale-hunting ban no doubt helped, perhaps along with rehabilitation of some polluted feeding areas.

But the humpbacks face the same numerous risks as other whales, from shipping, industrial activity and more. More protection measures will be needed to ensure their continued survival.

7. VANCOUVER RENEWABLE CITY AND GREENEST CITY PLANS: Green buildings and transportation, zero waste, local food, access to nature and a goal to get 100 per cent of energy from renewable sources by 2050—Vancouver is showing that cities are on the forefront of environmental protection and climate solutions.

8. MARINE PROTECTED AREAS FOR GLASS SPONGE REEFS : Marine protected areas are too small and isolated. But protecting the unique glass sponge reefs off the B.C. coast was an important first step. Glass sponges build their skeletons from silicon dioxide, or glass. They provide important habitat for rockfish and other species. Trying to protect rare sponge reefs in isolation without an ecological perspective is not enough. We still have much to learn about their biology and interactions with the larger ecosystem before we can truly ensure their survival.

9. NORTH COAST TANKER MORATORIUM: A voluntary tanker exclusion zone has been in place since 1985. In 2017, the federal government introduced the Oil Tanker Moratorium Act. If passed, it would prohibit oil tankers carrying more than 12,500 metric tonnes of crude or persistent oil products from stopping, loading or unloading in the area from the B.C.-Alaska border to the mainland point across from the northern tip of Vancouver Island, including Haida Gwaii. It would also protect the coastline around Dixon Entrance, Hecate Strait, and Queen Charlotte Sound.

10. GRIZZLY BEAR TROPHY HUNT BAN: The big question after the B.C. government banned grizzly bear trophy hunting in late 2017 was "Why did it take so long?" Scientific evidence showing the iconic animals were at risk had been available for years, and a ban had wide public support. But a small group of guide-outfitters managed to keep the hunt going for many years. Even with the ban, grizzlies are far from being protected, as populations continue to decline and we still don't have solid measurements of numbers or territory.

8 MADE-IN-B.C. INVENTIONS

1. HELI-SKIING: Heli-skiing, which involves being carried onto a mountain by helicopter rather than, say, hiking or taking a gondola, was invented in 1965 by Hans Gmoser, and has since become a popular way to go off-piste on hills around the world. Not everyone is a fan, however—the practice has been banned in parts of Europe over environmental concerns.

2. THE EGG CARTON: The egg carton was invented in 1911 by Smithers resident Joseph Coyle, who is said to have overheard a hotel owner griping about receiving what you might call "prematurely scrambled" eggs from a local farmer. Coyle, who was a newspaper man, fastened the first cartons out of newsprint, and they functioned much the way they do to-day, keeping each egg snugly separated for safety. He wasn't as good at naming as he was at inventing, however, which is why it was once dubbed "The Coyle Egg-Safety Carton."

3. AMBROSIA APPLE: The firm, sweet Ambrosia apple made its debut in B.C.'s Similkameen Valley on a farm owned by the Mennell family. In the Mennells' telling, the apple's seedling "magically appeared" one day among a row of Jonagolds, and was so delicious that pickers stripped it clean. The family named it after a term from Greek mythology—it means "food of the gods."

4. RETROREFLECTIVE BACKPLATES ON TRAFFIC LIGHTS: You see them all the time, but you might not know the yellow rectangular retroreflective borders surrounding traffic lights debuted in B.C. in 1998. Research found that crashes dropped by 15 per cent at intersections where the test borders were installed, and they are now commonly used across North America.

5. LONDON FOG: Despite what the name might suggest, a London Fog—a latte made with Earl Grey tea—was invented right here in the Lower Mainland. A few websites even claim Scottish cafes call the drink Vancouver Fog in recognition of its origin, although we couldn't find a Scot familiar with the drink. After hearing the description, a few of them called it "bog-gin," whatever that means.

6. THE CALIFORNIA ROLL: The California roll was invented by chef Hidekazu Tojo in the 1970s, back when the very idea of eating raw fish wrapped in rice and seaweed made many squeamish restaurant-goers squirm. Tojo decided to use cooked crab and, in a stroke of bril-liance, to conceal the seaweed inside the rice. And why call it a California roll? Tojo says he named the dish in honour of his L.A. patrons who gobbled them up.

7. NANAIMO BARS : This one is actually the subject of debate, with some claiming the deli-cious desserts actually originated in Alberta, where they were supposedly called Smog Bars. This dish has also, coincidentally, been known as a London Fog Bar over the years. But all that really matters at the end of the day is that you can reliably purchase and eat them on BC Ferries.

8. HAART THERAPY: Last but certainly not least is this life-saving treatment for HIV patients. The pioneering work of Dr. Julio Montaner and the B.C. Centre for Excellence in HIV/AIDS brought about what's now known as Highly Active Anti-Retroviral Therapies, which have become the gold standard of treatment around the world—and allowed countless patients to live long and full lives.

Indigenous people in a dugout canoe circa 1890.

10 PRE-COLONIAL INNOVATIONS FROM B.C. FIRST NATIONS

1. CEDAR EVERYTHING: This really could just be a list of all the amazing things Indigenous peoples across B.C. created using the wood and bark of cedar trees. The Coast Salish Nations braided the roots into cords that could be woven into watertight, heat-proof baskets. Slender branches were used as rope. The Kwakwaka'wakw used rope made from cedar bark to create armour, but the inner bark could also be used for softer purposes like diapers and bedding. The wood itself went into everything from fishing gear to bentwood boxes to building materials for homes.

2. CLAM GARDENS: This is an ancient practice used by Indigenous peoples up and down the coast. The gardens were created by building rock walls along the low tide line to trap seawater and create beach terraces where shellfish could thrive. Some of these gardens could be more than a kilometre long. The Hul'q'umi'num and W̱SÁNEĆ are now involved in a project to restore two clam gardens in the Gulf Islands that are believed to date back thousands of years.

3. DEEP-WATER DENTALIUM SPEARS: Dentalium shells were used as currency and to make jewelry in pre-colonial times, but these mollusks lived deep below the ocean's surface, so they weren't easy to catch. The Nuu-chah-nulth could harvest dentalium from 10-20 metres below their fishing boats using a long, broom-like tool, weighted down by rocks, that could pluck these sea creatures from the sea floor.

4. TLINGIT ARMOUR: The Tlingit of Alaska, Yukon and northern B.C. made their armour from wooden slats and rods, bound together with plant fibres and animal hides. The typical suit included a cuirass that covered the upper body, as well as a helmet. Later, the armour was plated with Chinese coins the Tlingit earned from trading with the Russians.

5. REEF NETS: Reef-netting was actually banned in B.C. a century ago, but it's having a revival now, prompted in part by the research of a W̱SÁNEĆ academic at the University of Victoria. The Coast Salish peoples invented this form of salmon fishing, which involves stringing a net between two boats and sitting in wait along spawning routes in the summer or fall. Colonial authorities derided the reef net as a "fish trap," but it's now considered one of the most sustainable ways to fish.

6. DUGOUT CANOES: Hollowing out a tree to build a canoe is the oldest method of boat construction on the planet, and dugouts are built by peoples around the world. But this was a technique that West Coast Indigenous peoples took to new levels. B.C.'s massive red cedar trees made it possible for coastal Nations to build dugouts that were up to 24 metres long—these huge vessels were used for trading, whaling and hunting seals. There's even a theory that these canoes made it possible to travel all the way from Hawaii to B.C., a distance of thousands of kilometres.

7. STONE SALMON TRAPS: These traps were a simple but elegant innovation used mainly by Indigenous peoples along the northern coast. Fishers created U-shaped stone walls in the intertidal areas just offshore—the walls were hidden at high tide, and trapped water as the tide flowed out. Any fish that were left inside at low tide would be trapped, making them easy prey.

8. FISHING WEIRS: The concept is pretty similar to stone traps, but these structures are placed in rivers instead of on the shoreline. Weirs are essentially fences that are placed in shallow, slow-moving water to block the salmon as they try to swim upstream. The fish are either speared, netted or directed into traps.

9. PIT HOUSES: This is a purely B.C. invention, limited to the First Nations who lived in the Plateau region in the centre of the province. Pit houses were mainly used in the winter months, and were built by digging a wide, round hole in the ground, one or two metres deep, then using logs to construct a conical roof above. The roof was filled in with pine needles, grass and sometimes cedar bark, and then covered with earth. The people who lived inside entered using a ladder fitted into a hole on top.

10. HERRING RAKES: The fact that this invention ever existed will give you an idea of just how plentiful herring used to be in B.C. waters. Herring rakes were an incredibly simple invention—a long hardwood stick with sharp teeth made of bone or wood drilled into the side. During the spring herring run, all that was necessary to bring in a big haul was to sweep the rake through a school of fish, impaling the tasty little morsels on the spikes.

(Opposite) A group of half-dressed Doukhobor men and women are loaded into a police vehicle.

CULTURE AND COMMUNITY

SHANDA LEER'S LIST OF 10 B.C. DRAG QUEENS WHO COULD DRAIN THE STRAIT OUT OF GEORGIA

These mostly fictional drag names are served by Shanda Leer, diviner of East Vancouver's third most accurate horoscopes and everyone's favourite tipsy aunt at a wedding.

Shanda Leer.

1. GROUSE MOUNT-HIM
2. BELLA COOLIT
3. COCKSWELL DAY
4. JOYCE COLLINGWOOD
5. LISA CONDO
6. HIM CATTRALL
7. HAMELA MANDERSON
8. WANDA FUCA*
9. PACIFIC RIMMER
10. VICTORIA HARBOUR(S A LOT OF RESENTMENT)

* Wanda is a true queen and a legend in the West Coast drag scene. Back in the '90s she was crowned the 26th Empress of Vancouver by the Dogwood Monarchist Society.

10 OUTDATED, UNNECESSARY, OR DOWNRIGHT DISTURBING B.C. LAWS

1. NO THROWING SNOWBALLS: Victoria's 1887 Street By-Law contained a number of commonsense regulations, including that you couldn't ride your horse on the sidewalk, or "at a gallop or pace exceeding six miles an hour."

But to the dismay of schoolchildren, it also outlawed throwing snowballs and a lot of other fun mischief. It barred the use of "any bow and arrow, catapult or slingshot," and the throwing of "any stone, snowball or other missile."

2. NO DUELLING BAGPIPES: Speaking of Victoria, the city currently has a bylaw that prohibits any street performer from playing bagpipes "at the same time as another street performer whose performance also includes bagpipes." Bagpiping is also forbidden before 11 a.m. on weekdays and 10 a.m. on weekends. (This law actually makes a fair bit of sense.)

3. NO MORE THAN FOUR SNAKES: The City of Port Coquitlam has a bylaw banning people from keeping more than four rats or four non-venomous snakes as pets. (Don't even bother asking about venomous ones.) Graciously, the city's snake and rat limits do not apply to pet stores or schools.

4. NO YELLOW MARGARINE: It's deliciously salty and spreads like a dream, but margarine isn't butter—and in the late 1940s, B.C. wanted to make sure everyone could tell the difference.

That's why the province decided companies should only be able to sell ivory-coloured margarine. The strange policy was pushed by anxious butter producers, which led to a scathing *Vancouver Sun* editorial mocking the notion of a "colour monopoly."

"We see no reason why the housewife should be required to mix her margarine to the desired shade of yellow before putting it on her table," it read. The law was repealed just a few years later, and cow-milking butter farmers somehow managed to squeeze by.

5. NO BARE KNEES IN ENGLISH BAY: Vancouver's vagrancy bylaw used to ban people from bathing in English Bay unless they were modestly dressed in a swimsuit "covering the body from the neck to the knees." And though thigh-concealing swimwear was fashionable in the early 20th century, the law inexplicably remained on the books until 1986—a full 22 years after the debut of the bikini-heavy *Sports Illustrated* Swimsuit Issue.

6. NO SPITTING IN THE LAUNDRY: Another repealed Vancouver bylaw banned laundromat workers from using the cleaning power of saliva. It outlawed the use of "any water or other liquid that has been in the mouth of any person."

7. NO LOUD PARROTS: The citizens of Oak Bay appreciate their peace and quiet. The scenic Victoria suburb's Anti-Noise Bylaw prohibits people from riding loud motorcycles, shouting on a wharf or playing a phonograph at an unreasonable volume.

And don't think they forgot about your noisy-ass parrot. Any bird owner whose pet squawks loud enough to disturb the "rest, enjoyment, comfort, or convenience" of an Oak Bay resident can face a fine of up to $1,000 a day.

8. NO HAPPY HOUR: Until 2014, it was illegal for bars and restaurants across the province to switch booze prices back and forth over the course of a day—effectively outlawing happy hour specials.

And there have been plenty of other oddball liquor laws in B.C. over the years. The Liquor Act of 1921 made it illegal to sell booze on election day, but allowed veterinarians to "administer or cause to be administered liquor to any dumb animal."

9. NO HAVING BABIES: One of the darkest and most ill-conceived of B.C.'s now-defunct laws is the Sexual Sterilization Act of 1933. It legislated the creation of a Eugenics Board, which was given the authority to order forced sterilization of inmates who were "likely to beget or bear children who by reason of inheritance would have a tendency to serious mental disease or mental deficiency."

Other provinces considered similar laws, but B.C. and Alberta were the only ones to actually implement them—and they weren't repealed until the *1970s*.

10. NO VOTING WHILE CHINESE OR INDIGENOUS: Another shameful law was the one that restricted voting rights for non-white British Columbians. The 1875 Qualifications and Registration of Voters Act decreed "No Chinaman or Indian shall have his name placed on the Register of Voters for any Electoral District, or be entitled to vote at any election of a Member to serve in the Legislative Assembly of the Province." And legislators weren't fooling around—the punishment for adding Chinese or Indigenous names to the register included potential jail time.

BONUS: NO KILLING A SASQUATCH: A number of websites claim there's an old B.C. statute that specifically outlaws the killing of a Sasquatch—sadly, Courthouse Libraries BC tried to track down the source of the claims and found it as elusive as the Sasquatch itself.

That said, it probably is technically illegal to *hunt* a hypothetical Sasquatch—the province is very particular about who can hunt what species, particularly when it comes to big game animals.

8 TIMES SOMEONE TRIED TO CREATE A UTOPIA IN B.C.

Beginning in the 19th century, groups across North America attempted to build ideal societies within self-contained communities. These utopian communities usually didn't last for long, but the people who built them typically tried to achieve perfection through collective living. It should come as no surprise that B.C. was a hotbed for these attempted utopias.

1. SOINTULA: Journalist Matti Kurikka travelled all the way from Finland to establish the small town of Sointula, a "place of harmony" on Malcolm Island, which is now just a short ferry ride from Port McNeill. It was 1901, and about 200 Finnish miners were attracted to the community by promises of communal living and equal wages and voting rights for women.

But the utopian promise began to dissolve after a massive fire in 1903 destroyed the three-storey structure where many community members ate and slept. Eleven people were killed. By 1905, the dream was over, but many of the Finns remained, and their descendants still live on Malcolm Island.

2. SAMMON TAKOJAT (A.K.A. WEBSTER'S CORNERS): Matti Kurikka didn't give up on finding a utopia in B.C. when Sointula failed. He left Malcolm Island in 1904, taking with him about half of Sointula's men. They began clearing land in the Vancouver area and soon earned enough money to buy a farm near Maple Ridge. This time, Kurikka's idea was to build a socialist utopia strictly for bachelors.

But he only lived in this masculine paradise for a few weeks before leaving on a lecture tour. While he was on the road, he received a letter from the colonists, who told him not to bother coming back. Women soon moved into the colony, and by 1913, the community had been subdivided into private homesteads.

3. METLAKATLA: The concept for Metlakatla came from an Anglican lay minister named William Duncan, but the residents were hundreds of Tsimshian people from Lax Kw'alaams and other villages near Prince Rupert on the far northern coast. The utopian Christian community was established in 1862, and it definitely helped Duncan attract followers when a smallpox epidemic that devastated Lax Kw'alaams skipped over Metlakatla.

Duncan demanded that his followers follow 15 strict rules, including renouncing their Indigenous "devilry"—a.k.a spiritual beliefs—and traditional medicine. The experiment brought in financial support from across North America and as far away as England. By 1879, 1,100 people lived in Metlakatla.

But eight years later, after a dispute with church authorities, Duncan left with the majority of the town's residents to found a new village in Alaska.

4. STAND FAST BIBLE STUDENT COLONY: The Stand Fast Bible Students Association was founded in Portland, Oregon not long after the last soldiers were killed in the First World War. Pacifism and conscientious objection to war were among its most important founding principles.

The B.C. colony, founded in Sooke in 1924, began with about 300 people who wanted to live simple lives and await the second coming of Christ. They gave up all their possessions and put their minds and backs to running communal businesses like a cheese factory and a fish reduction plant.

But within just a few years, money became an issue and everyone abandoned the community.

5. RAINBOW VALLEY COLONY: When the Stand Fast Bible Student Colony broke up, a few dissatisfied former members founded this tiny, remote colony near Port Renfrew in the late 1920s. Everyone lived in tents, and the children were homeschooled. Within just a few years, the colony met the same fate as its predecessor and was disbanded.

6. RUSKIN: At the centre of this settlement in Maple Ridge was a sawmill, managed cooperatively by the workers. The people who established Ruskin in 1895 were inspired by the English art critic John Ruskin, who denounced modern capitalism and believed in wholesale social reform that emphasized the arts. The founders of Ruskin formed a group called the Canadian Cooperative Society to experiment with profit-sharing and joint ownership.

The community had a few homes, a school, a general store and a vegetable farm, but it depended almost entirely on the timber trade for its survival. By 1899, the society was facing bankruptcy, and all of its assets had to be surrendered to a lumber company.

7. DOUKHOBOR SETTLEMENTS: More than 8,000 Doukhobors moved to the Kootenay and Boundary regions between 1908 and 1912. These spiritual Christian believers were ardently pacifist, which had put them at odds with the church authorities and the tsarist government in their native Russia.

When they first arrived in Canada, they were welcomed. The Doukhobors had no interest in individual land ownership, and instead lived in agricultural communes. Over three decades, they prospered through keeping orchards and producing jams and honey.

But the community and its reputation were severely damaged by a radical splinter group called the Sons of Freedom, who committed hundreds of acts of violence, including bombings of homes, schools, and churches.

The Doukhobors also faced persecution from the B.C. and Canadian governments. They were disenfranchised in 1917 and then again from 1934 to 1955. In 1939, the province foreclosed on their land and seized it—the Doukhobors weren't able to buy it back until the 1960s.

8. ARGENTA: The settlement of Argenta actually dates back to a silver boom the 1890s, but the community on the shore of Kootenay Lake took on its enduring counterculture feel in the 1950s, when a group of Quakers settled in town. They established a cooperative association and a boarding school, where students learned how to milk cows and chop wood. Later, anti-war protesters and hippies would be added to the mix.

Quakers still make up the majority of community members, and there is no commercial activity in town, but the population of Argenta has never gotten much bigger than about 100 people.

7 NEW RELIGIONS, SECTS, AND STRAIGHT-UP CULTS IN B.C.

1. THE AQUARIAN FOUNDATION: It's safe to say Brother XII was a straight-up cult leader. The man formerly known as Edward Arthur Wilson began as something of a utopian with plans for a perfect society, but over the years, his B.C. interlude took on a much darker tone.

Brother XII was a theosophist—a member of an occult spiritual movement developed in the 19th century—who claimed to be the reincarnation of the Egyptian god of the underworld, Osiris. He founded the Aquarium Foundation in 1927 and built his first colony near Nanaimo with plans to create an entirely self-sufficient society. Thanks to donations from wealthy American disciples who'd been entranced by the guru, the group also bought property on Valdes and De Courcy islands as Brother XII built his following to more than 8,000 people.

What was happening inside the colony was so fascinating and disturbing that the *Nanaimo Free Press* would call it "The most amazing story ever told in a Canadian court" in a 1933 article. When some followers sued to recover their money from Brother XII, their testimony revealed that he maintained control over his followers by turning them against each other. They said they were treated like slaves, and forced to work in the fields in exchange for meagre rations and a place to sleep.

The cult leader and his mistress eventually settled on De Courcy Island, where they kept armed men on patrol and fortified the shoreline to keep "government boats" at bay. Intruders were held captive, according to court testimony. Brother XII asked one follower to dynamite trees so they fell across the passages between the islands, impeding any vessels that might wander too close.

The legal action by some of Brother XII's core disciples put an end to the cult, but he and his mistress somehow managed to slip out of the colony, taking all the gold they'd collected with them.

2. KABALARIAN PHILOSOPHY: What's in a name? Just about everything, according to adherents of the Kabalarian Philosophy. The philosophy was developed in Vancouver in 1930 by a man named Alfred J. Parker, and it combines numerology with a bit of astrology, tossing in some ideas about spirituality from eastern and western religions. The end result? A tiny but enduring movement that claims "your name is your destiny."

Followers believe that changing your name to something more "balanced"—according to numerological principles—will lead to a happier, healthier life. Today, you can enter your name and birthdate into the group's website (kabalarianphilosophy.org) to see what they reveal about your future, health, and personality. You can also read real-life stories from people who say they changed their names to things like Daken and Daorcey and suddenly found themselves in better jobs with higher salaries. It could happen to you, too—all for the low, low price of $195 per name.

3. EMISSARIES OF DIVINE LIGHT: He called himself Uranda. Travelling salesman Lloyd Arthur Meeker had a spiritual awakening one late summer day in 1932, while he was living in Nashville. For three straight nights, he wrote about his new insights, later claiming the room filled with a silvery cloud as he worked. According to the website of the modern-day Emissaries, "It astounded him that the answers didn't come from anything separate from him, but from a reality that dwelt deep within him." The central idea was very New Age and very difficult to pin down—the theory that everyone has the potential for deeper connection with the spirituality inside them. Or something like that.

In 1948, the Emissaries came to B.C., forming a community in 100 Mile House under the leadership of Lord Martin Cecil, a local rancher who also happened to be the Marquess of Exeter. Members flocked to the Cariboo to live on Bridge Creek Ranch, many giving everything they had to the Emissaries. Cecil helped the new religion grow to about 4,000 members.

But after Cecil died in 1988, his son Michael temporarily took over and failed to keep the flock together—he says the numbers dropped by more than two-thirds in response to his attempts to make the Emissaries more democratic. Nonetheless, the religion continues to this day, and still has a spiritual centre in Abbotsford.

William Franklin Wolsey, head of the Canadian Temple of the More Abundant Life in Burnaby.

4. THE CANADIAN TEMPLE OF THE MORE ABUNDANT LIFE: It advertised itself as "The Church of Living Christians and Happy Souls." When the group appeared in Burnaby in the early 1950s, the local newspapers touted it as a place of charity, where the sick and poor could find succor. Leader William Franklin Wolsey styled himself as the Archbishop John I of Burnaby and claimed to be a "biopsychologist." The church ran a private school, and the most ardent followers claimed Wolsey had cured their illnesses.

Then, in 1959, the *Vancouver Sun* ran a series of articles exposing Wolsey as a convicted bigamist with phoney credentials who had a record of embezzlement and abandoning his children. He used the church to take in an estimated $1.5 million from his followers—amassing a personal fortune that would be worth nearly $13 million today.

Graduates of the church's school said they learned nothing useful in their classes and were "brainwashed" instead. They learned that meals should never be eaten off blue plates, for example, because blue vibrations interfered with the nutrients in the food, and that teachers needed beards or moustaches to act as antennae for the vibrations of the universe, according to the *Sun*. Wolsey taught the students sex ed.

For a while after the exposés were published, Wolsey was defiant, telling his flock in sermons, "No amount of persecution stops the work of Jesus Christ." But he eventually fled to the U.S. and set up a new church after a government investigation was launched.

5. CHILDREN OF GOD/THE FAMILY INTERNATIONAL: It began as a counterculture Christian church that attracted hippies and non-conformists, but today the legacy of The Children of God is child abuse and sexual misconduct. River and Joaquin Phoenix and Rose McGowan were all members as children. The movement didn't start in B.C.—it was founded in California by David Berg in 1968—but Berg and his followers appeared in Vancouver in the early 1970s, making a short-lived alliance with a local sect called the Jesus People's Army. The Children of God later made the city their headquarters for few years.

Berg's teachings originally blended fundamentalist Pentecostal Christian elements with hippie rebellion, but during his time in Vancouver, he began promoting himself as something of a prophet. Allegations of child sex abuse began popping up, and the B.C. government took at least a dozen children from the homes of cult members, later returning them when the parents promised to seek counselling.

Internal documents from the cult seized during a 1993 raid in Argentina revealed followers were told they could have sex with anyone at any time—including children. Police also seized videos of children being forced to perform sex acts with adults. Berg's former followers allege that women were required to sleep with multiple members of the group. The cult leader also encouraged something called "flirty fishing," where female followers were required to use sex to attract new members.

Berg died in 1994, but the group still exists. The movement is now called The Family International, which claims it has converted 18 million people over the years.

6. BOUNTIFUL: This tiny settlement in the Creston Valley is home to one of the most enduring and controversial religious groups in B.C. history. The polygamous Mormon fundamentalist community has strong connections to the U.S.-based Fundamentalist Church of Jesus Christ of Latter-Day Saints, led by convicted child rapist Warren Jeffs. The church teaches that men need to have multiple wives to achieve salvation, and girls are often married off as young teenagers. Women are taught to be subordinate to men in every way, and must keep their hair long and wear long dresses.

About 1,000 people live in Bountiful, but because of polygamy, most can trace their ancestry back to just six men. Leader Winston Blackmore married 27 women and had 149 children at last count. He and another community leader, James Oler, were convicted of polygamy in 2017, Canada's first conviction for that offence in more than a century. Two other community members have been found guilty of taking a 13-year-old girl across the border to marry Warren Jeffs.

7. NXIVM: NXIVM was marketed to women as a self-help group where everyone from homemakers to actresses could learn to be confident in themselves. Women paid thousands of dollars for courses on self-improvement produced by the leader of the secretive organization, Keith Raniere.

Then, in the fall of 2017, disturbing allegations began pouring out about what Raniere was really up to. The group was based in New York but had a following of about 1,200 people in its Vancouver chapter. Women were allegedly branded with Raniere's initials, and entered into slave-like sexual relationships with him.

In early 2018, Raniere was arrested and charged with a raft of criminal offences, including sex trafficking and conspiracy to commit forced labour. He'd later be charged with child exploitation and possession of child pornography, too. Actress Allison Mack, Seagram's liquor heiress Clare Bronfman, and several other people have pleaded guilty for their roles in helping to recruit and groom sex partners for the NXIVM leader.

10 WORDS FROM THE WITSUWIT'EN LANGUAGE AND THEIR MEANINGS

Provided by the Witsuwit'en Language and Culture Society. Fluent speakers: Helen Nikal and Mary Alice Namox.

Note: The phonetic pronunciations provided are close approximations and do not accurately convey Witsuwit'en sounds.

1. WITSUWIT'EN (WUT-SOO-WUH-T-EN): "People of the lower drainage" of the Widzin Kwah. Witsuwit'en people have inhabited the Bulkley Valley since the last ice age. Witsuwit'en society is matrilineal, meaning that children are recognized as members of their mother's house and/or clan. The Witsuwit'en are organized in five clans and Houses.

2. WIDZIN KWAH (WUH-DZUN/KWAH): This is the traditional Witsuwit'en name for what is now known as the Bulkley River, which in Witsuwit'en geography includes the Morice River. This river is the main salmon source in Witsuwit'en territory, feeding an entire watershed. It flows from Widzin Bin (Morice Lake), a major salmon spawning area, into the Skeena River and all the way to the Pacific Ocean. Father Adrien G. Morice, a French Catholic missionary who arrived in the late 1880s, renamed the southwestern parts of the river and lake after himself, while the Bulkley River was renamed after Charles Bulkley, engineer of the failed Collins Overland Telegraph line. Bulkley never actually saw the river.

3. DÏDIKHNÏ (DEE-DUH-NEE): "A Clan," which consists of several family groupings that trace their origins to a common ancestor. Each clan is represented by a crest, an animal, or an element of nature, which recalls its history and often has spiritual significance. The Witsuwit'en's rich oral history recounts innumerable events that reveal a depth of connection between the people and the land, based on gratitude and reciprocation. They also detail hard lessons learned when nature is not respected. The five clans are: C'ilhts'ëkhyu (Big Frog Clan, also known as the Unistot'en), Likhsilyu (Small Frog Clan), Gidimt'en (Bear/Wolf Clan), Likhts'amisyu (Fireweed Clan), and Tsayu (Beaver Clan).

4. YIKH (YUH): Though this word means "house" as a physical dwelling, socially it refers to a smaller family group, biologically related on the mother's side, who traditionally lived together in a communal cedar plank smokehouse in summer or pithouses dispersed throughout Witsuwit'en territory in winter. A clan can have two to three houses, each of which is led by a hereditary chief, male or female. One of these house chiefs serves as a spokesperson for the clan. House chiefs attain their position in part through inheritance on the mother's side, but also by merit, developed through training and demonstrated skill.

Providing for the house, organizing work, mediating conflict, and consulting with house members, particularly matriarchs, to reach consensus in decision-making was and continues to be essential. A house chief must be knowledgeable about the land, physically and spiritually, as well as house and clan histories, which are represented by crests that are owned and exclusive to particular houses and clans. A prospective house chief is expected to have a thorough understanding of feast business, proper etiquette, and be able to cooperate with other house chiefs to ensure the nation's prosperity. Wing chiefs and other high-ranking people with feast names have varying degrees of status and serve as consultants to the house chiefs.

5. YIN TAH: Meaning: "Witsuwit'en territory." Consisting of numerous house territories, Witsuwit'en territory spans 22,000 square kilometres from Burns Lake to about halfway to Hazelton, northwest of Witset (formerly Moricetown). Witsuwit'en territory is steeped with language and oral stories of their spiritual connection to the land. It is the source of their identity. Most Witsuwit'en houses have multiple territories from which foods and materials are harvested. Territorial boundaries were and continue to be strictly guarded and protected. Trespassing, poaching, and land degradation endangers not only the physical survival of house groups, but also their spiritual and cultural survival.

Traditionally, Witsuwit'en people returned to their house territories in the fall and gathered together in the summer villages to harvest salmon and hold feasts. A house would move to its other territories every few years to avoid over-harvesting. House territories were linked by a well-worn network of trails. Many trails are still visible, while many others became roads through the Bulkley Valley.

6. DINÏ DE'AS (DUH-NEE/DAY-AHS): Meaning: "Feast." Often referred to as the potlatch (or balhats, the Witsuwit'enized version of this Chinook word), the feast is the Witsuwit'en's governing system. After thousands of years of contact and intermarriage with coastal Indigenous peoples, the Witsuwit'en saw the merit of the clan system to organize their lands. The feast is the mechanism by which Witsuwit'en laws regarding land use are validated and upheld, how boundaries are delineated, protected and recognized within and beyond nations, as well as how work on how the land is organized.

Clan membership is a form of kinship across nations. Wolf Clan members attending another nation's potlatch would sit with their Wolf Clan. It is the mechanism by which disputes are resolved and trade is facilitated. Traditionally, it governed all aspects of Witsuwit'en social life such as birth, adolescent rites of passage, marriage, death, widowhood, inheritance of feast, and chiefly names. Many of these important stages of life are still vital to the Witsuwit'en feast today.

7. DIYIK (DUH-YUK): Meaning: "Canyon." The Widzin Kwah canyon in Witset was and continues to be an important summer salmon harvesting location. It is considered sacred and has been inhabited for over 5,500 years. Fishing sites in the canyon are often treacherously perched on the steep cliffs and rocks. Each clan has its own fishing sites. The canyon in Tsë Cakh (Hagwilget), located in Gitxsan territory, became an important Witsuwit'en fishing site after a landslide in the 1820s that blocked salmon from reaching the Widzin Kwah canyon. After commercial fishing on the Northwest Coast began, there was a significant decline in sockeye salmon. Interior Indigenous peoples were blamed and their traditional fishing technologies banned. The Department of Fisheries then blasted rocks in the canyon in Witset in 1928 and later installed fish ladders hoping to increase the number of salmon reaching spawning grounds. Rocks in the Hagwilget canyon were also blasted in 1959, destroying all traditional fishing sites. The Witsuwit'en resisted these interventions and continue to fight for salmon conservation.

8. LHOK (HLOKE): Meaning: "Salmon, fish." There are five salmon species in the Widzin Kwah: sockeye, coho, spring (Chinook), steelhead, and pink. The Witsuwit'en prize sockeye, but jar, smoke, and freeze all species except pinks for the winter. Salmon continues to be a main staple for Witsuwit'en people. Widzin Kwah sockeye has been endangered for almost 100 years due to various government policies and commercial overfishing in coastal waters.

9. HIDA (HUH-DAH): Meaning: "Moose." In the last century, the moose has been an important meat source for Witsuwit'en people; however, caribou were once the dominant species in the Bulkley Valley. The Grand Trunk Pacific Railway's construction in the early 20th century cleared an easy path for the moose through a large, densely forested region. Caribou began to decline and almost all caribou herds in the Bulkley Valley are now extinct.

10. 'ANU NIWHKINIC (AH-NOO/NOH-KUH-NIK) : Meaning: "Our language." Linguists categorize Witsuwit'en as belonging to the Na-Dene or Athabascan Language Family, which includes many Indigenous languages in British Columbia, the Yukon, the Northwest Territories, as well as Apache and Navajo in the southwestern United States. It is one of the largest language families in North America. As of 2019, only 3.2 per cent of the nation's population speaks Witsuwit'en fluently because generations of children were removed and sent to Indian residential schools and foster care or were punished for speaking their language in the public school system. The average age of fluent speakers is 70. Witsuwit'en organizations are making strong efforts to revitalise the language in hopes of avoiding extinction. Immersion programs and language classes have been initiated to help younger generations learn Witsuwit'en.

Textual renditions of Witsuwit'en oral and traditional knowledge belong solely to the Witsuwit'en Nation and therefore no claim of copyright or exclusive rights is made upon them in this publication.

10 FAMILIAR (OR JUST PLAIN FUN) CHINOOK JARGON TERMS

Chinook Jargon, or Chinuk Wawa, was a pidgin language originally used by B.C. First Nations and Native Americans as they traded with each other up and down the Pacific coast, all the way from California to Alaska. When white colonists arrived, the language evolved to become easier for Europeans to pronounce, and by the end of the 1800s, the jargon had become the working people's language. It faded away with the arrival of the railroad and floods of English-speaking people.

Source: the *Chinook Jargon Phrasebook*.

1. SKOOKUM - big, mighty, genuine, solid or strong

2. TYEE - chief, leader or boss

3. HIGH MUCKAMUCK - bigwig; the boss or leader who sits at the head of the table

4. TILLIKUM - friend or people

5. CHUCK - water or liquids

6. POTLATCH - give or gift

7. CULTUS - ordinary, meaningless or broken

8. WAWA - speech, to speak, language

9. HYAK - fast or swift

10. KWEESH! LAW MAN CHAKO - Watch out! The cops are coming!

10 GUINNESS WORLD RECORDS SET IN BRITISH COLUMBIA

Some Guinness World Records represent monumental achievements, such as Neil Armstrong's record for being the first man to walk on the moon.

The records on this list aren't quite so iconic. Some of them, however, are the result of very dedicated people working very hard to leave their mark on history. And that's astronomically cool in our books.

Or as Armstrong himself might have said, "That's one small step for man, one giant unicycle backflip for mankind."

1. LARGEST UNDERWATER PRESS CONFERENCE: Author Eric J. Pittman nabbed the record for largest underwater press conference—yes, that's a record—after somehow convincing 61 journalists to attend the launch of his book *Emails from a Nut!!!* at a pool in Victoria. The book might not have been an international bestseller, but the launch definitely made a splash.

2. OLDEST CURLER: Lola Holmes was 25 when she first tried curling back in the 1940s. Little did she know she'd later take the Guinness World Record for oldest curler at the ripe old age of 100. Given that stones can weigh close to 20 kilograms, partaking in the sport at her age is nothing to take for *granite*.

3. FASTEST VIDEO GAMING: Fred Vasquez, who goes by the nickname "Thanatos," earned his place in the record books by completing the first level of *Demon's Soul*—a notoriously difficult video game—in just four minutes and 44 seconds back in August 2010. You probably have to take our word for it, but that's actually pretty impressive.

4. BIGGEST CHERRY PIE: Back in 1990, before Oliver became known as the "Wine Capital of Canada," it earned a different title: home of the world's largest cherry pie. The massive undertaking, which was organized by the local Rotary Club, required 16,700 kilograms of pie filling and 414 kilograms of pastry, and the final product measured a whopping 5.5 metres across. If that description makes you feel both hungry and full at the same time, you're not alone.

5. FASTEST WOMAN TO CROSS CANADA ON FOOT: Ann Keane ended her record-setting trek across Canada by foot on September 8, 2002 in Tofino. It took her 143 days, of which she ran on all but three—a feat as impressive as her feet were sore.

6. MOST MOTORBIKES ON A BED OF NAILS: All that Burnaby Q. Orbax, of the gross-out "Monsters of Schlock" duo, had to do to earn his Guinness World Record back in 2015 was lie on a bed of nails and let 70 motorbikes drive over his body. Where's the challenge?

7. LONGEST BASKETBALL SPIN ON A TOOTHBRUSH: Sandeep Singh Kaila set his world record on New Year's Day 2019 by spinning a basketball on a toothbrush for one minute and eight seconds. Not impressed? Wait, did we mention the toothbrush was in his mouth?

8. HEAVIEST PEACH*: Kelowna orchardist Robert Hague grew a surprisingly plump Autumnstar peach that weighed in at a whopping 810 grams, breaking an existing Guinness World Record. While the fleshy fruit was a welcome surprise for Hague, it's safe to assume that for the previous record-holder, it was the pits.

Sadly, this record was broken in 2018 by farmers in Georgia. Seems like they probably had an unfair advantage.

9. LONGEST BEARD: Towering basketball legend Shaquille O'Neal is 7'2" tall, which makes him a full foot shorter than Sarwan Singh's beard. The fantastic facial hair was measured at 2.495 metres long and looks like it could come alive at any moment (though that last part has nothing to do with the record).

10. CONSECUTIVE UNICYCLE BACKFLIPS (ON A TRAMPOLINE): How many consecutive unicycle backflips did Cameron Fraser have to complete on a trampoline at Vancouver's PNE to earn his record? Only two. But we'd like to see you do better.

(Opposite) The name sasquatch comes from the Sts'ailes Tribe of B.C.

THE PARANORMAL

GREG MANSFIELD'S LIST OF B.C.'S 10 MOST HAUNTED PLACES

Greg Mansfield is a Vancouver-based researcher, writer, and award-winning adult educator. He's the author of the Ghosts of Vancouver *website and book.*

The following are the top 10 most haunted places in British Columbia, based on the number of ghostly residents and frequency of encounters with them.

1. RIVERVIEW HOSPITAL, COQUITLAM: Like many psychiatric institutions of its day, the care provided at Riverview Hospital was often cruel and abusive. This left its decaying buildings awash in negative energy and riddled with ghosts. It's currently a location for movie and television productions. Crew members and security guards see shadow figures, apparitions of former patients and staff, a phantom dog, strange lights, and objects moving on their own. Some hear disembodied footsteps and voices, doors and windows banging, and patients' bells ringing in vacant wards. Others are touched, poked, pushed, and pulled by invisible hands or sense they're being watched or followed as the atmosphere goes icy cold.

2. BASTION SQUARE, VICTORIA: All eight of the historic buildings that line this outdoor mall have ghosts. The old Supreme Court building is the most haunted. It sits on the site of Victoria's first jail, where the guilty were hanged and many still lie buried. Footsteps and unexplained voices are heard in the former courtrooms, and a slender apparition is seen on the main staircase. He's believed to be the ghost of Victoria's infamous "Hanging Judge," Sir Matthew Begbie. The ghost of a woman in white is seen outside. In another building at the entrance to Helmcken Alley, phantom organ music plays. In the alley itself, the clanking of chains is heard, and the ghost of a prisoner is seen.

3. WATERFRONT STATION, VANCOUVER: Thousands of commuters pass through Waterfront Station every day without knowing that it's Vancouver's most haunted building. Built during the heyday of rail travel, the station is home to many spirits. They include a woman in a flapper dress who dances in an upstairs hallway, a mournful grey lady, a kindly woman in blue who appears in a ladies' washroom, three little old ladies who sit on a bench waiting for a train that never comes, and other spectres who bang on doors, move furniture, touch the backs of people's necks, and cause cold spots and phantom footsteps.

4. BURNABY ART GALLERY, BURNABY: The gallery is situated in an old mansion with a chequered history. After the original owner, Grace Ceperley, died, the house became a priory for Benedictine monks. It later served as a schoolhouse for a Christian cult; its students were mentally and physically abused. The ghosts include an elderly woman believed to be Mrs. Ceperley, a well-dressed man, a monk, a young woman in white, various children, and shadow figures. Phantom footsteps are heard, as are loud bangs, disembodied voices, screams, and children crying. Doors open, close, lock, and unlock by themselves. Paintings are moved by unseen hands, and objects mysteriously disappear and reappear elsewhere.

5. HYCROFT MANOR, VANCOUVER: This stately home, built for General Alexander McRae and his wife, became a convalescent hospital for veterans following the Second World War. Today it's owned and operated by a women's club. Seven ghosts haunt this opulent building. One is an older man in an officer's uniform who's assumed to be General McRae. Another is a well-dressed lady, believed to be Mrs. McRae. The others include a woman in a nurse's uniform, three army veterans known as "The Pranksters" because they open and close doors and cause lights to flicker, and a "Crying Man" whose loud sobs are heard coming from a room on the lower floor.

6. HAT CREEK RANCH, CACHE CREEK: Visitors flock to historic Hat Creek Ranch to learn about B.C.'s Gold Rush era of the 1860s. The ranch has many historic buildings; the roadhouse is the most haunted. On the main floor, drinking glasses move by themselves in the bar and people have their clothes tugged. Upstairs, phantom footsteps walk the halls, doors are slammed, and a female voice cries out for help. The ghosts of an elderly woman and a long-dead cook sometimes appear. In the granary, the apparition of a man who hanged himself is seen. The spirit of a little girl plays in the grounds. A blacksmith's hammer is heard clanging in the forge. And unseen horses are heard trotting along a road, where they turn and enter a barn.

7. TRANQUILLE SANATORIUM, KAMLOOPS: Before tuberculosis was banished in the 1950s, many of B.C.'s afflicted were sent to Tranquille Sanatorium. It later became a place for housing mentally ill people. Today it serves as a farm and museum. In the sanatorium's old B-wing, the sound of crying children is heard on the eighth floor, where the pediatrics unit was housed. The apparition of a woman wails as she looks for her child. And an electrician who died while doing repairs is sometimes seen in the basement. In underground tunnels where the dead were transported, muffled moans are heard, and people are pushed by unseen hands. Strange mists and lights are seen throughout the complex.

8. HOTEL VANCOUVER, VANCOUVER: The Hotel Vancouver is one of several chateau-style hotels built across the country by railway companies in the early 1900s. Most of them are haunted. This hotel's best-known ghost is the elegantly dressed "Lady in Red." She's seen gliding through elevator doors, floating along the hallways, and lingering in certain guest suites on the 14th floor. Other ghosts include a man dressed in a fedora hat and trench coat in The Roof (a dinner-party venue on the 15th floor), invisible children heard playing in a guest elevator, and a shadow apparition in a room so frightening that they'll never let you stay in it.

9. CRAIGDARROCH CASTLE, VICTORIA: Built for coal baron Robert Dunsmuir, this imposing, castle-like mansion is designated as a National Historic Site. Unfortunately, Dunsmuir died before the house was finished in 1890. It later became a hospital, school, and office building. Several ghosts inhabit its opulent rooms, including a woman dressed in a Victorian-era maid's uniform, a man in a bowler hat, and a little girl. The partial apparition of a woman's satin slipper on a disembodied foot with the hem of a ballgown was once seen walking down the main staircase. Similarly, a pair of men's black dress pants from the knees down to the ankles was observed walking up a different set of stairs on a separate occasion. Inexplicable piano music is heard, strange odours are smelled, and cold drafts are felt throughout the house.

10. EMPRESS HOTEL, VICTORIA: A landmark on Victoria's inner harbour, the Empress Hotel is another of Canada's iconic railway hotels. Like many of them, it's haunted by several ghosts. One is a maid in an old-fashioned uniform who's seen on the sixth floor. Another is an elderly woman who died in an eighth-floor room that's now taken up by an elevator shaft. She knocks on guest room doors on that floor and asks for help to find her room. When people try to assist the confused lady, she leads them toward the elevator and then vanishes. The apparition of a thin, moustached man with a cane is also seen walking along the hotel's halls.

UFO*BC'S 10 MOST COMPELLING CLOSE ENCOUNTERS

*Written by David Pengilly, director of the non-profit UFO*BC society, with additional details gathered from the UFO*BC website.*

1. THE VANCOUVER ISLAND PHOTOGRAPH: This picture of a disc-shaped craft was taken on the east coast of Vancouver Island back in October 1981, and has received more notoriety than any other case on our website.

The photographer, a 25-year-old woman, was on holiday with her family when she turned her lens toward an eye-catching cloud formation above a mountain. It wasn't until they developed the film that the family noticed the UFO—but the high-quality image has since been analyzed by experts and cited in books.

Based on the craft's size in the image and distance from the camera, one analysis determined it would have been several hundred feet wide—an estimate that puts it in line with many other UFO sightings.

2. THE PRINCE GEORGE PHOTOGRAPHS: An 11-year-old boy was playing with a camera in his family's backyard near Prince George when he spotted this UFO on June 24, 1997. He managed to snap two quick photos of the craft, which was also in the classic flying saucer shape, before it disappeared from sight. The boy's photos are of excellent quality, much like the Vancouver Island photograph. Unlike the Vancouver Island photograph, however, they have received little attention.

3. WEST VANCOUVER AND BEYOND: Sightings of tiny dots in the sky, or nocturnal lights, are quite common, but close-range encounters are rare. One witness who sought out UFO*BC had three such encounters, including one in 1976 at West Vancouver's Whytecliff Park.

While gazing out toward Bowen Island, he noticed two distinct lights that appeared to touch down and land on the water. After briefly skimming the surface, the bright objects then submerged into the depths of the ocean.

4. THE JACKO LAKE INCIDENT : This encounter took place in May of 2000, when two friends were fishing just north of Kamloops at Jacko Lake. They were still out on the water when darkness fell, and were stunned to suddenly witness a large light lingering in the sky. A second, smaller light then emerged from some trees and floated up toward the larger one. Panicking, the men decided to rush back to shore, only to realize they were surrounded by thousands of loons in the water.

I met with one of the witnesses in this case. He was very sincere and believable, and assured us they had not been impaired in any way. His description of the lake covered in loons is one I will never forget.

5. BOOMERANG-SHAPED CRAFT OVER NORTH VANCOUVER : This May 15, 2000 sighting is notable in part for the credibility of its witnesses: two automotive technicians who are intelligent, educated, and share a long history of skywatching.

At around 10:50 p.m. that night, they were using a telescope on the rooftop patio of a North Vancouver condo building when they saw a boomerang-shaped craft lined with seven triangles. It was moving quickly, but they were still able to see it for several seconds—an encounter neither man could rationally explain, and which left them both with the "heebie-jeebies."

6. SIGHTINGS IN TELKWA/HOUSTON: A man was winding down in a chair at his Telkwa farm the night of July 29, 2002 when he saw a round, white light shoot across the sky through his window. Though the initial report sounded like it could have been a mere meteorite, more and more witnesses came forward until it became apparent that something very strange had taken place.

One corroborating report came from a forklift operator in nearby Houston, who saw, on the very same night, a phosphorescent ball of white light that appeared to hover before slowly crawling across the skyline.

7. VANCOUVER AIRPORT UFO: This report is also of particular interest because of the witnesses, who were mechanics at Vancouver International Airport and very familiar with planes and normal airport traffic.

The first witness was servicing an aircraft in the early afternoon of July 22, 2001 when he saw a metallic, highly reflective object shaped like a ball bearing that was slowly rotating in the sky. He watched in awe for several minutes before calling two others to look. The craft moved from side to side before descending into the tree line, and possibly down into the Fraser River.

8. MYSTERY OVER THE HIGHWAY: On June 15, 1994, four young siblings returned home before dinner buzzing with stories about an aborted abduction attempt involving a flying saucer and a "green man" with a blue light on his forehead. Though the case is baffling on many levels—there were no corroborating reports of the UFO, which would have been hovering near the Second Narrows Bridge during rush hour—the details are compelling nonetheless.

Their parents said the encounter altered the children's behaviour in different ways. One formerly nervous little girl had a newfound confidence. Another no longer felt safe going anywhere without company, including the bathroom.

9. A MCDONALD'S VISIT OF A DIFFERENT KIND : This sighting dates back to April 1982, and involves three friends who had stopped their car on an isolated back road near Richmond's

McDonald Park late at night. A craft suddenly emerged with three intensely bright lights that rapidly alternated in colour between red, green, and blue. Shortly after, a second UFO arrived. As the witnesses watched in stunned silence, the two craft began passing white beams back and forth, like Morse code.

We met one witness at the location of the sighting. He was very believable, and his description of the passing beams has remained with me for more than 20 years.

10. NOW, JUST WATCH THE BIRDIES : This very unusual case, witnessed on December 15, 1996 in Richmond's Steveston Village, involved green "balls of light" that put on an incredible aerial display for three young boys, all around 11 years old.

The boys eventually called for their parents, who caught just brief glimpses of the unexplainable encounter—memorable to me was the description by the father of seeing his son's face "illuminated" by one of the balls. It is details like this that add credibility to the case.

10 FACTS ABOUT THE OGOPOGO—MOST OF THEM TRUE

Before discussing the Ogopogo, it's important to acknowledge some cultural context. Long before the cryptid captured the imagination of white settlers, the syilx / Okanagan people spoke of n̓x̌aʔx̌ʔítkʷ (n'ha-a-itk), the sacred spirit of the lake. The stories of n̓x̌aʔx̌ʔítkʷ and the meaning behind them are powerful and fascinating, but they aren't ours to tell—you can learn about them at the Sncewips Heritage Museum in Westbank.

1. The name Ogopogo, which is a palindrome, came from an English music hall song that was popular in the 1920s. The lyrics are about a man searching for a banjo-playing creature whose "mother was a polly" and "father was a whale."

2. Though the Ogopogo is sometimes referred to as B.C.'s Loch Ness Monster, the sightings predate those of the actual Loch Ness Monster. The first settler to report witnessing a serpentine creature in Okanagan Lake was Susan Allison in 1872, and the n̓x̌aʔx̌ʔítkʷ stories date back much further.

3. A crew from Japan's Nippon TV spent tens of thousands of dollars searching for the Ogopogo in 1990 and 1991, employing divers, sonar-equipped boats and a helicopter. They managed to pick up one unidentifiable object on sonar, but didn't find anything that would convince a skeptic.

4. Okanagan Lake is 232 metres deep—plenty of space for an elusive cryptid to hide—and contains a cave near Rattlesnake Island that's sometimes referred to as "Ogopogo's Lair."

5. According to a recent Insights West survey, more British Columbians believe Princess Diana was murdered than believe the Ogopogo is real—27 per cent to 16 per cent, respectively.

6. One of the most famous Ogopogo videos was captured by Art Folden in 1968. An investigation decades later found he had, in fact, seen a living creature off in the distance... but that it was possibly just a beaver.

7. Much of the visual evidence pointing to the existence of a long, be-humped creature in Okanagan Lake is dismissed by skeptics as being either unusual wave activity or floating logs.

8. The best time to spot the beast is between the last week in August and the first week in October, according to local Ogopogo hunter Bill Steciuk.

9. The Ogopogo was once featured on a stamp in Canada Post's commemorative folklore collection, which also paid tribute to the Kraken, Sasquatch, and werewolves.

10. It's real, I tell you! *Real!!*

THOMAS SEWID'S LIST OF 8 FACTS ABOUT B.C.'S RICH SASQUATCH HISTORY

Thomas Sewid is a renowned Kwakwaka'wakw Sasquatch investigator and First Nations Sasquatch stage performer. He also runs the Facebook group Sasquatch Island.

1. The name Sasquatch comes from the Sts'ailes Tribe of B.C., also known as the Chehalis. Canadians prefer the term Sasquatch over Bigfoot, which is more common among Americans.

2. Vancouver Island has the highest concentration of wooden Sasquatch carvings on Earth, many of which can be found in Campbell River.

3. The Kwakwaka'wakw First Nations tribes of Northeastern Vancouver Island have the deepest ties to Sasquatch, for Tzoonakwa (Wildwoman of the Woods) is their highest ranked crest for a family to own and display.

4. Vancouver Island also has the highest number of Sasquatch encounters of anywhere in the world, and is sometimes referred to as Ape Island or Sasquatch Island.

5. Harrison Hot Springs has a Sasquatch Days festival every year in June.

6. B.C. has produced many well-known Sasquatch investigators, such as John Green, Dr. John Bindernagel, Thomas Steenburg, Rene Dahinden, Dave and Grace Williams, Kerry Kilmury, and myself.

7. B.C. beer brand Kokanee uses Sasquatch as their mascot. In the 1980s, Johnny Carson was so impressed with this that he brought a bottle of beer on stage and spoke about the Sasquatch.

8. Every Indian tribe in B.C. has a name and stories about Sasquatch.

(Opposite) Actor Seth Rogen and producer Evan Goldberg sit in Robson Square, which has been decked out to look like North Korea for the 2014 film The Interview.

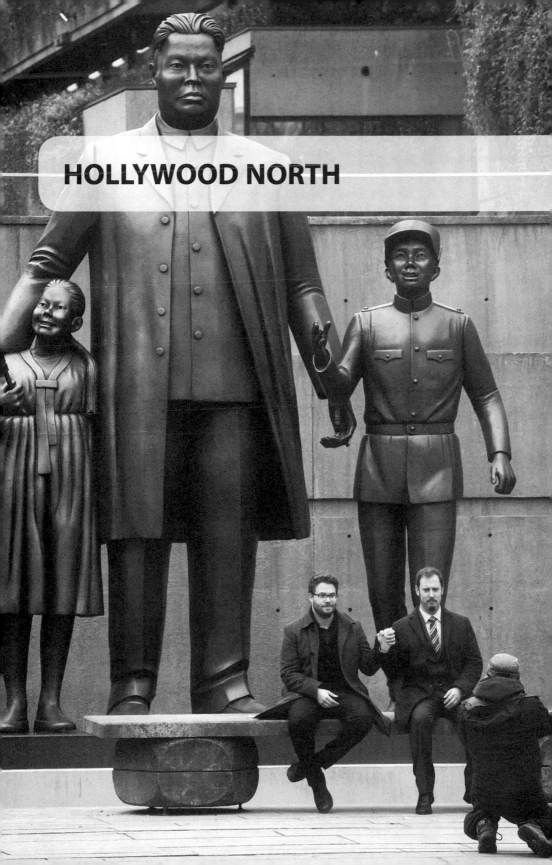

HOLLYWOOD NORTH

LAINEY'S LIST OF 4 CELEBRITY SCANDALS THAT HAPPENED IN B.C.

Elaine "Lainey" Lui's blog, LaineyGossip.com, started as an email newsletter to a small group of friends and colleagues in 2003. The Vancouver-based website quickly grew to become one of the most popular celebrity gossip blogs in North America. Today, she also works as a reporter for CTV's etalk, *and is a co-host on the network's daily talk show* The Social.

1. BEN AFFLECK'S TRIP TO BRANDI'S, 2013: While in town shooting a movie, Ben Affleck met up with Tara Reid and Christian Slater for a night out at Brandi's Exotic Show Lounge, a strip club in downtown Vancouver. He was engaged to Jennifer Lopez at the time. *The National Enquirer* reported that Affleck had "sex in the back room" of the club and cheated on Lopez with another dancer later on at Slater's house. He denied the allegations and threatened to sue. A couple of months later, he and Lopez postponed their wedding. And a few months after that, they ended their relationship for good.

2. EDISON CHEN'S HACKED PICTURES, 2008: Vancouver-born Edison Chen was one of the biggest celebrities in Hong Kong when his computer was hacked and intimate photos of him having sex with a number of young Hong Kong starlets were released online. Authorities launched an investigation but Chen refused to return to Hong Kong to testify, fearing retribution, and gave his testimony at B.C. Supreme Court instead. The scandal ruined his career, and those of many others in Hong Kong, for almost a decade.

3. KJ APA'S CAR ACCIDENT, 2017: *Riverdale* star KJ Apa fell asleep at the wheel and crashed into a light pole after working a 16-hour day. He was treated for minor injuries. The accident prompted SAG-AFTRA, the actors' union, to launch an investigation into working conditions and some cast and crew members were said to have lobbied executives to have production policies and procedures changed to account for the long hours.

4. CORY MONTEITH'S OVERDOSE, 2013: Cory Monteith was found dead in his hotel room at the Fairmont Pacific Rim Hotel in Vancouver. Monteith had recently spent a month in rehab for substance addiction. A coroner's report subsequently revealed that he died from a combination of heroin and alcohol. *Glee* was a hit show at the time, and Monteith was one of its biggest stars. His death made headlines around the world as international media descended on Vancouver.

THE STAR TREATMENT: 8 ACTORS WHO HAD A BAD TIME IN VANCOUVER

1. SHIA LABEOUF: Stories about Shia LaBeouf's oddball behaviour were only just starting to trickle out back in 2011 when the *Transformers* actor was filmed going toe-to-toe with a shirtless gentleman on Vancouver's Granville Strip. Or as TMZ put it, "LABEOUF … PUMMELED TO THE GROUND ON VANCOUVER SIDEWALK." The fight didn't noticeably hurt LaBeouf's career, but the wave of strange stories that followed—including the time he showed up to a movie premiere with a bag over his head that read "I am not famous anymore"—might have done a teensy bit of damage.

2. DJ QUALLS: Fans of raunchy early-2000s comedies might remember DJ Qualls as the lanky college student who eats soiled French toast in *Road Trip*. Some Vancouverites also know him as the guy who got his clock cleaned by a local cop. Qualls said the officer roughed him up during a late night brawl on Granville Street back in 2014, even though he was, by his account, just an innocent bystander. "(Police) tackled me, busted my face and handcuffed me," the actor tweeted. To make matters worse, Qualls also claimed he was stuck with an $800 bill for his ambulance and stitches.

3. DOMINIC PURCELL: Many proud Vancouverites like to think of their home as a world-class city. *Prison Break* actor Dominic Purcell had a different term: gulag.

In a searing Instagram post published in May 2016, Purcell made it crystal clear how he felt about filming in Vancouver. He slammed the soggy weather, locals' obsession with the Great Outdoors, and the "blind eye" turned to the homeless and people suffering from mental health issues.

He ended with a taunting "Can't wait to read the hate comments I get," and upset fans didn't disappoint. Purcell's post was later taken down.

4. KIRK ACEVADO: *Arrow* actor Kirk Acevado may not be the biggest name on this list, but his story was as embarrassing a blemish on the city as any. The Brooklyn native, who was born to Puerto Rican parents, said he was waiting for the Coach store on Burrard Street to open when an employee looked him up and down, asked if he intended to buy anything, and then locked the door—only to open it up when a white woman approached moments later.

The incident was especially ironic, Acevado said, because of what he was wearing at the time: a T-shirt of baseball player and civil rights icon Jackie Robinson.

5. DAVID DUCHOVNY: Many Vancouver *X-Files* fans remember when Judas, née David Duchovny, decided to mock the city's soggy weather during a 1997 interview on *Late Night with Conan O'Brien*. The actor called Vancouver "kind of like a tropical rainforest without the tropics," and a "very nice place if you like 400 inches of rainfall a day," which clearly cut too close to the bone for some rain-soaked wet blankets. People wrote letters to the *Vancouver Sun* calling Duchovny a "wussy" who needed to "ship his ass out of here." And the actor did just that shortly after, moving the show's production down to sunny Los Angeles, where he could be closer to his then-wife, Téa Leoni.

6. KJ APA: KJ Apa, who plays Archie on Netflix's hit series *Riverdale*, was born the same year David Duchovny put his foot in his mouth. And just two decades later, he stepped in the same minefield while trying to offer a perfectly reasonable criticism of Vancouver. During an appearance on *LIVE with Kelly and Ryan*, Apa described the city as "kind of boring" because "everything kind of shuts early"—not an altogether unfair an assessment of "No-Fun City." Some people were mad, although the backlash was nothing compared to Duchovny's drubbing.

7. WESLEY SNIPES: Whether Wesley Snipes enjoyed Vancouver during the filming of *Blade: Trinity* is hard to say, but he certainly despised working on the movie—at least enough to sue the production company and director.

Among the complaints in Snipes's lawsuit: that there were too many white people in the cast and crew (a departure from the previous two *Blade* films, which made an effort to employ diverse teams) and that the film's humour, much of which came from co-star Ryan Reynolds, was "juvenile." It was not the chummiest of sets.

8. ERROL FLYNN: Over the course of his career in the Golden Age of Hollywood, Errol Flynn became known as much for his off-screen scandals as he was for his leading roles. Without going into too much detail, let's say the myriad allegations against him would make any modern #MeToo supporter queasy. (He was also posthumously accused of being a Nazi sympathizer, though there was little evidence to back it up.)

But however you feel about the swashbuckling actor, he arguably had a worse time in Vancouver than anyone—at least on the day in 1959 when he suffered a heart attack and croaked.

11 CITIES (AND 1 PLANET) VANCOUVER HAS PLAYED IN THE MOVIES

With its frequent TV and movie shoots, Vancouver is said to be one of the most-filmed cities in the world—but rarely does Vancouver actually play itself. Here are some of the most far-fetched roles the city has pulled off over its long and illustrious career in front of the cameras.

1. SAN FRANCISCO: Vancouver is a common stand-in for the City by the Bay, including in the recent *Planet of the Apes* prequels and 2014's *Godzilla*. It even played the titular role of San Francisco in *Homeward Bound II: Lost in San Francisco*.

2. TOKYO: Speaking of *Godzilla*, the globe-trotting creature feature gave Vancouver a chance to play another world-class city: Tokyo. The Vancouver Convention Centre appears very briefly as an unspecified "Tokyo Airport," while the waterfront in Richmond's Steveston neighbourhood stands in for a Japanese village.

3. FUTURE CHICAGO: The Will Smith sci-fi action film *I, Robot* subbed Vancouver for a futuristic vision of Chicago from the year 2035. Though computer animation did much of the scene-setting, the city's Ovaltine Cafe makes a notable appearance, complete with automaton waiters.

The Jackie Chan action-comedy *Rumble in the Bronx* is one of many film productions that have substituted Vancouver for the Big Apple.

4. NEW YORK: While New York City has a personality all its own, Vancouver has doubled for the Big Apple on several occasions, including the 2014 comedy *The Interview* and Jackie Chan's 1995 action brawler *Rumble in the Bronx*. The latter elicited a few eye-rolls for having multiple shots where the North Shore Mountains could be seen in the background, but Chan once told an interviewer the filmmakers didn't bother thinking too hard about the scenery—the stunts were supposed to be the star of the show, anyway.

5. PYONGYANG: Given that *The Interview* revolves around an assassination attempt on Kim Jong Un, much of it is also set in North Korea. But the Seth Rogen and James Franco production was unlikely to receive a warm welcome in the Hermit Kingdom, so they filmed those scenes here as well.

6. DANCING ELK, MINNESOTA: Diablo Cody's 2007 Oscar-winner *Juno* is set in the sleepy town of Dancing Elk, Minn. And while there is no such town, the film was still supposed to conjure the *feeling* of Minnesota, and the location scouts found plenty of appropriate backdrops in Vancouver.

7. MOSCOW: The climactic bout between Rocky Balboa and Ivan Drago in 1985's *Rocky IV* supposedly takes place in Moscow, but the production never came within 1,000 kilometres of Soviet Russia. The PNE Agrodome provided an ample fight venue, while a property in snowy Wyoming doubled for the rural Russian cabin where Balboa trained.

8. SEATTLE: Vancouver also commonly plays Seattle, recently in the cancer-diagnosis comedy *50/50* and all three *Fifty Shades of Grey* films. Given the cities' similar vibes and geographic proximity, this one is a no-brainer for productions looking to save a little cash—just superimpose a Space Needle here and there, and you're good.

9. VANCOUVER, WASH.: On that note, the first *Fifty Shades* film also gave Vancouver the rare chance to play Vancouver—albeit the one next door in Washington state. The University of British Columbia doubled for Washington State University, where lead character Anastasia Steele was a student.

10. MUMBAI: Tom Cruise's *Mission Impossible: Ghost Protocol* manage to convincingly portray Vancouver as several exotic locations, including Moscow and Mumbai. Using some colourful lights and a lot of honking cars, the production simulated Mumbai's bumper-to-bumper traffic right outside the Vancouver Convention Centre for a frantic chase scene. That led to the big finale, which takes place in a futuristic parking garage that's actually just a Vancouver soundstage.

11. WATERBURY, CONNECTICUT: The plot of Adam Sandler's 1996 comedy *Happy Gilmore*, so much as it has one, revolves around Happy's efforts to prevent his grandmother's home from being repossessed by the IRS—and that home sits in the heart of Vancouver's Shaughnessy neighbourhood.

BONUS: THE PLANET ALTAMID: In *Star Trek Beyond*, the U.S.S. Enterprise crash lands on the planet Altamid, leaving the crew in hostile territory and giving Vancouver a rare opportunity to play an alien world. The exotic crash site was constructed at Kent Hangar Field, while other parts of Altamid's terrain, which looked suspiciously like Earth forests, were filmed around Squamish.

Squamish: The Final Frontier.

10 B.C. ACTORS WHO HIT IT BIG

1. KIM CATTRALL (BORN AUGUST 21, 1956): Though megastar and author Kim Cattrall was born in Liverpool, England, her parents crossed the pond when she was an infant and she spent her formative years in the small Vancouver Island community of Little River. She eventually moved to New York City in 1972, and scored her first on-screen acting role in *Rosebud* three years later. But it wasn't until the 1980s that she'd become a star, appearing in some of the best cult classics of the decade, including *Big Trouble in Little China*, *Mannequin*, and, yes, *Porky's*.

2. MICHAEL J. FOX (BORN JUNE 9, 1961): Michael J. Fox was born into an army family in Edmonton, but after moving from place to place his parents eventually planted roots in Burnaby. He was still living in B.C. when he made his acting debut on the CBC sitcom *Leo and Me* (not *The Beachcombers*, as is sometimes misreported) but his career didn't take off until he moved to Los Angeles. That's where he landed his star-making role as smarmy young Republican Alex P. Keaton on *Family Ties* in 1982.

3. PAMELA ANDERSON (BORN JULY 1, 1967): Pamela Anderson's B.C. breakout story is the stuff of legend. A few years after graduating from Highland Secondary School in Comox, she threw on a cropped Labatt T-shirt and headed out to a BC Lions game, where her image was broadcast onto the jumbotron—eventually leading Labatt to offer her a job as spokesmodel. She went on to star as C.J. Parker on *Baywatch* and its accompanying wall posters, which turned her into the Farrah Fawcett of adolescent boy bedrooms in the 1990s.

4. CARRIE-ANNE MOSS (BORN AUGUST 21, 1967): Carrie-Anne Moss was born in Burnaby, but the ambitious youngster commuted to Vancouver's Magee Secondary School for its drama program. Her career took a more zig-zagging path than most; rather than heading straight to California, she first ditched B.C. to pursue a modelling career in Europe. Interestingly, while everyone remembers Moss as Trinity in 1999's game-changing blockbuster *The Matrix*, few know she previously appeared in plain-old *Matrix*, a 1993 Canadian fantasy series.

5. RYAN REYNOLDS (BORN OCTOBER 23, 1976): International superstar Ryan Reynolds was born in Vancouver, where he attended Kitsilano High School. And before going on to portray at least three different comic book characters, Reynolds got his first acting job playing Billy Simpson on the Canadian teen drama *Hillside*. (Google it, trust us.) It wasn't until a few years later, when he moved to L.A. and was cast in the infinitely less angsty *Two Guys, a Girl and a Pizza Place*, that his star potential would shine through.

6. EVANGELINE LILLY (BORN AUGUST 3, 1979): Evangeline Lilly was born next door in Alberta, but raised in B.C. Her slow rise to stardom also began here—she was discovered by an agent from the Ford Modelling Agency while out walking in Kelowna. But before her big break on 2004's *Lost*, there was a string of non-speaking roles and commercials, including an ad for the Live Links chat service that you may remember seeing on late-night TV.

7. TAYLOR KITSCH (BORN APRIL 8, 1981): Taylor Kitsch had a humbler beginning than most of the stars on this list. The *True Detective* star was born in Kelowna, then raised in a trailer park by a single mom (he's even referred to his younger self as "white trash"). He attended Gleneagle High School in Coquitlam, and, like his brooding character Tim Riggins on *Friday Night Lights*, was a young athlete, playing junior hockey for the Langley Hornets before being forced off the ice by a knee injury. He moved to New York, then L.A. before finally landing that iconic role in 2006. Kitsch later went on to play Gambit in the critically lambasted, but B.C.-filmed *X-Men Origins: Wolverine*.

8. SETH ROGEN (BORN APRIL 15, 1982): Gravel-voiced funnyman Seth Rogen was born in Vancouver, and was still living in the city when Judd Apatow gave him his first acting job on the fantastic, but doomed *Freaks and Geeks* in 1999. Though Rogen, too, moved to L.A. in search of stardom, he drew on his West Coast upbringing for inspiration; he and co-writer Evan Goldberg based the hit comedy *Superbad* in part on their awkward coming-of-age years at Point Grey High School. They even named their production company Point Grey Pictures.

9. COBIE SMULDERS (BORN APRIL 3,1982): Cobie Smulders shares a few things with Robin Scherbatsky, her breakout role from the hit CBS series *How I Met Your Mother*: they were both born in Vancouver to English mothers, and both starred in questionable TV series (Scherbatsky in the fictional *Space Teens*, and Smulders in the unfortunately real *Veritas: The Quest*). Of course, Smulders's career eventually took off, with roles in the B.C.-shot series *The L Word* and *Smallville*, leading to a regular gig in the Marvel Cinematic Universe. But once upon a time, she was a regular teenager attending Lord Byng Secondary School and dreaming of being a marine biologist.

10. FINN WOLFHARD (BORN DECEMBER 23, 2002): Get ready to feel old and unaccomplished. Vancouver's Finn Wolfhard launched his child acting career when he was about 12 years old, and won a Screen Actors Guild award at 14 for his role as Mike Wheeler on Netflix's smash hit *Stranger Things*. He followed that up with another starring role in 2017's *IT* remake, which broke box office records. Beyond that, Wolfhard is the lead singer and guitarist for Vancouver-based rock group Calpurnia, which, unlike your high school band, is actually signed to a record label. So he's doing OK.

Honourable mentions: Jennifer Tilly (born September 16, 1958 in California but raised on Texada Island); Jason Priestley (born August 28, 1969 in North Vancouver); Thomas Middleditch (born March 10, 1982 in Nelson); Cory Monteith (born May 11, 1982 in Calgary but raised in Victoria); Kristin Kreuk (born December 30, 1982 in Vancouver).

The *Deadpool* movies are two of the top-grossing movies filmed in B.C.

10 HIGHEST-GROSSING MOVIES FILMED (AT LEAST PARTLY) IN B.C.

Worldwide gross, in U.S. dollars, from BoxOfficeMojo.com.

1. **TITANIC, 1997:** *$2.19 billion*

2. **THE TWILIGHT SAGA: BREAKING DAWN PART 2, 2012:** *$829.7 million*

3. **PIRATES OF THE CARIBBEAN: DEAD MEN TELL NO TALES, 2017:** *$794.9 million*

4. **DEADPOOL 2, 2018:** *$785 million*

5. **DEADPOOL, 2016:** *$783.1 million*

6. **2012, 2009:** *$769.7 million*

7. **THE TWILIGHT SAGA: BREAKING DAWN PART 1, 2011:** *$712.2 million*

8. **DAWN OF THE PLANET OF THE APES, 2014:** *$710.6 million*

9. **THE TWILIGHT SAGA: NEW MOON, 2009:** *$709.7 million*

10. **THE TWILIGHT SAGA: ECLIPSE, 2010:** *$698.5 million*

10 BOX-OFFICE BOMBS FILMED IN B.C.

Estimated losses adjusted for inflation to 2019 U.S. dollars. Source: Wikipedia.

1. MONSTER TRUCKS, 2016: *Estimated losses: $114-$129 million*
This is literally a movie about a monster living inside a truck, filmed in Chilliwack, Kamloops, and Surrey. As a reviewer for *Time Out* wrote, "It was never going to be Citizen Kane."

2. THE 13TH WARRIOR, 1999: *Estimated losses: $104-$199 million*
The rare flop based on a Michael Crichton novel, this movie implausibly starred Antonio Banderas as a Baghdadi poet taking refuge among Vikings in the 10th century. "I can hardly say what it's about, other than people killing each other," one reviewer wrote. It was filmed in Vancouver, Campbell River, Williams Lake, and Pemberton.

3. BALLISTIC: ECKS VS. SEVER, 2002: *Estimated losses: $98 million*
Poor Antonio Banderas—he just has a knack for filming duds in Vancouver. This time, he played a former FBI agent forced to team up with his nemesis, a former DIA agent played by Lucy Liu, to take down a common enemy. "For many viewers, the big question may be not whether Ecks and Sever will get together, or why they are fighting in the first place, but why am I sitting here, anyway?" a writer for the *Associated Press* said.

4. DUDLEY DO-RIGHT, 1999: *Estimated losses: $98 million*
Another entry in the very specific genre of live-action cartoon remakes starring Brendan Fraser, this story about a bumbling Mountie somehow managed to waste a cast that included Sarah Jessica Parker, Alfred Molina, and Eric Idle. It was mainly filmed in locations across the Lower Mainland, and earned terrible reviews—although the *Washington Post* called it "surprisingly pleasant."

5. DRIVEN, 2001: *Estimated losses: $95 million*
Vancouver was just one of at least 13 locations where this globe-trotting Sylvester Stallone car-racing flop was filmed. Maybe if the producers didn't insist on flying the cast between B.C., Ontario, Quebec, Chicago, Detroit, California, Florida, Germany, Japan, and Australia, it would have been a wee bit more financially viable.

6. SEVENTH SON, 2014: *Estimated losses: $90 million*
Jeff Bridges as a monster hunter, Julianne Moore as an evil witch, a war between supernatural forces and humankind, and yet somehow it "manages to be both ridiculous and bland," according to *New York* magazine. The movie was partly filmed in Vancouver, along with locations in Alberta and California.

7. FANTASTIC FOUR, 2015: *Estimated losses: $85-$106 million*
It wasn't the first *Fantastic Four* movie to be filmed in Vancouver, but by all accounts it was the worst—even with Michael B. Jordan playing one of the titular four, it was still "lightweight and basically unnecessary," according to Richard Roeper. The B.C. filming locations included Cypress Mountain in West Vancouver.

8. TOMORROWLAND, 2015: *Estimated losses: $80-$159 million*
This movie was the cause of much excitement while it was filming in Vancouver. For a time, trying to catch a glimpse of George Clooney was the hottest game in town. At its heart though, *Tomorrowland* was a film based on a Disney theme park, and critics couldn't stand its preachy tone.

9. POWER RANGERS, 2017: *Estimated losses: $78 million*
Maybe someday we'll get an Oscar-worthy movie about the Mighty Morphin Power Rangers, but alas, it didn't happen with this attempt, filmed in Vancouver, Kamloops, and Richmond. The *Globe and Mail*'s film critic called it "a work of soulless indifference," and the box office numbers proved audiences felt much the same.

10. THE BFG, 2016: *Estimated losses: $74-$104 million*
This was a remarkable failure for an adaptation of a Roald Dahl book directed by Steven Spielberg. Critics didn't seem to mind it, but it just couldn't find an audience. The movie was shot in Vancouver as well as locations in New York and the U.K.

10 B.C.-FILMED TV SHOWS THAT DIDN'T MAKE IT TO SEASON 2

1. WOLF LAKE (2001-02): Sometimes, success is all about the timing. If we told you that Lou Diamond Phillips and Graham Greene briefly starred in a TV thriller about werewolves living outside Seattle, you'd probably assume it was a cheap attempt at a *Twilight* rip-off. But it's not! *Wolf Lake* actually predated Stephenie Meyer's first vampire romance novel by four years. Sadly, the visionaries who created it were too far ahead of their time, and CBS yanked the show after just five episodes. Another four aired the following year on another channel.

2. CHORUS ANYONE (1964): People had strange ideas about what constituted an entertaining half hour of television back in the 1960s. Or maybe it was just the CBC. For one sweet summer, Canadians could tune into the national broadcaster every Sunday night to watch a Vancouver men's choir sing 30 minutes of songs on a particular theme—campfire music this week, maybe tunes about the ocean the next. For extra fun, sometimes there might be a piano duet!

3. FREQUENCY (2016-17): Buckle up and pay attention, because this one is complicated. This CW show was about an NYPD detective who discovered she could communicate with her long dead father through his old ham radio. (There was some lightning involved). No, he wasn't a ghost—don't be stupid. The ham radio was also a time machine, of course, and the dad was speaking to his daughter from the year 1986. Now, try to stay with me, because that's not all. The detective understandably tried to use this remarkable ham radio to save her father's life, but that set off the butterfly effect, and the present began to change. Oh no! Obviously, the only way for father and daughter to fix things was to work together across time and space to solve a murder.

4. THE MOUNTAIN (2004-05): Sometimes, you've got to let the setting decide what the show will be. Looking back, it seems a bit strange that there haven't been more B.C.-filmed shows set at ski resorts, but the fate of *The Mountain* proved it's not exactly a guaranteed formula for success. This show used the classic dramatic formula of relatives squabbling over the family business after the death of a patriarch. This time, the central character was the irresponsible youngest son who inexplicably inherits a family ski resort and has to learn to get along with his siblings while fighting off a scheming developer. I guess we'll never know how that all worked out.

5. PALACE GUARD (1991): Why don't they make shows about jewel thieves anymore? The slick individual at the centre of *Palace Guard* was Tommy Logan, recently back on the streets after a term in the slammer. Naturally, he was the perfect fit for the job of security expert at a chain of luxury hotels—Palace Hotels, to be specific, but I probably didn't need to tell you that.

Now for the twist. Tommy didn't know it, but he was also the illegitimate son of the tycoon who owned the hotels. Toss in a sexy female boss who had no patience for Tommy's shenanigans, and you've got the perfect formula for a TV show that was cancelled after three episodes.

6. ENDGAME (2011): Another entry in the inexhaustible genre of Brilliant But Troubled _____ Solves Mysteries In His Spare Time. This time, the quirky but ingenious hero is a chess master with agoraphobia. To pay the growing bills for the luxury hotel where he's been staying, he agrees to use the crime-solving skills he's learned from chess to help the police with their most difficult cases. Even on Canadian TV, the concept couldn't survive past the first season.

7. MIRACLES (2003): If people loved watching David Duchovny and Gillian Anderson investigating aliens on *The X-Files* so much, then surely they'd be just as psyched to see Skeet Ulrich looking into Catholic-tinged mysteries. That was the logic behind *Miracles*, and it turned out to be a bit faulty. Ulrich played a modern miracle investigator with the church who went rogue after a cynical monsignor dismissed his findings about a small boy with healing powers. Tagline: "Some miracles have nothing to do with angels."

8. MERCY POINT (1998-99): Sick of medical dramas? Well, what about a medical drama … in space? This short-lived show was set in the 23rd century, in a hospital space station called, you guessed it, Mercy Point. With a staff made up of humans, aliens, and androids, the narrative possibilities seemed endless. Sadly, that presumption was never tested—*Mercy Point* was placed on hiatus after just three episodes. The final four were later aired in two-hour blocks in the middle of summer.

9. PITFALL (1981-82): In the years before Alex Trebek was Alex Trebek, he took a turn as the host of this bizarre Canadian game show. *Pitfall* had some elements of *Family Feud*, a little bit of *Jeopardy!* and a tiny taste of *Wipeout*, plus some elevators and lots of flashing lights. It was all very complicated, but the game culminated with a bonus round where the champion had to try and cross a bridge while answering trivia questions and avoiding "pitfalls" that would send them plummeting downward. The show ended when the production company went bankrupt—Trebek has said he was never paid for the hosting gig, and many contestants didn't receive their winnings.

10. THE HEIGHTS (1992): There was exactly one successful thing about this TV show, and that's its theme song. If you've ever scrambled to switch radio stations when the syrupy chords of "How do you talk to an angel" begin, you can blame *The Heights*. It was meant to be something like a modern-day version of *The Monkees*—a musical show about a bunch of attractive young people who form a band. The theme was a big hit, reaching number 1 on the Billboard charts, but the rest of the show was a dud, and it was cancelled as soon as the song starting slipping out of the top position.

(Opposite) Carly Rae Jepsen's "Call Me Maybe" spent longer on the top of the Billboard charts than any other song by a B.C. artist.

THE ARTS

BEST OF THE WEST: TERRY DAVID MULLIGAN'S
10 FAVOURITE B.C. MUSICAL ARTISTS

Terry David Mulligan has been in broadcasting for 55 years. He programmed Canada's first FM rock station, CKLG-FM, later called CFOX, hosted CBC's first music video series Good Rocking Tonight, *and then became host and producer of* MuchWest *on MuchMusic and later Bravo! He's also an actor with credits in* Fantastic Four, Looking Who's Talking Too, *and* The X-Files. *Today and for the last 23 years, Mulligan hosts and produces* Mulligan Stew *on the CKUA radio network, creates and produces the food, wine and travel show* Tasting Room Radio, *and hosts the* Mulligan Stew Podcast. *He's been inducted into the B.C. Entertainment Hall of Fame and named Broadcaster of the Year.*

1. SPIRIT OF THE WEST: I was once told by Alan Doyle, after he left Great Big Sea and started his solo and writing career, that the biggest influence on his music, performances, and career started when he saw SOTW on MuchMusic. Nobody was combining Celtic roots with a punk/indy attitude.

They had a profound influence on bands from coast to coast—especially the Maritimes. Now, sadly, leader John Mann battles with Alzheimer's, but their legacy lives on.

2. COLIN JAMES: Many years ago, I was asked to judge Juno recommendations—a list of 10-12 names that would be narrowed down to four or five finalists. Colin James was on that list. He really had just started his career. Someone in the room said, "He can play, but he sure can't sing." I threw my pen.

Colin had it all: talent, smarts, and pure commitment to his craft. Many years forward, he's now established and an icon. In the blues world, his profile and reputation are going straight up. His guitar work is world class and man, can he sing! (Thank you, Regina.)

3. JIM BYRNES: The first time I saw Jim Byrnes, I was at a country club over an old pier in Vancouver's inner harbour. The band that was supposed to play was missing in action. The owner asked Jim to headline as a favour, and out he walked.

Normally the walking out part is routine, but not when the guy walking out has clearly lost the use of his legs and is supported by solid walking sticks. Then he opened his mouth and out came the blues—big, greasy, and growly.

Jim had grown up in St Louis. The blues is all he listened to on the radio and when he snuck into the clubs and Sunday gospel sessions. Jim went on to become a singular artist—also an actor, radio host, and award-winner. (Thank you, St. Louis.)

4. BARNEY BENTALL : Part cowboy, part rocker, and supporter of whatever charity you have, Bentall led one of the hottest rock acts in Canada in the late '80s and early '90s: Barney Bentall and the Legendary Hearts.

Then he stepped off the crazy train. Now he's a singer, songwriter, and leader of a handful of bands, including the all-star collectives known as Cariboo Express (like a stage full of Nashville) and The High Bar Gang (country swing and gospel from many, many years ago).

And he's still touring perhaps once a year with the original band. Barney Bentall and the Legendary Hearts are currently planning a 30th anniversary tour. Barney's in for the long haul—love him. (Thank you, Toronto.)

5. SARAH MCLACHLAN: She was discovered in the Maritimes by the founders of Nettwerk Records in Kitsilano, and they knew they had a voice and performer who could become someone special. But her parents wouldn't let her travel all the way across Canada to the other coast. She was too young. When the day came, off Sarah went to Vancouver and her destiny.

I did the first TV interview with her. Q: "What do you want to do here, Sarah?" A: "I want to sing and play and write my own songs and hope someone listens."

Oh, they listened all right. Sarah became world famous and fully earned every award that came her way. She not only changed her life, she changed listeners' lives as well. I got to travel with her to Cambodia and Thailand for World Vision. She's someone special—love her. (Thank you, Halifax.)

6. BRYAN ADAMS: The fun part was I got to watch from the very beginning of his career. Talk about determined. It was as though nothing was going to get in his way—and nothing did. He and his manager Bruce Allen kicked down all the doors, and best of all, when his break came, Bryan had the songs and the voice.

He's a very talented photographer, always lending his profile to fundraising around the planet. He's now a star all over the world, but it all started in North Vancouver.

Michael Buble

7. MICHAEL BUBLÉ: A world class crooner, but again, when he hooked up with Bruce Allen, all hell broke loose.

This was no overnight success. Bruce had Michael out on the road, and when he was at home, playing rooms all over Vancouver. Many rooms later, Michael was ready and so were music fans. Honoured with many of the biggest awards music can offer, Michael Bublé became the artist he'd always dreamed of becoming.

8. DIANA KRALL: She earned her chops playing bars and rooms first in Nanaimo, then around Vancouver Island, then Vancouver, Toronto, NYC and LA, and then the world. She studied with the best jazz musicians and teachers. Perhaps *the* teacher was Ray Brown, the boss of the bass, the guy who held down the bottom line for Oscar Peterson. And there were many others.

When the time came for Diana to show her talents, she was as prepared as anyone I'd ever seen or heard. What a voice—truly gifted piano skills. Boom! Hello, world.

9. ROY FORBES: Some know him as Bim, or Rockin' Roy Forbes. He's been part of at least three generations of music fans, with a voice like no other. He's a student of pop music history, can talk about turn of the century singers or today's folkies, and does so in his weekly CKUA radio show *Roy's Record Room*.

He always had impaired vision, but an accident several years ago blinded him completely. He's dealing with all that beautifully, thanks to his love Lydia. And nobody anywhere sings a better version of Hank Williams'"I'm so lonesome I could cry."

10. DAN MANGAN: For all of his amazing success, gaining audiences first in Vancouver, then all of Canada, then the USA, and now Europe, Dan Mangan continues to fly just under the radar of many music fans. Radio has no idea where to place him. He refuses to be squeezed into a format or style box.

What Dan Mangan does so well is consistently compose outstanding songs and perform them with an enormous amount of heart. As a result, he connects with audiences seeking just that kind of performer and just that kind of music. Dan's audiences are growing in leaps and bounds. His current album is "More or Less." He's won Junos, scored a number of film soundtracks, and co-founded Side Door, which matches performers with people who want to host shows in their homes or small venues. It's fair to say Dan Mangan is working on leaving a loving legacy—for his family and for all of us.

FROM STRIP CLUBS TO SHOPPING MALLS: 8 GIGS MICHAEL BUBLÉ PLAYED ON HIS LONG PATH TO STARDOM

Michael Bublé is one of B.C.'s most talented and successful singers, but the Burnaby native was hardly an overnight success. When he started performing in the mid-'90s, teenagers crooning like Frank Sinatra weren't exactly tearing up the charts. As Bruce Allen once said of the struggling singer, "I don't know what I'd do with him."

But what Bublé lacked in trendiness he made up in heart and determination. Here are a few of the many gigs he took while waiting to finally catch his break.

1. STRIP CLUBS: When Bublé was first starting out, his grandfather Mitch Santaga helped him book gigs at nightclubs, and even strip joints—despite the fact that he was underage. Bublé told *The Tennessean* newspaper Santaga used to have to barter their way into the seedy venues by promising to do odd jobs: "The drinking age was 19, and my grandfather would say, 'You let my grandson sing, I'll go fix the crappy toilets you have.' They went for it."

2. SINGING SANTA CLAUS: At one point, Bublé donned a fake beard and red coat to perform as a singing Santa Claus at a shopping mall—and he did it for an elf's wage. Bublé said he made a whopping $80 for the gig.

3. A PRIVATE EVENT AT A PEBBLE BEACH GOLF RESORT: Nothing to scoff at here, Pebble Beach has some world-class accommodations. But Bublé wasn't a big enough star to get a tee time, no matter how many times he asked his manager Beverly Delich to try.

"Who do you think I am, Houdini? You can't just play Pebble Beach," Delich told him, according to her memoir, *Come Fly With Me: Michael Bublé's Rise to Stardom*.

4. PLAYING ELVIS IN A MUSICAL REVUE: In 1997, Bublé was hired to perform in a musical revue based on the career of legendary DJ Red Robinson. He had to dress up like Elvis, sing "Jailhouse Rock," and, much to his initial discomfort, mimic the King's signature dance moves.

5. SINGING TELEGRAM: Bublé wasn't one to turn down work. He accepted gigs in hotel lobbies and on cruise ships, and even worked as a singing telegram—all experiences that helped turn him into the professional he is today.

"I wouldn't give that struggle up for anything. It gets you ready and gives you seasoning," he told the *Tennessean*. "I played for so many years to people sitting getting drunk. How refreshing to have people pay money to see you."

6. BILL AND MELINDA GATES' HOUSE: Back in 2000, years before his first studio album, Bublé was invited to perform at a private fundraiser at the Seattle home of Bill and Melinda Gates. The singer and his accompanying pianist were "surprised and delighted" when the hosts came by to say hello, according to Delich, and were particularly impressed by the technology at the Microsoft founder's guest house, where they were invited to relax.

"It was full of computers like nothing they had ever seen, all of the monitors encased in hardwood frames. And there was food, quite a spread," Delich wrote.

7. THE PACIFIC NATIONAL EXHIBITION: One of Bublé's first breaks was winning the PNE's youth talent contest back in 1995. Six years later he returned, and even though he was headlining and had made a few high-profile connections in the industry, he was still struggling to score a record contract.

"It wasn't lost on either one of us how odd it seemed that one weekend he would be … hobnobbing with the Hollywood elite and the next be on stage playing his hometown agricultural fair," Delich said.

8. CAROLINE MULRONEY'S WEDDING: One of Bublé's independent CDs eventually ended up in the hands of Brian Mulroney, who was so impressed he hired the crooner to perform at his daughter's wedding in Montreal. It ended up being a major moment in Bublé's career trajectory; one of the guests was famed music producer David Foster, and years later, after some cajoling, Foster would agree to produce Bublé's first studio album.

11 SONGS BY B.C. ARTISTS THAT TOPPED THE BILLBOARD CHARTS

1. "CALL ME MAYBE" BY CARLY RAE JEPSEN: *Nine weeks, 2012*
Your undefeated champion of the charts, a beloved gay icon and Canada's sweetheart, CRJ is the pride of Mission.

2. "(EVERYTHING I DO) I DO IT FOR YOU" BY BRYAN ADAMS: *Seven weeks, 1991*
He was actually born in Kingston, ON, but Adams got his start as a teenager in Vancouver, working as a background musician.

3. "PROMISCUOUS" BY NELLY FURTADO FEAT. TIMBALAND: *Six weeks, 2006*
Victoria's Portuguese-Canadian queen has repped B.C. hard on the pop charts, selling more than 40 million records over the years.

4. "BAD DAY" BY DANIEL POWTER: *Five weeks, 2006*
It's true, some guy from Vernon really did have the number 1 song in North America for a whole month.

5. "HAVE YOU EVER REALLY LOVED A WOMAN?" BY BRYAN ADAMS: *Five weeks, 1995*
Adams' first real gig as a singer was fronting for the Vancouver glam rock band Sweeney Todd, beginning in 1976.

6. "HOW YOU REMIND ME" BY NICKELBACK: *Four weeks, 2001-2002*
Looking back, it feels like Nickelback must have been a bigger deal than this in the aughts, but it turns out this was their only number 1 single.

7. "ALL FOR LOVE" BY BRYAN ADAMS, ROD STEWART, AND STING: *Three weeks, 1994*
Kevin Costner couldn't be bothered to even attempt an English accent for *Robin Hood: Prince of Thieves*, but these three superstar singers put everything they had into the movie's cheesy theme song.

8. "SEASONS IN THE SUN" BY TERRY JACKS: *Three weeks, 1974*
Legend has it that "Seasons in the Sun" was meant for the Beach Boys, with Vancouver's Jacks serving as producer. When the band turned it down, Jacks released it himself, and the song became the most successful single by a Canadian to date.

9. "GIVE IT TO ME" BY TIMBALAND FEAT. NELLY FURTADO AND JUSTIN TIMBERLAKE: *Two weeks, 2007*
Long before she was famous, Furtado proved her work ethic by spending eight summers working as a chambermaid alongside her mother, brother, and sister.

10. "SAY IT RIGHT" BY NELLY FURTADO: *One week, 2007*
Today, Furtado is essentially a Portuguese knight. She was named a Commander of the Order of Prince Henry by Portugal's president in 2014.

11. "HOT CHILD IN THE CITY" BY NICK GILDER : *One week, 1978*
Fun fact: Gilder was the original lead singer for Vancouver's Sweeney Todd, but he left the band to find fame and fortune after scoring a big hit with "Roxy Roller." Bryan Adams was his replacement.

NATHAN SELLYN'S LIST OF THE 8 UNQUESTIONABLY GREATEST VIDEO GAMES DEVELOPED IN B.C.

Nathan Sellyn is the chief creative officer of FlowMotion Entertainment, the studio behind the hit mobile game Cook It! *Nathan was originally cast in the role of Grandson in 1987's* The Princess Bride, *but was replaced by Fred fucking Savage just prior to filming.*

1. DEF JAM: FIGHT FOR NY (EA VANCOUVER): EA Vancouver is one of Electronic Arts' most successful studios, delivering their parent company massive cheques every year due to their work on various sports and racing franchises. However, they are *unquestionably* best known for 2004's *Def Jam: Fight for NY,* the sequel to the vastly inferior *Def Jam: Vendetta. Fight for NY* allows players to either create a character or choose from a vast array of Def Jam legends, including such icons as Warren G, Flavor Flav, or Carmen Electra, who released an epony-mous album more than a decade prior to the game's publication. That album was produced by Prince! Prince is not in this game.

2. FLOOR KIDS (HOLOLABS): Developed by Victoria's Hololabs, *Floor Kids* is unquestionably the best breakdance battle game in history. That may seem like a victory by acclamation, but there have actually been many breakdance battle games throughout history. This lineage begins with the cleverly titled *Break Dance* for the Commodore 64, which benefited from breakdancing's pole position in that era's zeitgeist, and more or less ends with 2006's *B-Boy.* Unfortunately, the latter title was developed by a British studio, and it is widely understood that the British know nothing about breakdancing. This left the video game breakdancing crown wide open for 2018's *Floor Kids*, which features both music by Kid Koala (43 years old at the time of the game's release) and hundreds of the freshest moves. Get funky.

3. MARIO STRIKERS (NEXT LEVEL GAMES): One of the various sports franchises devel-oped by EA Vancouver is *FIFA*, a title that some critics claim raises the standard for soccer games with each of its annual releases. Those critics are wrong, because the greatest soccer video game of all time is unquestionably *Mario Strikers*, which removes "real life" soccer stars (boring, mostly Italian) and replaces them with your favourite Nintendo characters (ador-able, only one Italian). While *Mario Strikers* is simply superior to *FIFA* in every way, its most notable advantage is its verisimilitude. For years, players around the world have begged EA to include a "Super Strike," which (as every true soccer fan knows) allows a team's captain to

Floor Kids is unquestionably the best breakdancing battle game to come out of B.C.

release a special shot that—if perfectly timed—results in two goals. *Mario Strikers* not only includes this critical feature, it also avoids the annoyance of diving, because *Mario Strikers* has no penalties.

4. BULLY (ROCKSTAR VANCOUVER): In 2002, global gaming behemoth Take-Two Interactive purchased Barking Dog Studios, one of Vancouver's most celebrated gaming companies. While many employees left as a result of the acquisition, those who remained formed Rockstar Vancouver, a studio that released only one independently developed titled over its 10-year existence. So while *Bully* is by default unquestionably the greatest game in Rockstar Vancouver's history, they sure made their only shot count. Surrounded by understandable controversy for what detractors saw as a promotion of school violence and bullying, *Bully* actually possesses a heartwarming, anti-bullying storyline. Also, players restore their healthy by drinking soda and kissing.

5. COMPANY OF HEROES (RELIC ENTERTAINMENT): Relic Entertainment is one of the pillars of Vancouver's gaming industry, releasing several high-quality titles across multiple genres over its more than 20-year history. However, their reputation was cemented in 2006 when they were named "Best Developer" by IGN.com and released *Company of Heroes*, a World War II RTS game that not only sold millions of copies, but was also adapted into a film starring *Passenger 57*'s Tom Sizemore. *Passenger 57* is unquestionably the greatest action movie of all time, and one can only hope that at some point Hollywood realizes this and releases 56 sequels. Similarly, *Company of Heroes* was one of the greatest RTS titles ever, matching the best elements of the genre's gameplay with what at the time were new standards for sound and graphics. Plus you kill Nazis.

6. CLUB PENGUIN (NEW HORIZON INTERACTIVE): British Columbia's gaming industry extends beyond just Vancouver. In 2005, Kelowna-based developer New Horizon Interactive released *Club Penguin*, unquestionably the most well-known game to ever emerge from B.C. *Club Penguin* was the culmination of several penguin-themed titles from creator Lance Priebe who had developed at RocketSnail Games, and the result of his team's desire to provide their children with a game "that had some social components but was safe, and not just marketed as safe." They likely never expected that their penguin persistence would result in one of the most popular massively multiplayer online games of all time, eventually reaching more than 200 million registered accounts, spawning roughly a billion memes, and introducing an entire generation to both the delights of online gaming and the wrath of a language filter.

7. THE SIMPSONS: ROAD RAGE (RADICAL): Vancouver has one of the most highly regarded video game development industries in the world, and many of its leaders trace their roots back to Radical Entertainment, a company that got its start developing games for the original NES. Their work includes some of Mario's lesser-known adventures (*Mario is Missing*, *Mario's Time Machine*) and a variety of sports titles, but their greatest title is unquestionably 2001's *The Simpsons: Road Rage*. Players adopt the role of a taxi driver and ferry notable *Simpsons* characters between destinations. Their services are in high demand, because Mr. Burns has purchased all of Springfield's buses…and made them radioactive.

8. DARKEST DUNGEON (RED HOOK STUDIOS): The release of *Spelunky* in 2008 sparked a decade of evolution for the roguelike genre, spawning countless titles and innovations. *Darkest Dungeon*, developed by Vancouver indie Red Hook Studios, was unquestionably the most innovative of the bunch. Foremost among the game's innovation was the introduction of the "Affliction System," through which the player's characters gain stress and eventually afflictions (Paranoid, Abusive, Masochistic, among others) as a result of battling a Lovecraftian menagerie of gothic horrors. Following its release, *Darkest Dungeon* transformed from Kickstarter success story into commercial breakout, and was voted Original RPG of the Year by the National Academy of Video Game Trade Reviewers. It's also really hard, and I'm ashamed to say I never beat it.

KEVIN CHONG'S LIST OF 10 ESSENTIAL BOOKS OF FICTION SET IN VANCOUVER

Kevin Chong is the author of six books, including *The Plague*, a retelling of the Camus classic set amidst the rising inequity of modern-day Vancouver.

1. WAYDE COMPTON, *THE OUTER HARBOUR*: Short stories, 2015

2. TIMOTHY TAYLOR, *STANLEY PARK*: Novel, 2001

3. CAROLINE ADDERSON, *ELLEN IN PIECES*: Novel, 2014

4. MADELEINE THIEN, *SIMPLE RECIPES*: Short stories, 2002

5. LEE HENDERSON, *THE MAN GAME*: Novel, 2009

6. GURJINDER BASRAN, *EVERYTHING WAS GOOD-BYE*: Novel, 2012

7. HELEN POTREBENKO, *TAXI!*: Novel, 1975

8. ZSUZSI GARTNER, *BETTER LIVING THROUGH PLASTIC EXPLOSIVES*: Short stories, 2012

9. MICHAEL TURNER, *THE PORNOGRAPHER'S POEM*: Novel, 2001

10. CARELLIN BROOKS, *ONE HUNDRED DAYS OF RAIN*: Novel, 2015

3 BOOKS BY B.C.-BASED AUTHORS THAT WON THE GILLER PRIZE

1. *WASHINGTON BLACK* BY ESI EDUGYAN, 2018

2. *DO NOT SAY WE HAVE NOTHING* BY MADELEINE THIEN, 2016

3. HALF-BLOOD BLUES BY ESI EDUGYAN, 2011

4 BOOKS BY B.C.-BASED AUTHORS THAT WON THE GOVERNOR GENERAL'S AWARD FOR FICTION

1. *DO NOT SAY WE HAVE NOTHING* BY MADELEINE THIEN, 2016

2. *BURNING WATER* BY GEORGE BOWERING, 1980

3. *THE RESURRECTION OF JOSEPH BOURNE* BY JACK HODGINS, 1979

4. *HEAR US O LORD FROM HEAVEN THY DWELLING PLACE* BY MALCOLM LOWRY*, 1961

*Lowry was an Englishman who also spent time in the U.S. and Mexico, but his most productive writing years took place while he lived in a shack in Dollarton on the North Shore.

11 BOOKS BY B.C.-BASED AUTHORS THAT WON THE GOVERNOR GENERAL'S AWARD FOR NON-FICTION

1. *MAMASKATCH: A CREE COMING OF AGE* BY DARREL J. MCLEOD, 2015

2. *BEE TIME: LESSONS FROM THE HIVE* BY MARK L. WINSTON, 2015

3. *THE END OF ABSENCE: RECLAIMING WHAT WE'VE LOST IN A WORLD OF CONSTANT CONNECTION* BY MICHAEL HARRIS, 2014

4. *JOURNEY WITH NO MAPS: A LIFE OF P.K. PAGE* BY SANDRA DJWA, 2013

5. *THE GOLDEN SPRUCE: A TRUE STORY OF MYTH, MADNESS AND GREED* BY JOHN VAILLANT, 2005

6. *EMILY CARR* BY MARIA TIPPETT, 1979

7. *THE CRYSTAL SPIRIT: A STUDY OF GEORGE ORWELL* BY GEORGE WOODCOCK, 1966

8. *CANADA: TOMORROW'S GIANT* BY BRUCE HUTCHISON, 1957

9. *THE INCREDIBLE CANADIAN* BY BRUCE HUTCHISON, 1952

10. *THE UNKNOWN COUNTRY* BY BRUCE HUTCHISON, 1942

11. *KLEE WYCK* BY EMILY CARR, 1941

(Opposite) Tojo Maki, better known as a California roll, helped popularize sushi among westerners.

FOOD AND DRINK

Sockeye salmon wrapped in Haida Gwaii kelp prepared by chefs at Salmon n' Bannock.

INEZ COOK'S LIST OF 9 FRIGGIN' DELICIOUS INDIGENOUS FOODS TO TRY IN B.C.

Inez Cook (Snitsmana) belongs to the Nuxalk Nation of Bella Coola, and is the cofounder of Salmon n' Bannock, a popular First Nations bistro in Vancouver.

1. SOAPBERRIES: These look like burnt orange capers, and taste a bit like Aperol or Campari, though I can't really compare it to anything. We whip these up with a little bit of sugar and water. It looks like pink fluffy clouds, but then you bite into it and it's like nothing you've ever tasted. In the old days we called it Indian ice cream, even though there's no milk in it. It's really delicious—it's a delicacyand I love it a lot.

2. SMOKED OOLICHANS: These little fish are also known as candlefish and they were traded like gold in certain parts of the province. For thousands of years, they were traded up and down the Grease Trails, named for the oolichan grease that would drip out of the traders' boxes. They're seasonal in the springtime and up north they're smoked for 14 hours. They're friggin' delicious.

3. HERRING ROE ON KELP: This is a traditional food for some of the coastal First Nations and it's a big hit for us. It's harvested in Bella Bella by placing the seaweed or hemlock branches in the water while the fish are spawning.

4. HUCKLEBERRIES: Of course, I'm talking about the purple ones. The ladies who get them for us, they usually have to go with a gun to scare off the bears.

5. WIND-DRIED SALMON: If you ever get out to any of the communities, you have to try this. It's like jerky. You bite it right off the skin when it's ready, and it's so good. It's got a very unique flavour and it's delicious.

6. CANDIED SALMON: Our communities have so many different ways of preparing fish, but this is a classic. Ours is hot smoked with maple and pepper.

7. SMOKED BARBECUE SEA LION: This one's a bit harder to find, but it comes from the Nisga'a territory near Terrace. Honestly, when you first bite it, you'd think it tastes like a black cod, but then when you start eating it, it's much meatier.

8. SUN-DRIED HALIBUT: It's funny, it's like a jerky, but one of my staff is from Haida Gwaii and she said you have to eat it with butter. I was skeptical, but it was amazing. You just put a piece of butter on it and eat it like you would a piece of toast.

9. SALAL BERRIES: I had salal berry jam for the first time recently, on a trip to Haida Gwaii. It was amazing! Three of us bought all the jam they had.

CHEF TOJO'S TOP 10 DELICIOUS SUSHI INGREDIENTS FROM B.C.

Chef Hidekazu Tojo opened his iconic Vancouver restaurant, Tojo's, in 1988, and is widely credited with kicking off the city's sushi craze. He's known as the inventor of the California roll, and was appointed a goodwill ambassador of Japanese cuisine by the Japanese government in 2016.

1. ALBACORE TUNA: Albacore is creamy, tender, and melts in your mouth, but it's also sustainable and available in abundant numbers along the West Coast. Try it as tataki—marinated in lemon juice, seared and served with ponzu sauce, and garnished with ground ginger, daikon with red chilli, and green onion.

2. SABLEFISH: Another great sustainable B.C. seafood that's caught around Haida Gwaii and Tofino. It's delicious marinated with rice vinegar and smoked, or served as nigiri, temari, or battera. It goes especially well with pickled ginger and shiso leaf.

3. WILD PACIFIC SALMON—INCLUDING THE SKIN AND ROE: Salmon goes well in any type of sushi, including nigiri, rolls, temaki, battera, temari, and aburi, and it's delicious smoked. Chef Tojo created the B.C. roll using barbequed salmon skin. Salmon roe (ikura) is also delicious marinated in sake, soy, mirin, and served as gunkan sushi.

4. SPOT PRAWNS: These crustaceans are sweet and tender, and best eaten fresh and raw. They're in season in the springtime.

5. DUNGENESS CRAB: They're abundant along the West Coast, and readily available all year around. The sweet, briny and delicate flavour works best in sushi rolls and temaki. Chef Tojo created the Tojo maki (a.k.a California roll) pairing Dungeness crab with avocado, egg, and spinach, and topping with sesame seeds.

6. GEODUCK: These huge clams have a crunchy texture and a briny taste, and they're a B.C. delicacy. Geoduck is delicious in nigiri or cut in cubes and incorporated in temaki with cucumber. They're available all year. This is what Chef Tojo served Kate Middleton and Prince William during their visit to B.C.

7. SEA URCHIN: They're creamy and briny, and best served as gunkan style sushi. B.C. urchins are caught by divers, and the ones from Haida Gwaii are especially sought after. They're best in the winter, and would make a great pasta sauce.

8. SEA ASPARAGUS: These succulent plants are salty and crunchy, and a great source of minerals. Add them to rolls or temaki for seasoning and texture. They can be foraged and are plentiful from spring to fall.

9. PINE MUSHROOM: This wild fungus has an aromatic, delicate flavour with an almost crunchy texture. Try grilling, then serve as nigiri, in rolls or as temaki—it goes especially well with yuzu sauce. Pine mushrooms are usually available in the fall.

10. BEETS: A great vegetarian option—bake, slice, then serve in rolls or nigiri. Beets pair well with other vegetables and fruits including yam, asparagus, and pineapple, and they're available all year round.

MUST-TRY DISHES FROM B.C.'S TOP 10 RESTAURANTS

The 2018 Canada's 100 Best Restaurants ranking includes a whopping 22 restaurants from B.C.—more than any other province except Quebec. Here are the signature dishes and reviewer favourites from the top 10 on the list.

1. KISSA TANTO, VANCOUVER (#10) Whole fried fish with daikon soy dipping sauce.

2. HAWKSWORTH RESTAURANT, VANCOUVER (#11) Hamachi ceviche with sea buckthorn, jalapeño and pumpkin seed.

3. SAVIO VOLPE, VANCOUVER (#14): Half chicken with rosemary and grilled lemon.

4. CIOPPINO'S MEDITERRANEAN GRILL, VANCOUVER (#19): Veal shank braised with saffron risotto "alla Milanese" and peas.

5. ST. LAWRENCE, VANCOUVER (#20): Tourtière de ville au cerf (traditional venison meat pie).

6. L'ABATTOIR, VANCOUVER (#21): Baked Pacific oysters with whipped garlic butter and winter truffle.

7. MAENAM, VANCOUVER (#23): Crispy eight spice ling cod, with caramelized palm sugar-tamarind sauce, fried Thai spices and aromatics.

8. ANNALENA, VANCOUVER (#34): Buttermilk fried chicken with lemongrass aioli, chili lime, and nam jim pickles.

9. MASAYOSHI SUSHI BAR, VANCOUVER (#48): Omakase—chef's choice of nigiri and other Japanese creations.

10. VIJ'S RESTAURANT, VANCOUVER (#50): Wine-marinated lamb "popsicles" in fenugreek cream curry.

AND SELECTIONS FROM 4 NON-VANCOUVER RESTAURANTS THAT MADE THE TOP 100

1. PILGRIMME, GALIANO ISLAND (#79): Galiano potatoes in kelp oil, salmon roe, buttermilk, and smoked and pickled bull kelp.

2. THE PEAR TREE, BURNABY (#83): Pan-roasted Lois Lake steelhead, served with pommes dauphine and butternut squash.

3. WOLF IN THE FOG, TOFINO (#85): Potato-crusted oyster with leek and truffle.

4. AGRIUS, VICTORIA (#93): Lamb tartare mixed with preserved Meyer lemon and tossed with sourdough croutons sautéed in rendered lamb fat.

Mike the bartending dog delivers a beer to thirsty patrons at Victoria's Bowser Hotel bar in 1940.

GLEN MOFFORD'S LIST OF 10 STRANGE BUT TRUE STORIES FROM B.C. BARS

Glen A. Mofford is a Nanaimo-based historian and the author of Along the E&N: A Journey Back to the Historic Hotels of Vancouver Island *and* Aqua Vitae: A History of the Saloons and Hotel Bars of Victoria, 1851-1917.

From the sweet and cute to the dangerous and tragic, B.C.'s drinking establishments have a long and chequered past. The following are 10 examples, in no particular order, of events that took place in or because of the drinking establishments of British Columbia over the years.

1. MIKE THE BAR DOG: Patrons at the Bowser Hotel bar on Vancouver Island from 1938 to 1941 were surprised and delighted when their waiter turned out to be a black and white English sheepdog-terrier cross. Mike was trained to carry a bottle of beer to customers, collect their money, and bring back their change with a bottle opener in his mouth.

2. LIKE FATHER, LIKE SON: Another Mike, this one in human form, walked into the Barclay beer parlour in Port Alberni in April 1961, took off his coat, stood on a chair and cried out to the waiter, "One small beer please." The understanding waiter coolly made his way over to the table and asked his name and his age. "Mike, and I'm three years old," came the reply. Apparently Mike had walked nearly 2 miles from his home to the hotel beer parlour to order a beer just like dad.

3. BURIED DOWN THERE: In 1888, while tearing down the old Pony Saloon on Johnson and Government streets in Victoria, a worker made a gruesome discovery when he pried up the floorboards in the saloon office—human remains. It was later determined the skeleton was that of an adult male who, in the 1860s, was murdered, his body unceremoniously stuffed under the back office floor in order to conceal the dastardly deed. The murder was never resolved but the newspapers of the day reported that the proprietor of the Pony Saloon and a mysterious lady in a red dress were seen making a hasty exit, boarding a steamer to San Francisco.

4. SOMETHING FISHY: In the 1890s at 1080 Main Street (then known as Westminster Avenue) in Vancouver was the Bridge Hotel, built near False Creek many years before much of False Creek was filled in. The owners of the hotel coined the slogan "Fish off the veranda into False Creek," and many guests did just that. But they didn't stop there, they also fished from their rooms and some patrons fished from the windows of the bar. Fish was taken off the menu.

Eventually the hotel name changed to the Globe Hotel and then in 1921 it shut down, in part due to lack of business brought on by Prohibition. It was replaced with the Hugh Baillie, W. Jack and Co., asbestos manufacturers and suppliers.

5. EASY RIDER, OR THE FIRST DRIVE-THROUGH BEER PARLOUR: On a warm June evening in 1969, a group of people were sitting in the King's Hotel beer parlour in Victoria, enjoying a few beers and chatting, when suddenly through the front swinging doors came a man on a motor-cycle who proceed to drive through the bar, only to exit out the back door without saying a word. Stunned patrons and staff watched as he continued down the back alley and out of sight.

6. HORSE SENSE: The first u-drive service could be attributed to Henry Simpson, the innova-tive proprietor of the first Prairie Inn Tavern, built in 1859 in Saanichton on Vancouver Island. Simpson's tavern was a popular social hub in the farming community where, on occasion, a customer would imbibe too much. Simpson's solution was to help the tipsy patron onto one of his trained horses and point it in the right direction to get the person home, and sooner or later the horse would return riderless to Simpson's stables.

7. MURDER AND MAYHEM IN THE MANHATTAN: The normally peaceful Kootenay town of Nelson was the location of one of the bloodiest murders that took place in a B.C. bar. Headlines in the *Omineca Miner* for January 6, 1912 shook Nelson and the province to its core as details of the murders were made public. In the wee hours of Saturday morning, two burglars attempted to rob the popular Manhattan Saloon in Nelson. They were interrupted by Caleb A. Barton and Jack Gould, who heard the break-in and rushed to the saloon. A gun fight ensued which saw one of the thieves fleeing from the scene and the lifeless bodies of Barton and Gould lying in a pool of blood on the saloon floor. The remaining burglar was gravely injured from gunshot wounds but lived to stand trial and hang for murder.

8. PRACTICAL JOKER: Charles H. Dickie was a large man who, in 1891, leased the Alderlea Hotel in Duncan and decided to clean it up. He fired a few slackers on his staff and took the bar back from some of the regulars who thought they owned the place. Dickie didn't put up with any non-sense and those who opposed him found themselves out the door, onto the street and barred.

But Dickie also proved to be a practical joker. When one troublesome customer checked out of the hotel, Dickie took the 60-pound cannonball that acted as a doorstop, put the heavy object into the man's valise, then watched with hilarity as he attempted to lift it. Another departing guest would be distracted as his bag was nailed to the floor with similar humorous results. On another occasion a customer left on the train to Victoria with a sheepskin in place of his tailored suit in his suitcase. When his lease was up, Dickie then lent his unique talents to his new job as Member of Parliament for the Cowichan District.

9. LITTLE ANNIE ROONEY: The California Saloon that once graced lower Johnson Street in Victoria during the Gold Rush era was a rough and tumble place. The infamous saloon had more than its share of fistfights, robberies, and illegal gambling, as the police records attest. But one rare calming influence was the piano player. Whenever Annie Rooney played, the pa-trons listened and a temporary truce was observed by the rowdy patrons as she tickled the piano keys and sang. What most patrons did not know was that Annie Rooney, born female, had lived as a man for many years. She must have been very convincing, because she served six months as a sailor in the United States Navy before her birth sex was discovered.

10. CARR'S CLOSE CALL: In the 1880s, a young Emily Carr was visiting one of her sisters in downtown Victoria when a herd of cattle rushed down Fort Street where she was standing. If it wasn't for the quick actions of an employee of the Bee Hive Saloon, who snatched her off the street at the last minute, she would have been trampled to death. Emily watched the cattle go by to the Hudson's Bay Company marshalling yard, and later wrote about the experience and the description of what she saw inside the Bee Hive Saloon in her *Book of Small*.

JOHN SCHREINER'S LIST OF 10 WINERIES THAT PUT B.C. ON THE MAP

John Schreiner is author of Icon: Flagship Wines from British Columbia's Best Wineries *and* John Schreiner's Okanagan Wine Tour Guide.

It took the British Columbia wine industry just a generation to go from mediocre to world class.

There now are more than 300 wineries, a 10-fold increase from 1990. The rise in the quality of the wines has been even greater, the result of much better viticulture, better equipped wineries and a vast expansion in numbers of soundly trained winemakers.
The leadership from certain wineries stands out. Here are 10 wineries that have been putting British Columbia on the world map.

1. MISSION HILL FAMILY ESTATE WINERY: Anthony von Mandl, who has owned this winery since 1981, had previously recognized the Okanagan's wine potential while doing a feasibility study for a German winery briefly considering investing in B.C. In 1992, Anthony recruited a talented winemaker from New Zealand, John Simes. The chardonnay John made in that vintage won a major award at a London wine competition.

That confirmed Anthony's vision. Since then, he has never stopped investing in vineyards, wineries, and talent, and has become the owner of the largest privately-held wine growing business in the Okanagan. It is one of the best and includes prestigious labels such as Checkmate, Martin's Lane, CedarCreek, and Road 13.

2. BLUE MOUNTAIN VINEYARD & CELLARS: The Mavety family began farming their Okanagan Falls vineyard in 1972, initially with hybrid grape varieties. By 1986, they began replanting with the vinifera vines that make superior quality wines. Blue Mountain's pinot noir and chardonnay wines, along with traditional method sparkling wine, quickly established a following and inspired Blue Mountain's peers.

3. BURROWING OWL WINERY: In 1994, Burrowing Owl (along with Sumac Ridge and Tinhorn Creek Vineyards) redeveloped dormant land on Black Sage Bench by planting Bordeaux reds and syrah. The winery recruited Bill Dyer, a winemaker from the Napa Valley. He made the seven initial vintages and the big, bold wines established the reputation of both Burrowing Owl and Black Sage Bench.

4. NK'MIP CELLARS: This Osoyoos winery created an immediate sensation when it opened in 2002 because it was the first North American winery with Indigenous ownership. It is a joint venture between the Osoyoos Indian Band and the wine group now called Arterra (formerly Vincor International). Nk'Mip makes outstanding wines because it gets some of the best grapes from vineyards the Band has farmed since 1968.

5. QUAILS' GATE ESTATE WINERY: The Stewart family, which has been active in Okanagan agriculture since the early 20th century, began growing wine grapes in the mid-1960s on the

Mission Hill was established in 1966, and has grown to become one of B.C.'s most recognized wineries.

slope of Boucherie Mountain in West Kelowna. They pioneered pinot noir in 1975; the variety has since become one of the Okanagan's signature wines. The winery opened in 1989. The cellar has almost always been managed by well-trained winemakers from either Australia or New Zealand.

6. TANTALUS VINEYARDS: This winery is on a historic East Kelowna vineyard in which the superior Mosel-developed clone 21B riesling was planted in 1978. The predecessor winery here, then called Pinot Reach Cellars, made an Old Vines Riesling that was the first Okanagan wine to attract positive critical notice by Jancis Robinson MW, a leading British wine writer. The winery's name changed under new ownership and Tantalus became a leading producer of riesling, another of the Okanagan's signature wines.

7. OSOYOOS LAROSE WINERY: Now operated by Groupe Taillan, a major Bordeaux wine company, the winery was launched in 1998 as a joint venture between Vincor International and the French. The objective of Donald Triggs, then Vincor's chief executive, was to bring seasoned French expertise to the Okanagan. The Osoyoos Larose winemakers all have come from France; several are now with other Okanagan wineries.

8. PAINTED ROCK ESTATE WINERY: John Skinner, a former investment dealer, has been a leader among a group of wineries offering Okanagan wines to European consumers. The wines now are in both British and French markets and are well received. (The King of Sweden once ordered a Painted Rock wine after a tasting at a Stockholm dinner.) Painted Rock's meticulous vineyard was planted in 2005 on a bench overlooking Skaha Lake. Both the viticulture and the winemaking are supervised by Alain Sutre, a leading consultant from Bordeaux.

9. FOXTROT VINEYARDS: Widely regarded as the producer of the Okanagan's most coveted Pinot Noir, Foxtrot has a remarkably high profile internationally for a small winery. That is because Torsten Allander, the founder and former owner, cultivated sophisticated consumers in the United States. When he sold Foxtrot in 2018, it was acquired by two New York experts on Burgundy. Their decision to bring in consulting winemaker Veronique Drouhin from one of Burgundy's top producers has raised Foxtrot's profile even higher.

10. LASTELLA WINERY and **LE VIEUX PIN:** These sister wineries in the South Okanagan have consistently marketed their wines to prestige clients in Europe and the United States, setting them apart from most B.C. wineries, which seldom export. The wineries are managed by Severine Pinte, a superb French-trained winemaker. LaStella focuses on merlot, the signature red in the South Okanagan, while Le Vieux Pin is focussed on syrah.

THE 10 MOST EXPENSIVE LOCAL WINES AT THE B.C. LIQUOR STORE

1. MISSION HILL FAMILY ESTATE OCULUS 2014 (WEST KELOWNA): $135 for 750 mL
"This wine is just getting started, but the early prognosis is excellent. Cellar a decade before you begin to assess the full charm of this wine."—wine writer Anthony Gismondi

2. MISSION HILL COMPENDIUM 2014 (WEST KELOWNA): $82 for 750 mL
"Beautifully balanced and voluptuous."—"The Wine Guy," Tony Aspler

3. CHECKMATE MERLOT END GAME 2013 (OLIVER): $80 for 750 mL
"It's concentrated and dark, with savory herbs and lush flavors of roasted black fruit, smoke, char, licorice, and espresso. Impressively, the tannins remain polished and proportionate."— Paul Gregutt, *Wine Enthusiast* magazine

4. CHECKMATE CHARDONNAY FOOL'S GOLD 2014 (OLIVER): $80 for 750 mL
"We love the complexity here and the perfumed, peachy, melon fruit flavours with a slice of toasted oak and lees. Best of all is the salty acidity giving the entire wine structure and grace and that classic south Okanagan sagebrush."—Anthony Gismondi

5. MISSION HILL FAMILY ESTATE QUATRAIN 2014 (WEST KELOWNA): $75 for 750 mL
"Intense and concentrated wine with lots of black fruit, plum, spice, and leather. It is ripe yet not overdone." - winemaker Rhys Pender

6. NK'MIP QWAM QWMT RIESLING ICEWINE 2015 (OSOYOOS): $70 for 375 mL
"A nose from which ginger and citrus aromas emanate. Sweet but expressing good vivacity. A creamy mouth that lingers."—wine consultant Sara d'Amato

7. BLACK HILLS NOTA BENE 2016 (OLIVER): $65 for 750 mL
"A remarkably well-made B.C. red wine from one of the province's top producers. Full-bodied, yet elegant and balanced with a long finish. Aromas of cassis, black currant, and dark spice."—wine reviewer Natalie MacLean

8. BURROWING OWL MERITAGE 2013 (OLIVER): $60 for 750 mL
"A well-rounded, five-grape Bordeaux-style blend, the emphasis here is on forward-fruit flavors that mix tart berry with lemon and orange-tinged acids. It's made for near-term drinking, a most pleasant wine, though without the gravitas for long cellaring."—*Wine Enthusiast* contributing editor Paul Gregutt

9. MISSION HILL RESERVE RIESLING ICEWINE 2015 (WEST KELOWNA): $57 for 375 mL
"This exceptional effort brings lush, candied apricot and orange peel fruits, wrapped in cinnamon, apple sauce, and butterscotch. Big and succulent, it coats the palate deliciously but never turns syrupy."—Paul Gregutt

10. POPLAR GROVE LEGACY 2014 (PENTICTON): $56 for 750 mL
"It's at its savoury best in 2014 with an almost voluptuous entry of black fruit, dried leaves, licorice, and sagebrush. A stylish red that just leaves me only wanting more in the finish."— Anthony Gismondi

January 2019 prices from B.C. Liquor Stores.

JOE WIEBE'S LIST OF 10 B.C. CRAFT BEER STORIES

Joe Wiebe, a.k.a. the "Thirsty Writer," is the author of Craft Beer Revolution: The Insider's Guide to B.C. Breweries, *the definitive guidebook to British Columbia's burgeoning craft beer industry, currently in its second edition.*

1. IT ALL STARTED IN 1982: Back in 1982, there was no such thing as a craft brewery in British Columbia, but two men managed to change all that when they built the first microbrewery in Canada in Horseshoe Bay. Frank Appleton and John Mitchell worked together to build the Horseshoe Bay Brewery using recycled dairy equipment and whatever else they could find. The brewery made only one beer at first: *Bay Ale* for the Troller Pub, which was managed by Mitchell. It was a big hit, and kicked off the craft beer revolution, which is still going strong today.

2. B.C.'S ORIGINAL SEASONAL: Back in 1987, Vancouver Island Brewing's original brewmaster Hermann Hoerterer made a special beer he called *Hermannator* as a seasonal gift for friends and family. The beer has been brewed annually since then, making it B.C.'s original seasonal beer. This special *Eisbock* takes over three months to mature, spending a significant time at subzero temperatures to create a rich malt body, with notes of chocolate, coffee, and brandied plums. Recently, VIB began aging some of the annual batch in bourbon barrels; this beer, which they nicknamed "Bourbonator" at the brewery, has an even richer flavour enhanced by whisky and barrel notes.

3. SEAN HOYNE'S JOB INTERVIEW: Sean Hoyne was a graduate student in English Literature at the University of Victoria and an avid home brewer in the late 1980s when Swans Brewpub was under construction. His then-girlfriend/now-wife Chantal encouraged him to apply for the position of brewer. He showed up at the job interview with Frank Appleton—who had built the brewery—with a six-pack of his homebrew. They chatted and tasted each of the beers, and by the time they were done the six-pack, Frank offered him the job. Hoyne has been brewing ever since; he moved over to the Canoe Brewpub a few years later and then opened his own brewery, Hoyne Brewing, in 2011.

4. THE BELGIAN CONNECTION: Belgium is the home of a legendary beer culture featuring Trappist monasteries, where brewing and drinking beer is part of the monks' day-to-day life, as well as the unique *Lambic* brewing process, which involves spontaneous fermentation, multi-year barrel-aging, and blending that results in world-renowned sour beers. In addition to Cédric Dauchot, the brewmaster at Townsite Brewing in Powell River, who was born and trained in Belgium, several other B.C. brewers have a connection to Belgium.

David Beardsell befriended a monk at Chimay in the 1980s and even brought back some of the abbaye's own yeast, which he uses to this day at Red Collar Brewing in Kamloops. Iain Hill, brewmaster at Strange Fellows Brewing in Vancouver, toured Belgium in the 1990s and learned about the brewing traditions in Flanders. His *Oud Bruin* is generally considered the best version of the style made in B.C. And Ben Coli built Dageraad Brewing just so he could recreate his favourite Belgian beers after multiple trips there. The brewery is named for the Dageraadplaats, a city square in Antwerp where he often sat with his Belgian friends sipping local beers.

5. THE FIRST SOUR BEER IN NORTH AMERICA?: Soon after Iain Hill (Strange Fellows Brewing) returned from a trip to Belgium in 1995, he visited his friend James Walton at Storm Brewing, who mentioned he had a couple batches of beer that had gone sour. "He was going to chuck them, but I said you should hang on to them," Hill recalls. "Time went by and he put them in barrels and the beer became incredible. To my mind it tasted like an authentic *Lambic*. We toasted with James's *Kriek* at our wedding instead of wine, and honestly it tasted like Cantillon. It was amazing."

In the early 1980s, Frank Appleton and John Mitchell built the first microbrewery in all of Canada.

Walton might even be the first brewer in North America to produce *Lambic*-style sour beers. An article about sour beers published in *The New Yorker* in 2013 identifies a beer brewed by William Reed at the Boston Beer Co. in 1996 as the earliest American sour, right around the same time as Walton's first forays. Hill began making sour beers himself later, and is now regarded as one of the best sour beer producers in B.C.

6. WHO BREWED THE FIRST IPA IN B.C.?: West Coast IPAs bursting with big hop flavours and aromas have been the most popular style of craft beer for more than a decade now. This updated take on the traditional British style first showed up in California and Oregon in the early 1990s. Here in B.C., the first IPAs were made at Sailor Hagar's Brewpub in North Vancouver by Gary Lohin, now the brewmaster at Central City Brewing in Surrey, and Bill Herdman at Tall Ship Ales in Squamish. Interestingly, the two often compared notes as home brewers in the '80s. Herdman says he brewed a draft version of *Tall Ship IPA* in 1993, and a bottled version followed a year later in 1994. Lohin says he brewed his *Bengal IPA*, which had a tiger face on the label, at Sailor Hagar's in 1994. Later, when Lohin released his *Red Racer IPA* in its signature green can in 2008, it was a trailblazing beer because of its aromatic dry hopping and aggressive hop bitterness, and it remains a favourite today.

7. THE LEGEND OF MATT PHILLIPS: When Matt Phillips wanted to open his own brewery back in 2001, all the banks turned him down for loans. Undeterred, he signed up for every credit card he could find and maxed them all out. He slept at the brewery, showering at a nearby gym, and did everything from brewing the beer to filling kegs and delivering them to local pubs and restaurants in an old blue milk truck. Bit by bit the brewery expanded until today Phillips Brewing and Distilling is the most successful craft brewery in B.C. and perhaps all of Canada.

8. NIGEL'S ALIBI: Back in 2006 when Nigel Springthorpe took over the management of the Alibi Room in Vancouver's Gastown neighbourhood, he didn't know much about beer, but he was interested in learning more. He started seeking out breweries that didn't normally ship their beer to Vancouver to put their beer on tap at his "modern tavern." The tap list kept expanding, finally reaching 50 lines, and the restaurant quickly became the city's headquarters for craft beer, where beer geeks regularly congregated and breweries begged to get their beer put on tap. For years, Nigel hinted that he wanted to open his own brewery and then finally in 2013, he did just that, teaming up with brewer Conrad Gmoser to open Brassneck Brewery on Main Street.

9. ROCK BAY MASH UP: Breweries often work together to produce special collaboration beers, but in reality these beers are always brewed at one of the breweries with the other brewery just symbolically participating. The exception to that took place in 2014 in Victoria. Driftwood Brewery and Hoyne Brewing, which share a parking lot in the Rock Bay industrial area, each brewed a batch of Baltic Porter with the same ingredients except for the yeast— Driftwood used an ale yeast and Hoyne used a lager strain. When the batches were ready, the breweries connected more than 60 metres of hose together to pipe the Hoyne batch to merge with Driftwood's in a big tank at Driftwood Brewery. The resulting *Rock Bay Mash Up Baltic Porter* (8% ABV) was released in 650-mL bottles by both breweries.

10. 100 NEW BREWERIES IN FIVE YEARS: The craft beer industry in British Columbia began in the early 1980s and grew steadily for three decades until it had reached a respectable size, with about 50 breweries at the end of 2012. Then, early in 2013, the provincial government announced that craft breweries were allowed to operate on-site tasting rooms, a move that ultimately created a new business model: small breweries that focus on retail sales by the glass and growler fill, rather than the traditional wholesale model that required them to be significantly larger in order to sell beer all across the province. Over the next five years, 100 new breweries opened, most following this new model, and the industry continues to expand at a dizzying rate: at the end of 2018, there were 167 craft breweries in the province, with many more set to open.

(Opposite) Teresa the Traveler has spent much of her life exploring B.C. and the world.

TOURISM

10 GIGANTIC B.C. ROADSIDE ATTRACTIONS

1. CANADA'S BIGGEST FISHING ROD, HOUSTON: If you've ever wondered why so many small towns in B.C. have gargantuan roadside attractions, the folks in Houston are upfront about it. As the town website explains, sometime in the 80s, tourism promoters were telling every town council that would listen that a surefire to put yourself on the map would be to install something comically oversized.

Houston's idea for a fishing rod came from local fisherman named Warner Jarvis, and the final product is 18 metres long. No worries if you're rolling through town late at night—Houston pays to keep it illuminated.

2. GIANT GOLD PAN, QUESNEL: It's a giant gold pan, what more can we say? There were outraged rumours a few years back that the town was planning to remove this beloved symbol of the Gold Rush years. The mayor was forced to make a public statement to calm everyone down. Oh, and there's also a giant shovel and pickaxe beside the pan.

3. WORLD'S LARGEST HOCKEY STICK AND PUCK, DUNCAN: There have been many challengers to this throne, but pay no attention to the pretenders with their puny twig in Eveleth, Minnesota, or the wannabes in Parry Sound, Ontario (they haven't even built theirs yet.)

The indisputable fact is that the 62.5-metre, 28-tonne hockey stick at the Cowichan Community Centre in Duncan still holds the Guinness World Record for biggest in the world. The stick and puck, 40 times the size of the real thing, were built for Expo 86, and when the fair was over, it took a barge and three flatbed trucks to motor them across the Strait of Georgia and up-island to their new home.

4. THE GREAT HOG OF FREEDOM, LYTTON: You'd be hard-pressed to find a more heroically named roadside attraction than this giant motorcycle on the property of artist Kenny Glasgow. It's 7.5 metres long, and took three years to build. Two other giant bikes sit nearby, but at just 1.5 and two times the size of the real thing, they're just nothing compared to The Great Hog.

5. WORLD'S LARGEST BURL, PORT MCNEILL: This one is pretty self explanatory. It's a great big wooden knot in a parking lot, and there isn't a bigger one on the planet (allegedly). This burl is 6 metres tall, and it was carved from a Sitka spruce on northern Vancouver Island in 2005.

As one recent online reviewer writes, "My second visit to the burl and I still don't understand why it's there or what it's about, but there is something great about the madness of the whole fact tourist information points you to a tree lump." Even better? Lucky Port McNeill is also home to the (allegedly) second largest burl in the world.

6. GIANT LAWN MOWER, ENDERBY: If you've already sunk your savings into transforming your home into a museum for antique tools, why not find an equally bonkers way to advertise it? Herb Higginbottom built this gigantic reel mower—the largest in the world—from scratch, even building the rollers needed to work the steel. It stands more than 6 metres high.

7. THE TRUCK FORMERLY KNOWN AS THE LARGEST IN THE WORLD, SPARWOOD: Don't feel sorry for the Terex Titan; it had a good run. For 25 years, this green behemoth was the biggest truck in the world, until it was beat out by younger, chunkier competitors. At 6.88 metres tall, 20 metres long and 260 tonnes, the 1974 prototype was designed to haul materials around open-pit mines. Sadly, the timing was all wrong. The Titan was produced just as the bottom was dropping out of the coal market, and this prototype was the only one ever built. Still, it worked the mines near Sparwood until 1991.

8. 12-METRE-HIGH CROSS-COUNTRY SKIS, 100 MILE HOUSE: According to TripAdvisor, looking at these skis is #2 on the list of the top 10 things to do in 100 Mile House. Take from that what you will. The skis are said to be the biggest in the world, and they come complete with 9-metre-tall poles. Find them outside the South Cariboo Visitor Centre.

9. WORLD'S BIGGEST PADDLE, GOLDEN: Golden is proud to point out that its landmark 18.5-metre paddle was built to scale, and it's the perfect size for a 24-metre tall giant canoeist. Believe it or not, it took just one Western red cedar log to complete this beauty.

10. GIGANTIC GARDEN GNOME, NANOOSE BAY: This smiling 8-metre-tall guy with his absurdly large thumbs-up used to be the mascot for a go-kart track, but he's spent most of his life standing beside a gas station. The gnome named Howard is the creation of local artist Ron Hale, who once described his creative process to a reporter like this: "I am not one of those people who look too far ahead. I just went and done it." In early 2019, Howard was offered a new home at a farm near Saanich, where the owners have planned an attraction built around him called Gnome Man's Land.

TERESA THE TRAVELER'S TOP 10 LIST OF HISTORICAL SPOTS TO VISIT IN B.C.

Kamloops' Teresa Cline—a.k.a. Teresa the Traveler—is the author of nine books about her adventures in B.C. The most recent is Hidden History, *part of her Discover British Columbia series. You can read more of her recommendations at* teresathetraveler.ca*.*

The province of British Columbia is not very old, but it certainly has some interesting history. Tucked away in numerous roadside museums and historical sites are stories of frontier life in the Wild West. From the days of fur trading to the Gold Rush and construction of the railway, the stories of the people who lived this history come alive when you visit these places.

1. HAT CREEK RANCH, NORTH OF CACHE CREEK: This 1860s roadhouse catered to miners, pack-train operators and wagon trains until the introduction of the automobile to the Cariboo in the early 1900s. The ranch was founded by Scottish fur trader Don McLean—father of the famous outlaw gang "The Wild McLeans." Today, guests can ride a stagecoach and learn the history of the ranch from actors dressed in period costumes.

2. MASCOT MINE, HEDLEY: The Mascot Mine operated between 1936 and 1949. This was one of the most unusual mining operations in the world. It was built on the side of a mountain, 5,000 feet above the tiny town of Hedley. At its peak, it employed 130 men, who commuted to work on a tram. The site has been restored and is managed by the Upper Similkameen Indian Band, who provide tours to the site throughout the summer months.

3. OTHELLO TUNNELS, EAST OF HOPE: The Othello Tunnels were part of the Kettle Creek Railway that operated from 1915 to 1989. The section of the railway called the Coquihalla Subdivision was the most difficult to construct and operate. It consisted of 43 bridges, 13 tunnels and 16 snow sheds. In 1959, heavy rains washed out sections of this line. The damage was never repaired and the subdivision was officially closed in 1961. Today, it is part of a trail network. People can walk through tunnels and bridges and see some of the locations where the iconic movie *Rambo* was filmed.

4. BARKERVILLE: Barkerville is one of B.C.'s most famous ghost towns. In the mid-1860s, this Gold Rush town had a population of 5,000. In 1868, a fire nearly destroyed the town, but amazingly no one was killed. Today, over 100 heritage structures still stand. Visitors can learn to gold pan, watch a show at the theatre, and watch the infamous Matthew Begbie, a.k.a. "The Hanging Judge," hold court.

5. O'KEEFE RANCH, VERNON: The O'Keefe Ranch is exactly the same age as Canada. It was founded in 1867 by Cornelius O'Keefe, an Irish immigrant. This was an operational cattle ranch until 1967, when the family decided to restore and rebuild the original structures. They transformed it into a tourist attraction that remains open to this day.

6. FORT LANGLEY: This fort has been called the birthplace of British Columbia. George Simpson, the Governor of the Hudson's Bay Company, came up with the idea of building a permanent trading post along the lower Fraser River, and four months later, on November 26, 1827, Fort Langley was complete. In 1866, this British colony merged with the British colony on Vancouver Island to form the backbone of what would be British Columbia. The fort became a national historic site in 1923 and was opened to the public in 1931.

7. FATHER PANDOSY'S MISSION, KELOWNA: This is the site where Oblate priest Father Pandosy established the first permanent European settlement in the Interior of British Columbia. The mission was established in 1859, and over the next 30 years became an important religious, social and cultural centre. At its peak, the mission covered 2,000 acres of land, where missionaries raised 550 head of cattle and planted fruit and vegetable gardens. In fact, they planted Okanagan's first apple orchard using a seedling from St. Mary's Mission in Mission.

8. FORT STEELE: Fort Steele was established in 1864 during the Gold Rush after John Galbraith set up a ferry across the Kootenay River. It was the only ferry for hundreds of miles, and generated such a lucrative income that a town sprung up around it. By the late 1890s, this fort was the heart of East Kootenay. It began to decline once the railway was extended to Cranbrook, bypassing Fort Steele. It was designated a historic site in 1967. Today, it is a tourist attraction with 60 heritage buildings. People can do a Wild West photo shoot, watch live theatre, and meet the actors dressed in period garb demonstrating such skills as dressmaking and blacksmithing.

9. ALEXANDRA BRIDGE, NORTH OF YALE: This historic bridge was built in 1861 and named after Princess Alexandra of Wales. It was built using Chinese and native labor as part of the Cariboo Road. It was destroyed by the Fraser flood of 1894, but with the dawn of the automobile, a new suspension bridge was built on the original pilings in 1926. It closed in 1964 when the current bridge was built 2 kilometres downstream. Today, this majestic bridge is open to tourists.

10. THE LAST SPIKE AND RAILWAY MUSEUM, CRAIGELLACHIE AND REVELSTOKE: On November 7, 1885, the ceremonial final spike was driven into the Canadian Pacific Railway at Craigellachie. It represented both the completion of the railway and a symbol of national unity. After visiting this historical site along the Trans Canada highway, stop in Revelstoke to visit the Railway Museum to learn about British Columbia's rich railway history.

10 WEIRD AND WONDERFUL B.C. MUSEUMS

1. SASQUATCH MUSEUM, HARRISON HOT SPRINGS: In case you hadn't heard of the Sasquatch, he's kind of a big deal in these parts. This museum traces the history of the big guy, whose name is an anglicized version of the Sts'ailes word Sa:sq'ets. The Sts'ailes people think of him as a caretaker of the land, but finding the Sasquatch has also become an obsession for non-Indigenous cryptozoology fans, and this museum shows off all purported evidence of his existence.

2. ALDER GROVE TELEPHONE MUSEUM, ALDERGROVE: As you might have guessed, this place is home to a whole lot of very old telephones. The quaint little house used to be a BC Tel building, and inside you'll find switchboards, phone repair tools, glass insulators from telephone poles, and a whole lot of other stuff that will look like artifacts from an alien planet to anyone born after the year 2000.

3. DEEP CREEK TOOL MUSEUM, ENDERBY: It took 50 years of collecting antique tools to get Herb Higginbottom to where he is today—welcoming visitors on a personal tour of his lifelong passion. He started piecing the museum together when his wife fell ill and he wanted to stay close to home. And then he built a gigantic lawn mower for the front yard to tie the whole thing together.

4. JIM'S FORD CORRAL MUSEUM, SORRENTO: This is another personal passion project, created by a transplanted Newfie who decided to get really, really into collecting antique gas station accoutrements. The museum is filled with old-timey gas pumps and ancient oil company signs. Outside, you'll find old cars, toys, and bikes—it's a glimpse at how B.C. used to be.

5. MINIATURE WORLD, VICTORIA: The name pretty much says it all—everything is very, very small here. They call it "The Greatest Little Show on Earth," so it's something like the Reno of Victoria. There are more than 85 tiny set pieces, including scenes from a circus, outer space, Camelot and a fantasy world. Amazing bonus? Miniature World also has the world's smallest working sawmill.

6. VICTORIA BUG ZOO: The provincial capital seems to have a bit of a thing for the very small. The Bug Zoo occupies just two rooms, but its inhabitants are so wee that there's space to display about 50 different species of insects and other arthropods. It hosts the continent's biggest ant farm, which displays a working colony of leaf-cutter ants, and aims to help visitors shed their fear of species like tarantulas, giant walking sticks, cockroaches, and scorpions.

7. VANCOUVER POLICE MUSEUM: To get into the right mood for this museum, you'll want to remind yourself that its Gastown digs were home to the coroner's court and city autopsy facilities until 1980. Now that you're properly creeped out, it's time to comb over evidence from the scenes of some of Vancouver's most brutal crimes, handle tools used by forensic investigators, and eyeball the outrageous items police have confiscated over the years. The museum also runs a Sins of the City walking tour to show off the seedier side of Vancouver's history, including drugs, sex, and discrimination.

8. CORKSCREW INN WINE MUSEUM, VANCOUVER: The Corkscrew Inn is just a wee, five-room bed and breakfast on the West Side, but its owners still make space for an exhibition of just about every device ever invented to remove a cork from a bottle. There's a steam-power corkscrew designed by proprietor Wayne Meadows, tiny tools used to open medicine bottles and cologne, and antiques dating back three centuries. One tiny catch—you have to get a room for the night if you want to see the collection.

9. HOME OF A THOUSAND FACES, RADIUM HOT SPRINGS: With his tie-dyed, wizard-like wardrobe, artist Rolf Heer is one of those characters you can only find in B.C. He carves faces—or really just different versions of his own face—from stumps and driftwood using a chainsaw, and his workshop is filled with woody self portraits. The house also contains a funhouse room filled with mystery doors inviting visitors to open wide and get pranked. Oh yeah, and there are goats.

(Sadly, the Home of a Thousand Faces was destroyed in a fire in November 2018)

10. EMBALMING FLUID BOTTLE HOUSE, BOSWELL: Less famous for what's inside its walls than what those walls are made of, the house built by David H. Brown in 1952 was meant to "indulge a whim of a peculiar nature," in the man's own words. That's putting it mildly. Brown was retired from the funeral business when he started building his collection of 500,000 empty embalming fluid bottles, contributed by like-minded pals across western Canada. The result is this castle-like structure overlooking Kootenay Lake. Visitors can tour the main floor and the landscape during the summer months.

5 B.C. TRANSPORTATION WRECKS TO EXPLORE

1. THE PESUTA, HAIDA GWAII: This 264-foot log barge was being towed by the tug Imbre-caria when it got caught in a gale in Hecate Strait in 1928. It wrecked on Haida Gwaii's East Beach, north of Tlell River, and settled with its wooden skeleton thrusting out of the shore-line, slowly sinking into the sand as the years went on. Now, visitors can reach the wreck by following a 10-kilometre hike—just be careful to go at low tide, or you may get stranded.

2. WHISTLER TRAIN WRECK: The stranded boxcars are covered in graffiti, which should come as no surprise considering they've been lying there since 1956. Now a popular destination for hikers in the Whistler area, the freight train wrecked when it hit a stretch of track under repair at more than double the local speed limit. The crash left three cars wedged into a rock cut. They were later moved away from the tracks by a logging firm, but have been left to rust nearby ever since.

3. ROYSTON WRECKS, COURTENAY: More than a dozen shipwrecks make up this ghostly display on the east coast of Vancouver. But they're not there because of some horrible tragedy or a dumb mistake that keeps getting repeated. These old ship hulls were placed along the shoreline intentionally in the 1930s as part of a breakwater to protect the area from winter storms. Some of the ships date all the way back to the 1800s, and a few have become nesting grounds for a wide variety of birds. The wrecks can be seen from land, but also explored by kayak or underwater.

4. CANSO BOMBER CRASH, TOFINO: After the attack on Pearl Harbour, the Canadian government thought it wise to build an airfield on the far West Coast to protect the country from the threat of a Japanese invasion. It was from this airfield that an ill-fated Royal Canadian Air Force Canso 11007 bomber took off on the night of February 10, 1945 with a crew of 12 on board. But the plane malfunctioned as it headed up-island, and crashed into a thick stand of trees near Tofino. Luckily, pilot Ron Scholes managed to stall the plane and slow its descent, saving the lives of everyone on board. Like most of the other wrecks on this list, the remains of the Canso bomber can be reached along a popular hiking trail.

5. SS *VALENCIA*, CAPE BEALE: There's a reason the stretch of ocean that hugs the coast from Oregon to northern Vancouver Island is nicknamed The Graveyard of the Pacific. The wild and unpredictable weather and rugged coastline have claimed many a ship over the years. The Valencia is one of the most famous and the most deadly of those wrecks—she was a 1,600-ton passenger steamer that sank off Cape Beale in 1906, killing more than 100 people. All of the women and children on board died in the wreck, and only a small number of men survived. Some of the detritus can still be seen on the beach just off the West Coast Trail, southeast of Pacheco Point. Even better, anyone with access to some scuba gear can explore the wreckage on the ocean floor.

(Opposite) From exploring the beaches to wetting your whistle at an award-winning brewery, there's plenty to do in Tofino.

THE CONCIERGE RECOMMENDS

KARIN SCHWAGLY'S LIST OF 10 THINGS TO DO IN VANCOUVER

Karin Schwagly is concierge at the Shangri-La Hotel in Vancouver.

1. BEST RAINY DAY ACTIVITY: LUCIDA BOARD GAME CAFE: Over 1,000 meticulously categorized board games and open flame-fired pizza.

2. BEST NEIGHBOURHOOD FOR A MICROBREW PUB CRAWL: HASTINGS SUNRISE, A.K.A THE EAST VILLAGE: Hastings Sunrise is a portside neighbourhood in East Vancouver. Use the map available at EastVillageVancouver.ca to take a self-guided tour of more than 10 microbreweries while you enjoy the murals and mountain views that make up this evolving industrial neighborhood.

3. BEST GASTRO PUB: BUCKSTOP: Late night (for Vancouver) cozy spot with a thoughtful beverage menu that serves barbecue. Fiona, the proprietor, is most often found tending bar. Their deep-fried pickles are the best.

4. BEST BREAKFAST/BRUNCH: FORAGE: Dedicated to serving locally sourced food and making most ingredients in house, including nutella, jam, and ketchup. Bonus: they take reservations if you don't fancy queuing, but make them in advance.

5. BEST MUSEUM: MUSEUM OF ANTHROPOLOGY: A carefully designed space showcasing artifacts of local Indigenous nations as well as thought-provoking international exhibits. Their complimentary guided tours are offered daily. Bonus: the museum is located on the University of British Columbia campus, a 20-minute drive from downtown Vancouver. The campus also offers many other parks, gardens, and noteworthy attractions.

6. BEST AUTHENTIC INDIGENOUS EXPERIENCE: TALAYSAY TOURS: A locally owned Indigenous tour company that offers walking tours in Stanley Park. Learn the scientific significance, history, and purpose that this area has for the first inhabitants of B.C.

7. BEST HOLE-IN-THE-WALL SUSHI RESTAURANT: MIKO: Not to be confused with the upscale and equally delicious Japanese restaurant Miku, Miko is located in Vancouver's West End at 1335 Robson St. They are a small, family-run restaurant serving cooked and raw Japanese classics. Reservations are accepted by phone. Open for dinner and weekday lunch. Closed on Sundays.

8. BEST WAY TO ENJOY GRANVILLE ISLAND: VANCOUVER FOODIE TOURS: A two-hour tour of Granville Island that offers VIP access to the most noteworthy vendors and restaurants. You will consume more than enough food to suffice for a meal while learning about the creative people and cuisine that make Granville Island one of Canada's most visited tourist destinations. This island is a sardine can stuffed with all things delicious and delightful. It is expedient to have a helpful guide to enable you to make the most of your time there. They will also give you individualized recommendations on how to explore the island after your tour.

9. BEST UNIQUE VANTAGE POINT OF VANCOUVER: THE VIEW FROM CRAB PARK: Located at the edge of Gastown, Crab Park is on the shores of Burrard Inlet. Its view encompasses Vancouver's port, the North Shore mountains, and the downtown skyline. The park's grassy field backs a rail yard and converted warehouse district. Great place for kids and dogs.

10. BEST PLACE FOR A DROP-IN YOGA CLASS: STRETCH YOGA: Loft yoga studio located in Chinatown with complimentary mat rentals and showers. Try their Yin class with live cello.

DEBORAH SLENO'S LIST OF 10 THINGS TO DO IN VICTORIA

Deborah Sleno is the concierge at The Fairmont Empress Hotel and a member of Les Clefs d'Or Canada

1. AFTERNOON TEA AT THE FAIRMONT EMPRESS: A tradition served daily since its opening in 1908, world-famous Tea at the Empress is served in the sophisticated Lobby Lounge. Featuring scones with clotted cream and jam, four different finger sandwiches, an assortment of pastries made in house and a choice of tea from the tea menu. Enjoy the sounds of the live piano music while enjoying your tea.

2. ROYAL BRITISH COLUMBIA MUSEUM: This is a world where you can experience the history of British Columbia in an afternoon. Considered one of the top museums in North America, you will not be disappointed. The adjoining National Geographic IMAX Theatre is also worth a visit.

3. BUTCHART GARDENS: Established in 1904, this 55-acre showpiece still maintains the gracious traditions of the past, from the exquisite Sunken Garden, to the charming rose, Japanese, and Italian gardens. Seasonally, there is daily entertainment, night illumination and fireworks displays, as well as two restaurants and a gift shop.

4. CVS CITY TOUR: This narrated tour includes Old Town, Chinatown, Antique Row, Uplands and Oak Bay, and the beautiful Scenic Marine Drive. You'll discover the best of Victoria's lovely homes, gardens and points of historic interest. Tours available from spring until September 30.

5. CRAIGDARROCH CASTLE : "Victoria's Legendary Landmark" was completed in 1890. Experience this lavish home, full of antiques and exquisite woodwork, which was originally owned by the fascinating Dunsmuir family. (Please note: climbing stairs is required to enjoy this attraction.)

6. WHALE WATCHING AND NATURE TOURS: Ready for an exhilarating trip? April through October are the ideal months to spot killer whales; however, you can view seals, sea lions, porpoises, eagles and much more marine wildlife year round. And you don't have to put on one of those orange survival suits if you'd rather not—an indoor cabin can be arranged if you prefer. This is possibly the most exciting way to spend a few hours. You'll have a great time!

7. VICTORIA HARBOUR FERRIES (SEASONAL): Take a leisurely 45-minute tour of our lovely Inner Harbour or a 50-minute tour of the historic Gorge Waterway. These "water taxis" are a unique and fun way to see the sights.

8. GOVERNMENT STREET: From the front of the Fairmont Empress Hotel, turn right and treat yourself to a stroll up Government Street. Enjoy a variety of unique shops, including Rogers' Chocolates, Murchie's Tea & Coffee, Lush cosmetics, Munro's Books, and many more. Visit Bastion Square, Market Square, and Chinatown for more interesting shopping experiences.

9. A TASTE OF VICTORIA FOOD TOUR: This is a two-hour guided food tasting tour through the historic districts of Chinatown, Old Town, and the Inner Harbour that includes visits to local businesses serving local products.

10. HORSE-DRAWN CARRIAGE TOUR: Majestic horses and professional guides escort you on a relaxing, entertaining tour through the city's historic, scenic beauty.

COAST INN OF THE NORTH'S LIST OF 10 THINGS TO DO IN PRINCE GEORGE

Recommendations from the front desk staff at the Prince George hotel.

1. BEST RAINY DAY ACTIVITY: BROWSING BOOKS OR ART: Choose either Two Rivers Art Gallery or Books and Company. Two Rivers Art Gallery has a variety of art styles in its permanent collection and unique rotating exhibitions that change every three months. Books and Company is a quaint local bookshop with a variety of events including chess nights, musical performances, Scrabble Sundays and more—you'll always find something interesting in the book shop.

2. BEST MUSEUM: THE EXPLORATION PLACE: The Exploration Place has both museum exhibits and an interactive science centre. Whether you are interested in seeing some of the massive dinosaurs that once roamed these lands or if you'd like to get up close and personal with some reptiles, there is something for everyone.

3. BEST HIKING TRAIL: TAKE YOUR PICK: Forests for the World or Cottonwood Island Nature Park—both of these local parks have a beautiful network of well-maintained trails where you can see a variety of wildlife.

4. BEST LOCAL SKI HILL: PURDEN SKI VILLAGE: Purden Ski Village celebrated its 50th year of operation in the 2018/2019 season. It has 26 named runs and the longest covers more than 3 kilometres of terrain. Located just 60 kilometres outside of Prince George, it's a short drive to some of the best skiing and snowboarding in central B.C.

5. BEST PLACE TO SEE WILDLIFE: GINTERS FIELD: Ginters Field is one of the city's designated off-leash friendly dog parks and is quite popular with the local moose population as well.

6. BEST DAY TRIP: THE ANCIENT FOREST: The Ancient Forest, which can be found approximately one hour east of Prince George, is home to the only inland temperate rainforest in the world. With a boardwalk winding nearly three kilometres through the forest, guests have the chance to see 1,000-year-old trees.

7. BEST LOCAL WINERY: NORTHERN LIGHTS ESTATE WINERY: Northern Lights Estate Winery has a year-round wine tasting bar and winery tours, as well as a quaint bistro with a riverfront patio. It is the perfect place to sit back, relax, and enjoy a taste of the local wine.

8. BEST VANTAGE POINT OF PRINCE GEORGE: CONNAUGHT HILL PARK: Connaught Hill Park has beautiful 360° views of the city as well as the Fraser River. It is the perfect place to relax and enjoy the outdoors.

9. BEST LOCAL HISTORIC SITE: HUBLE HOMESTEAD: Huble Homestead is a heritage site that was once a homestead and fur-trading post. It is open from May to October each year for guided tours. They also hold special events and demonstrations throughout the season.

10. BEST LOCAL DROP-IN SESSIONS: YMCA: The local YMCA has a variety of classes available. With everything from martial arts to yoga, there is something for everyone, and with the purchase of a day pass you can attend as many classes as you want for the day.

TOBY KOLADA'S LIST OF 10 THINGS TO DO IN KELOWNA AND THE OKANAGAN

Tony Kolada is the guest experience manager for the Grand Okanagan Resort in Kelowna.

1. STAY AT THE DELTA HOTELS BY MARRIOTT GRAND OKANAGAN RESORT: Enjoy complimentary bikes, kayaks, pedal boats and outdoor swimming pools equipped with a bar. Sleep in luxury and dine in the magnificent OAK + CRU Social Kitchen & Wine Bar. This experience is a destination must!

2. WINE TOURING: The Okanagan Valley is home to more than 300 wineries and is one of the best destinations, infrastructure-wise, to travel around and see as many as you'd like.

3. GET OUT ON LAKE OKANAGAN: Head down to the local Kelowna Downtown Marina and rent a jet ski or a boat and go surfing, skiing, tubing, wakeboarding, and more. Go parasailing and glide high over the lake or test your need for speed on the Kelowna Jet Boat Adventures high-speed boat charter.

4. GOLF IN THE GLORIOUS OKANAGAN SUN: Check out the abundance of beautiful, award-winning golf courses such as The Harvest, Gallagher's Canyon, Predator Ridge, and Tower Ranch Golf Club.

5. TAKE OVER THE MOUNTAINS WITH OKANAGAN ATV TOURS: Down in Peachland, this team has tons of terrain, amazing machines, and great staff that will help you explore our rugged mountains.

6. COME FLY WITH ME AT VALHALLA HELICOPTERS: Tour the region's beautiful lakes, mountains, and landscapes from the sky as you soar above the valley.

7. GET ON YOUR BIKES AND RIDE WITH MYRA CANYON ADVENTURE PARK: Take a ride along Myra Canyon's historic trestle trails, ride through tunnels and over large valleys. The sites will amaze you and the family.

8. EXPLORE ALL OF KELOWNA'S LOCALLY CRAFTED WINES, CIDERS AND BREWS: Get a group of friends together on Smile Cycle's downtown cultural district tour to really kick the experience up a notch!

9. SEIZE THE DAY AND EXPLORE THE BEAUTIFUL WATERFALLS OF FINTRY: This magnificent hike is doable for anyone and each view is worth a thousand words and more.

10. DINE THROUGHOUT THE OKANAGAN VALLEY: Explore the amazing culinary scene this valley has to offer from Lake Country to Osoyoos.

ANTOINE GAY'S 10 THINGS TO DO IN TOFINO AND PACIFIC RIM NATIONAL PARK RESERVE

Antoine Gay is the Clefs D'or Concierge at the Wickaninnish Inn in Tofino.

1. GET OUT ON THE WATER: Take a tour of the West Coast's famous wildlife. According to the tides, the season and the weather, that could mean whale watching, bear watching, or a private wildlife boat tour, and kayak or canoe trips. The concierge recommends Ocean Outfitters tour company, Remote Passages Marine Excursions, Browning Pass Charters, Tofino Sea Kayaking, and T'ashii Paddle School.

2. GET INTO THE WATER: Tofino is famous for water sports—especially surfing and stand-up paddleboarding. The concierge recommends Surf Sister Surf School and T'ashii Paddle School.

3. GRAB SOME MUNCHIES IN TOWN: For a vegetarian meal, try Bravocados, or if you're feeling like casual fusion, SoBo is the place to be. Wolf in The Fog is famous for a more sophisticated experience, and Shelter Restaurant is best if you've come with family in tow.

4. EXPLORE THE ARTS AND CRAFTS SCENE: Stroll Campbell Street and Main Street enjoying art galleries, local crafts, and shopping.

5. RELAX WITH PRE-DINNER DRINKS AND COCKTAILS: Try Tofino Brewing Co. for its award-winning Blonde Ale or settle into The Hatch Waterfront Pub for the view of the inlets

6. DIG IN FOR DINNER AT THE POINTE RESTAURANT: Before crashing into bed for a well-deserved sleep at The Wickaninnish, the concierge recommends reserving a space at the chef's table in Howard's Wine Cellar. And *The Wickaninnish Cookbook* is a great keepsake to remember your visit.

7. DROP BY THE CARVING SHED: The Carving Shed is a sanctuary that functions as a working gallery for local carvers and a place to continue the legacy of local carver Henry Nolla.

8. WALK OR RIDE A BIKE ALONG CHESTERMAN BEACH: Check out the scenery at one of the area's most famous beaches, including surfers catching a wave and colourful creatures in the many tide pools.

9. PACK LUNCH FOR THE ROAD: The locals love the tacos at Tacofino and the fish and chips at Wildside Grill.

10. TAKE A HIKE: Choose one of the many trails inside the Pacific Rim National Park Reserve. The concierge recommends Schooner Cove Trail, which includes a 2-kilometre hike through the rainforest to the beach.

THE FOUR SEASONS CONCIERGE'S GUIDE TO 10 THINGS TO DO IN WHISTLER AND THE SEA-TO-SKY CORRIDOR

Members of the team at the Four Seasons Resort and Residences in Whistler have each offered a favourite thing to do while visiting Whistler and the Sea-to-Sky corridor.

1. BOBSLEIGH: "Because it's fast and furious."—Jasmine (Jazzy) Stewart

2. SKIING: "It is the best feeling in the whole world."—Hannah Jones

3. HELISKIING: "Because there is nothing like soaring over a magical glacier before carving a perfect line."—Simon Boldireff

4. FUNGI FORAGING: "Because I'm a nerd and mushrooms are cool. The ice caves are also the most surreal experience you can have in Whistler. There is no place on Earth like it." — James Shaw, director of guest services

5. HELI-SNOWMOBILING ON THE GLACIER: "Unbelievable vistas, the freshest powder and an adrenaline rush to last a lifetime."—Lisa Cook

6. WHITE WATER RAFTING: "Great adrenaline rush going down the Elaho River hitting huge waves! A very thrilling experience for those that are not afraid to get completely soaked."—Darren King

7. HIKING: "I love exploring the hidden beauty of Whistler. You get a feeling of peace and relaxation from being in nature."—Shenalyn Esperitu

8. TOUR OF WHISTLER'S CRAFT BREWERIES: "It's an amazing way to see a different side to the town, while tasting all our local drops."—Ashley Pellegrini

9. SLOW FOOD CYCLE THROUGH PEMBERTON: "Cycle to Pemberton's best food places including Mile One, North Arm Farm, and the Pemberton Distillery."—Eleanor Gilkes

10. EAGLE FLOAT ON THE SQUAMISH RIVER: "Squamish is the bald eagle capital of the world, and the Eagle Float is an awesome way to watch them hunt from the water."—Anton Masich

FOR YOUR REFERENCE

8 OFFICIAL SYMBOLS OF B.C.

1. FLOWER: PACIFIC DOGWOOD: Don't be tempted by these simple white flowers, please—it's illegal to pick them.

2. BIRD: STELLER'S JAY: They're loud and squawky and they'll steal your lunch if you step away from your picnic table for even a second, but their electric blue feathers are also stunningly beautiful.

3. MAMMAL: SPIRIT OR KERMODE BEAR: Despite what many people assume, these nearly white black bears aren't albinos—they actually carry a single mutant gene that gives them white fur.

4. FISH: PACIFIC SALMON: This one seems like a bit of a given, considering the importance of salmon to this province's history and economy. There are five true salmon species in B.C.: Chinook, chum, Coho, pink, and sockeye.

5. TREE: WESTERN RED CEDAR: Fact: the Western red cedar isn't actually a true cedar, but it is closely related to another pretender, the northern white cedar. If you want to get technical about it, these fakers really belong in the cypress family.

6. GEMSTONE: JADE: It's B.C.'s jade, but Thailand seems to have perfected the art of carving it. Bangkok's Wat Dhammongkol temple is home to the world's largest sculpture made from B.C. jade—a Buddha carved from a 32-tonne boulder.

7. TARTAN: GREEN, RED, AND WHITE WITH HINTS OF BLUE AND GOLD: Look, no province worth its salt can exist without an official tartan. And each of the five colours in B.C.'s plaid, adopted in 1974, has meaning. Red is for the maple leaf, green is for the forests, white is for the dogwood, blue is for the ocean, and gold is for the crown and sun on the provincial flag.

8. MOTTO: SPLENDOR SINE OCCASU: Modesty has never been British Columbia's strong suit. This phrase means "splendour without diminishment," which is only slightly less bombastic than "The Best Place on Earth."

B.C. BY THE NUMBERS: 25 BASIC FACTS

1. POPULATION IN JANUARY 2019: 5 million

2. JOINED CONFEDERATION: 1871

3. POPULATION IN 1871: 36,000

4. TOTAL AREA: 944,735 square kilometres

5. LAND AREA: 922,503 square kilometres

6. POPULATION DENSITY IN 2016: 5 people per square kilometre

7. AVERAGE HOUSEHOLD SIZE IN 2016: 2.4 people

8. COASTLINE: 27,200 kilometres

9. **NUMBER OF FIRST NATIONS:** 198

10. **SHARE OF CANADA'S FIRST NATIONS:** 31%

11. **GDP IN 2017:** $282 billion

12. **SHARE OF CANADA'S GDP:** 13%

13. **SHARE OF B.C. GDP FROM REAL ESTATE, RENTALS, AND LEASING:** 18%

14. **PROVINCIAL PARKS, RECREATION AREAS, CONSERVANCIES, ECOLOGICAL RESERVES, AND PROTECTED AREAS:** 1,033

15. **NATIONAL PARKS:** 7

16. **NATIONAL HISTORIC SITES:** 95

17. **UNESCO WORLD HERITAGE SITES:** 3

18. **SHARE OF LAND BASE THAT'S PROTECTED:** 15.4%

19. **SHARE OF MARINE AREA THAT'S PROTECTED:** 3.2%

20. **TOTAL LENGTH OF ALL ROADS:** 719,000 kilometres

21. **U.S. BORDER CROSSINGS:** 19

22. **BC FERRIES ROUTES:** 25

23. **PORTS SERVED BY BC FERRIES:** 47

24. **HIGHEST TEMPERATURE EVER RECORDED:** 44.4° C (July 16 and 17, 1941 in Lytton and Lillooet)

25. **LOWEST TEMPERATURE EVER RECORDED:** -58.9° C (January 31, 1947 in Smith River)

B.C.'S 10 MOST VALUABLE HOMES

Real estate is king in British Columbia. Though we may not have the highest salaries or the most reliable job prospects, at least our housing is dependably overpriced. These are the most valuable residential properties from the 2019 B.C. property assessments—and bear in mind, most of these had actually fallen from their 2018 values.

1. **3085 POINT GREY RD., VANCOUVER $73.12 MILLION:** Chip Wilson, you've done it again. The bombastic Lululemon founder's gigantic 15,700-square-foot Kitsilano mansion consistently tops this list, though it lost more than $5.7 million in value in just one year. That's a piddling amount for one of B.C.'s richest people, but knowing Chip, it probably still bugs him a little.

2. **4707 BELMONT AVE., VANCOUVER $65.47 MILLION:** Including the basement, it measures nearly 29,000 square feet—enough space to fit about 100 of those micro lofts that so many average Vancouverites have had to settle for in recent years. This mansion overlooking Spanish Banks was designed by architect Russell Hollingsworth, but the owner on the land title records is reportedly a company called Pisonii (PTC) Ltd., which is not registered in B.C.

3. JAMES ISLAND $56.76 MILLION: This is the one entry on the list that makes something like objective sense. This private island, just off Saanichton in the Southern Gulf Islands, spans more than 300 hectares and includes white sandy beaches, an 18-hole golf course, a 5,000-square-foot main house, six guest cottages, a Western-themed village, an airstrip, and a pool house.

According to media reports, the Seattle billionaire Craig McCaw bought the island for $26 million in 1994, then put it back on the market in 2012 at an eye-popping asking price of $75 million. But it's failed to sell so far, and the exorbitant price likely isn't the only thing holding potential buyers back. The 900-member Tsawout First Nation has asserted rightful ownership of the island, and filed a lawsuit claiming it.

4. 4719 BELMONT AVE., VANCOUVER $41.20 MILLION: This stretch of Belmont Avenue is probably the richest city block in the province. If you don't have a private swimming pool and tennis court, it must be hard to show your face at the neighbourhood block party each summer. This 18,000-square-foot mansion, owned by Future Shop founder Hassan Khosrowshahi, has it all—plus six bedrooms, 10 bathrooms, and sweeping views of the beach and North Shore mountains.

5. 2815 POINT GREY RD., VANCOUVER $39.96 MILLION: This impressive 9,300-square-foot estate right on the shoreline of English Bay is the home of socialite Jacqui Cohen, the CEO and president of Army & Navy and granddaughter of the discount department chain's founder. Cohen has so much pull with City Hall that she can even commandeer its beloved bike lanes; in 2015, she managed to get a permit to let limos park in the lane outside her house while she was hosting a glitzy fundraiser.

6. 4743 BELMONT AVE., VANCOUVER $37.72 MILLION: Billionaire philanthropists Joe and Rosalie Segal bought the property for a reported $7 million in 2009. Eight years later, they put it up for sale at $63 million—the highest sale price Vancouver had ever seen. So far though, there have been no takers for the 21,000-square-foot mansion. But it remains an apt symbol of just how far Joe Segal has come in his 90-something years on the planet, beginning as a boy who sold frozen fish by bicycle and growing up to become the hugely successful head of a retail empire that once included Zellers and the Bay.

7. 4773 BELMONT AVE., VANCOUVER $35.88 MILLION: Built in 2010, this gleaming white two-storey house has five bedrooms, nine bathrooms and the same spectacular view of English Bay as every other unattainable property on the odd-numbered side of Belmont Avenue.

8. 4857 BELMONT AVE., VANCOUVER $35.62 MILLION: This 1986 single-storey home is one of the older properties on this list, but it occupies a prime piece of real estate right next to the UBC Endowment Lands.

9. 3489 OSLER ST., VANCOUVER $35.16 MILLION: Finally, an astronomically high assessment that isn't on Belmont Avenue or Point Grey Road. This lot in the very old-money Shaughnessy neighbourhood once belonged to the famously philanthropic Koerner family, but it was the Leungs who built the 16,600-square-foot home that's stood on the property since the 90s. It reportedly features an indoor pool and a 2,000-square-foot maid's apartment.

10. 2999 POINT GREY RD., VANCOUVER $35.01 MILLION: Well, this is interesting. This pricey 6,500-square-foot home shows up in the infamous leaked Panama Papers as the registered address of Robert Disbrow, a Vancouver executive whose name appears multiple times in the database of offshore entities. Disbrow has denied being involved in any improprieties. He was, however, disciplined by the B.C. Securities Commission way back in 1998 and fined $110,000 by the Toronto Stock Exchange for his role in a conflict of interest case involving a shell company in Alberta.

THE LIVING WAGE FOR 10 B.C. CITIES

British Columbia is full of infamously expensive places to live. Every year, the Living Wage for Families Campaign calculates the hourly wage that both parents of two young children would have to earn to meet their basic expenses, including rent, food, transportation and child care. Here are the results for 2018.

1. VANCOUVER: $20.91/hour

2. VICTORIA: $20.50/hour

3. TOFINO: $20.11/hour

4. REVELSTOKE: $19.37/hour

5. NELSON: $18.42/hour

6. DAWSON CREEK: $18.29/hour

7. KAMLOOPS: $17.31/hour

8. POWELL RIVER: $17.15/hour

9. COMOX VALLEY: $16.59/hour

10. PRINCE GEORGE: $16.51/hour

MOST POPULAR BABY NAMES OF 1918

BOYS:	GIRLS:
John	Mary
William	Margaret
Robert	Dorothy
James	Helen
George	Kathleen
Arthur	Elizabeth
Gordon	Ruth
Douglas	Jean
Charles	Irene
Thomas	Florence

MOST POPULAR BABY NAMES OF 1968

BOYS:
Michael
David
Robert
James
John
Richard
Kevin
Christopher
Steven
William

GIRLS:
Lisa
Michelle
Karen
Sandra
Susan
Jennifer
Tracy
Tammy
Laura
Kelly

MOST POPULAR BABY NAMES OF 2018

BOYS:
Liam
Lucas
Oliver
Benjamin
Ethan
Noah
Logan
William
James
Leo

GIRLS:
Olivia
Emma
Amelia
Charlotte
Chloe
Ava
Sophia
Isla
Emily
Hannah

CONTRIBUTORS

We'd like to extend a huge thank you to everyone who contributed. This book couldn't have happened without you.

Kevin Chong • Teresa Cline • Coast Inn Of The North • Inez Cook • Madeleine de Trenqualye • Four Seasons Resort And Residences Whistler • Antoine Gay and the Wickaninnish Inn • Rick Hansen • Stephen Hui • Rick James • Kat Jayme • Michael Kluckner • Toby Kolada And The Grand Okanagan Resort • Eve Lazarus • Fred Lee • Shanda Leer (Anthony Casey) • Elaine Lui • Greg Mansfield • Darcy Matheson • Justin McElroy • Ashleigh McIvor • Rod Mickleburgh • Glen A. Mofford • Terry David Mulligan • Bif Naked • John Schreiner • Karin Schwagly and the Shangri-la Hotel Vancouver • Nathan Sellyn • Thomas Sewid • Rob Shaw • Deborah Sleno and The Fairmont Empress Hotel • David Suzuki • Chef Hidekazu Tojo • UFO*BC • Roy Henry Vickers • Daniel Wagner • Joe Wiebe • Paula Wild • The Witsuwit'en Language And Culture Society • Richard Zussman

PHOTO CREDITS

Page 118: Credit: Charles S. Bailey, City of Vancouver Archive, AM54-S4-: Mi P2.

Page 123: Credit: Harry Braithwaite Abbot, City of Vancouver Archive, AM753-S1-. CVA 256 05.

Page 125: Credit: Jack Lindsay, City of Vancouver Archive, AM 1184-S3-: CVA 1184-495.

Page 126: Credit: Chase Hansen

Page 131: Credit: Credit City of Burnaby Archive, Columbian Newspaper collection, 480-1024.

Page 137: Credit: Thomas Sewid.

Page 145: Credit: The Canadian Press / Darryl Dyck.

Page 148: Credit: New Line Cinema, 1995.

Page 149: Credit: Paramount Pictures, 2016. Star Trek logos trademark of CBS Studios, Inc.

Page 151: Credit: Joe Lederer. Trademarks Marvel, Twentieth Century Fox Film Corporation.

Page 155: Credit: Anil Sharma.

Page 161: Credit: MERJ Media.

Page 165: Credit: Leila Kwok.

Page 166: Credit: Kaas Cross.

Page 169: Credit: Don Coltman, City of Vancouver Archive, AM1545-S3-: CVA 586-383.

Page 175: Credit: ronniecua, Adobe Stock.

Page 177: Credit: Teresa the Traveller.

Page 191: Credit: smjones, Adobe Stock